Exam Ref 70-744
Securing Windows
Server 2016

Timothy Warner
Craig Zacker

PHI Learning Private Limited

Delhi-110092

2017

This Indian Reprint—₹ 595.00
(Original U.S. Edition—₹ 2672.00)

EXAM REF 70–744: SECURING WINDOWS SERVER 2016
by Timothy Warner and Craig Zacker

Authorised reprint from the English language edition, entitled EXAM REF 70–744: SECURING WINDOWS SERVER 2016, 1st Edition, 9781509304264 by WARNER, TIMOTHY; ZACKER, CRAIG, published by Pearson Education, Inc, publishing as Microsoft Press, Copyright © 2017 by Timothy Warner.

ISBN-978-81-203-5353-4

Trademarks

Microsoft and the trademarks listed at *http://www.microsoft.com* on the "Trademarks" webpage are trademarks of the Microsoft group of companies. All other marks are property of their respective owners.

Warning and Disclaimer

Every effort has been made to make this book as complete and as accurate as possible, but no warranty or fitness is implied. The information provided is on an "as is" basis. The authors, the publisher, and Microsoft Corporation shall have neither liability nor responsibility to any person or entity with respect to any loss or damages arising from the information contained in this book or programs accompanying it.

This edition is authorised for sale in India, Pakistan, Bangladesh, Bhutan, Nepal, Sri Lanka, and the Maldives only.

The export rights of this book are vested solely with the publisher.

Published by Asoke K. Ghosh, PHI Learning Private Limited, Rimjhim House, 111, Patparganj Industrial Estate, Delhi-110092 and Printed by Mudrak, 30-A, Patparganj, Delhi-110091.

Contents at a glance

Contents

What do you think of this book? We want to hear from you!

Microsoft is interested in hearing your feedback so we can continually improve our
books and learning resources for you. To participate in a brief online survey, please visit:

www.microsoft.com/learning/booksurvey/

Chapter 4   Manage Privileged Identities   131

Chapter 6   Implement workload-specific security   245

What do you think of this book? We want to hear from you!

Microsoft is interested in hearing your feedback so we can continually improve our
books and learning resources for you. To participate in a brief online survey, please visit:

www.microsoft.com/learning/booksurvey/

Introduction

Many Windows Server books take the approach of teaching you every detail about the product. Such books end up being huge and tough to read. Not to mention that remembering everything you read is incredibly challenging. That's why those books aren't the best choice for preparing for a certification exam such as the Microsoft Exam 70-744, "Securing Windows Server 2016." For this book, we focus on your review of the Windows Server skills that you need to maximize your chances of passing the exam. Our goal is to cover all of the skills measured on the exam, while bringing a real-world focus to the information. This book shouldn't be your only resource for exam preparation, but it can be your primary resource. We recommend combining the information in this book with some hands-on work in a lab environment (or as part of your job in a real-world environment).

The 70-744 exam is geared toward IT professionals who have a minimum of three years of experience working with Windows Server. That doesn't mean you can't take and pass the exam with less experience, but it probably means that it will be harder. Of course, everyone is different. It is possible to get the knowledge and skills required to pass the 70-744 exam in fewer than three years. But whether you are a senior-level Windows Server administrator or just a couple of years into your Windows Server journey, we think you'll find the information in this book valuable as your primary exam prep resource.

This book covers every major topic area found on the exam, but it does not cover every exam question. Only the Microsoft exam team has access to the exam questions, and Microsoft regularly adds new questions to the exam, making it impossible to cover specific questions. You should consider this book a supplement to your relevant real-world experience and other study materials. If you encounter a topic in this book that you do not feel completely comfortable with, use the "Need more review?" links you'll find in the text to find more information and take the time to research and study the topic. Great information is available on MSDN, TechNet, and in blogs and forums.

Organization of this book

This book is organized by the "Skills measured" list published for the exam. The "Skills measured" list is available for each exam on the Microsoft Learning website: *http://aka.ms/examlist*. Each chapter in this book corresponds to a major topic area in the list, and the technical tasks in each topic area determine a chapter's organization. If an exam covers six major topic areas, for example, the book will contain six chapters.

Microsoft certifications

Microsoft certifications distinguish you by proving your command of a broad set of skills and experience with current Microsoft products and technologies. The exams and corresponding certifications are developed to validate your mastery of critical competencies as you design and develop, or implement and support, solutions with Microsoft products and technologies both on-premises and in the cloud. Certification brings a variety of benefits to the individual and to employers and organizations.

> **MORE INFO** ALL MICROSOFT CERTIFICATIONS
>
> For information about Microsoft certifications, including a full list of available certifications, go to *http://www.microsoft.com/learning*.

Acknowledgments

Timothy Warner I would like to thank my friend and Microsoft Press colleague Orin Thomas for making the introductions that resulted in my work on this book. Thanks to Karen Szall and Trina Macdonald for your professional editorial guidance. Thanks to Troy Mott for your awesome project management skills. As always, thanks to my family (Susan, Zoey, and the "animules") for your love and support.

Free ebooks from Microsoft Press

From technical overviews to in-depth information on special topics, the free ebooks from Microsoft Press cover a wide range of topics. These ebooks are available in PDF, EPUB, and Mobi for Kindle formats, ready for you to download at:

http://aka.ms/mspressfree

Check back often to see what is new!

Microsoft Virtual Academy

Build your knowledge of Microsoft technologies with free expert-led online training from Microsoft Virtual Academy (MVA). MVA offers a comprehensive library of videos, live events, and more to help you learn the latest technologies and prepare for certification exams. You'll find what you need here:

http://mva.microsoft.com

Quick access to online references

Throughout this book are addresses to webpages that the author has recommended you visit for more information. Some of these addresses (also known as URLs) can be painstaking to type into a web browser, so we've compiled all of them into a single list that readers of the print edition can refer to while they read.

https://aka.ms/examref744/downloads

The URLs are organized by chapter and heading. Every time you come across a URL in the book, find the hyperlink in the list to go directly to the webpage.

Errata, updates, & book support

We've made every effort to ensure the accuracy of this book and its companion content. You can access updates to this book—in the form of a list of submitted errata and their related corrections—at:

https://aka.ms/examref744/errata

If you discover an error that is not already listed, please submit it to us at the same page.

If you need additional support, email Microsoft Press Book Support at *mspinput@microsoft.com*.

Please note that product support for Microsoft software and hardware is not offered through the previous addresses. For help with Microsoft software or hardware, go to *http://support.microsoft.com*.

We want to hear from you

At Microsoft Press, your satisfaction is our top priority, and your feedback our most valuable asset. Please tell us what you think of this book at:

http://aka.ms/tellpress

We know you're busy, so we've kept it short with just a few questions. Your answers go directly to the editors at Microsoft Press. (No personal information will be requested.) Thanks in advance for your input!

Stay in touch

Let's keep the conversation going! We're on Twitter: *http://twitter.com/MicrosoftPress*.

Important: How to use this book to study for the exam

Certification exams validate your on-the-job experience and product knowledge. To gauge your readiness to take an exam, use this Exam Ref to help you check your understanding of the skills tested by the exam. Determine the topics you know well and the areas in which you need more experience. To help you refresh your skills in specific areas, we have also provided "Need more review?" pointers, which direct you to more in-depth information outside the book.

The Exam Ref is not a substitute for hands-on experience. This book is not designed to teach you new skills.

We recommend that you round out your exam preparation by using a combination of available study materials and courses. Learn more about available classroom training at *http://www.microsoft.com/learning*. Microsoft Official Practice Tests are available for many exams at *http://aka.ms/practicetests*. You can also find free online courses and live events from Microsoft Virtual Academy at *http://www.microsoftvirtualacademy.com*.

This book is organized by the "Skills measured" list published for the exam. The "Skills measured" list for each exam is available on the Microsoft Learning website: *http://aka.ms/examlist*.

Note that this Exam Ref is based on this publicly available information and the author's experience. To safeguard the integrity of the exam, authors do not have access to the exam questions.

## CHAPTER 1

Implement server hardening solutions

Server hardening refers to the process of improving the security configuration of a server. A Windows server is a soft target for attackers if:

- Operating system files are installed from a non-trusted source

- System is not current with patches and security updates

- Administrator accounts have weak passwords

- File systems don't use NTFS and are unencrypted

Of course, the previous list is incomplete and is meant only to get you thinking on the right track. In this chapter we'll examine a number of techniques intended to raise the security posture of your Windows Server 2016 infrastructure computers.

> **IMPORTANT**
> **Have you read page xvii?**
> It contains valuable information regarding the skills you need to pass the exam.

Skills in this chapter:

- Configure disk and file encryption
- Implement server patching and updating solutions
- Deploy and manage malware protection
- Protect credentials
- Create security baselines

Skill 1.1: Configure disk and file encryption

Our first 70-744 order of business is to review disk and file encryption in Windows Server 2016. The idea of whole-disk encryption is pretty simple—we want to scramble all disk contents to the sector level, such that only authorized parties can read the data.

To be effective, BitLocker Drive Encryption must be deployed alongside the IT security principle of least privilege. This means that server operators should be able to access only those resources that they need to do their jobs. After all, a local administrator can easily disable BitLocker and thereby circumvent its protections.

Determine hardware and firmware requirements for Secure Boot and encryption key functionality

In this section we'll tackle a host (pun intended) of hardware security features that aren't all specific to Microsoft Windows Server operating systems, but are fully supported. We'll cover UEFI, BitLocker Drive Encryption with and without the TPM chip, how Network Unlock works, and how we configure BitLocker Drive Encryption through Group Policy.

UEFI

Unified Extensible Firmware Interface (UEFI) is the successor to the older Basic Input Output System (BIOS) firmware interface we've had since the first PCs; any new server hardware you purchase nowadays uses UEFI firmware. Windows Server 2016 fully supports all UEFI features, especially Secure Boot.

The method for starting your server into UEFI setup depends entirely on the original equipment manufacturer (OEM). Consult your documentation or visit the vendor's website to find out which keystroke to use. Figure 1-1 shows the appropriate UEFI setup screen from a Lenovo notebook computer.

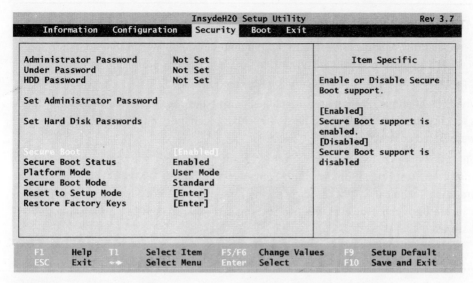

```
                        InsydeH20 Setup Utility                    Rev 3.7
      Information   Configuration    Security    Boot   Exit

   Administrator Password      Not Set                  Item Specific
   Under Password              Not Set
   HDD Password                Not Set            Enable or Disable Secure
                                                 Boot support.
   Set Administrator Password
                                                 [Enabled]
   Set Hard Disk Passwords                       Secure Boot support is
                                                 enabled.
                                                 [Disabled]
   Secure Boot                 [Enabled]         Secure Boot support is
   Secure Boot Status          Enabled           disabled
   Platform Mode               User Mode
   Secure Boot Mode            Standard
   Reset to Setup Mode         [Enter]
   Restore Factory Keys        [Enter]



    F1      Help     T1    Select Item   F5/F6   Change Values   F9    Setup Default
    ESC     Exit     ←→    Select Menu    Enter   Select         F10   Save and Exit
```

FIGURE 1-1 Configure Secure Boot and startup passwords from within UEFI setup

Secure Boot

Secure Boot is a UEFI feature that protects the server's startup environment. The UEFI firm-ware stores a database of trusted hardware, drivers, operating systems, and option ROMs. This database is structured by the server's OEM. In short, your server starts up only if its operating system boot loader files and device drivers are digitally signed and trusted by the Secure Boot database.

Secure boot can be disabled by starting the server into UEFI/BIOS setup. This may be necessary when some server hardware isn't recognized by the UEFI. You can also enable the UEFI's compatibility support module (CSM) to configure the server to boot using legacy BIOS mode, although this defeats the purpose of UEFI startup security.

> **NOTE   PREVENTING UNAUTHORIZED UEFI CHANGES**
>
> An important IT security truism is that an attacker with physical access to your server makes software-based protections far less effective. Make sure to place your servers in physically-secured areas, preferably monitored with security cameras.
>
> Your server's UEFI setup program should allow you to set one or more startup passwords that prevent the system from unauthorized startup. Because the UEFI/BIOS firmware set-tings are saved by battery power from the motherboard, you need to add physical locks to the server chassis.

TPM

A Trusted Platform Module (TPM) is a microchip that is installed on current-generation servers and desktop-class motherboards. The TPM's main function is protecting security-related data, particularly encryption and decryption keys.

What's great about TPM is that its functionality is tied to your server hardware itself. That is, its security "travels" with the host hardware, and is much more difficult to bypass than a software-based control.

Windows Server 2016 supports both the current-generation TPM v1.2 as well as the original TPM 1.0 specification. An often-confused point about TPM is its relationship to Secure Boot. Technically, TPM can provide the same type of boot-time protection that UEFI Secure Boot can. However, the two systems are separate and rely upon separate trust stores.

EXAM TIP

We must always remember why we enable controls such as Secure Boot and TPM security; namely, to prevent the injection of unauthorized boot code that can compromise our servers. Microsoft certification exams tend to put more emphasis on the "why" rather than the "how," although we do need to understand how to configure security controls in order to conquer the 70-744 certification exam.

Enable BitLocker to use Secure Boot and BCD integrity verification

BitLocker Drive Encryption (BDE) is Microsoft's native disk encryption solution for operating system and data drives. BitLocker, along with the Boot Configuration Database (BCD), was introduced originally in Windows Vista.

Specifically, the BCD is a firmware-independent database that stores Windows startup configuration data. In Windows Server 2016, the BCD is located on the unlettered, 500 MB System Reserved partition on your startup disk.

To prepare BitLocker to use Secure Boot for vplatform and BCD database integrity validation, enable the Allow Secure Boot For Integrity alidation policy found in the Group Policy path: Computer Configuration\Policies\Administrative Templates\Windows Components\BitLocker Drive Encryption\Operating System Drives.

You may get better performance and reliability configuring your Windows Server 2016 servers to use Secure Boot for BCD verification because, at least in my experience, benign changes to the BCD can sometimes trigger BitLocker Recovery, as discussed later in this section.

Deploy BitLocker Drive Encryption

Thus far, you've probably noticed the themes of (a) physical security; (b) least privilege; (c) Secure Boot; and (d) the TPM chip as essential elements of any contemporary Windows Server 2016 infrastructure server.

Having accomplished that, let's turn our attention to how to deploy BitLocker Drive Encryption. The deployment workflow is similar for Windows Server and Windows Client computers; however, the 70-744 exam objectives constrain our discussions only to protecting Windows Server 2016-based servers.

The first step is to install the BitLocker Drive Encryption feature. Fire up an administrative Windows PowerShell prompt and run the following command:

```
Install-WindowsFeature -Name BitLocker -IncludeAllSubFeature -IncludeManagementTools
-Restart
```

> **NOTE ALTERNATE WAYS TO INSTALL BITLOCKER**
>
> If you're more graphically minded, you can always install BitLocker on local or remote serv-ers by using Server Manager. By contrast, if you're accustomed to the Deployment Image Servicing and Management (DISM) command-line tool, you can still use it by running the EnableWindowsOptionalFeature wrapper cmdlet. The specific syntax for BitLocker feature installation is:
>
> ```
> Enable-WindowsOptionalFeature -Online -FeatureName BitLocker,
> BitLocker-Utilities -All
> ```

Configure BitLocker with or without TPM

BitLocker Drive Encryption can be configured to use a number of authentication methods called protectors. Table 1-1 sums up the options and their startup behaviors.

TABLE 1-1 BitLocker protectors and their startup behaviors

Protector configuration	Startup behavior
No TPM	Requires a BitLocker password or a startup key on a USB flash drive
TPM + startup PIN	Requires the presence of a TPM chip as well as a personal identification number (PIN)
TPM +startup key	Requires a TPM chip and a USB flash drive-based startup key
TPM + startup PIN + startup key	Requires TPM, PIN, and startup key

As you probably expect, we use Group Policy to specify our server BitLocker Drive Encryp-tion policy. The policy in question is called Require Additional Authentication At Startup, and it's located in the same GPO path we used earlier: Computer Configuration\Policies\Adminis-trative Templates\Windows Components\BitLocker Drive Encryption\Operating System Drives. You can see this policy in Figure 1-2.

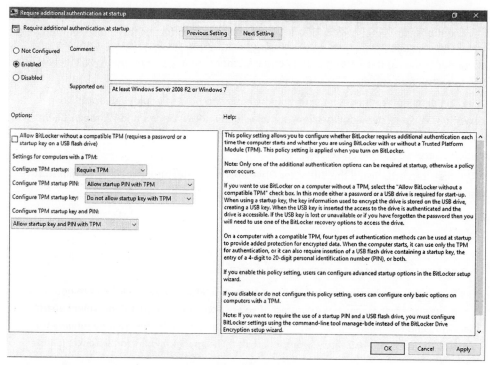

FIGURE 1-2 Establishing BitLocker Drive Encryption policy in Windows Server 2016

> **NOTE** **TPM STANDS ALONE**
>
> It's possible to leverage TPM security and BitLocker Drive Encryption without any addition-al protectors. In this case, the server starts normally and (at first blush) appears to offer no security benefit to the administrator. Upon deeper reflection, though, we understand that the TPM protects the server against offline attacks by validating the startup environment as we previously discussed.

Although it's certainly not recommended, you can configure Windows Server 2016 to use BitLocker without TPM protection by selecting the Allow BitLocker Without A Compatible TPM (Requires A Password Or A Startup Key On A USB Flash Drive) Group Policy setting.

After your new Group Policy settings have taken effect, it's time to actually encrypt our server's operating system volume. Follow these steps to get that job done:

1. Open Control Panel and start the BitLocker Drive Encryption item.

2. In the BitLocker Drive Encryption Control Panel interface beneath Operating System Drive, and click Turn On BitLocker.

3. Depending on how you've configured BitLocker policy in your domain, the specific options vary. As shown in Figure 1-3, our test server offers us the choice of using a USB startup key or using a password. Choose Enter A Password to continue.

FIGURE 1-3 Choosing a BitLocker authentication protector

4. Type and reenter a strong password in the Create A Password To Unlock This Drive dialog box and click Next to continue. A strong password is at least eight characters long and consists of a combination of (a) uppercase and lowercase characters; (b) non-alphanumeric characters; (c) numbers; and (d) absence in any dictionary in any language.

5. Back up your recovery key by choosing to save it in one of the following locations:
   - **USB flash drive** Note that this is not the same USB flash drive that you'd use as a startup key.
   - **File** Make sure to remove the file from the local server's file system!
   - **Printout** Once again, keep the printed key in a safe place, far away from its associated server.

6. Choose how much of your operating system drive to encrypt. By the way, you can (and should) encrypt your server's data drives as well; we're concerned with the operating system drive here for simplicity. Your choices here are to encrypt only used disk space or to encrypt the entire drive. For an existing server, choose the latter option and click Next to continue.

7. Choose which encryption algorithm to use. Windows Server 2016 supports the following four options:
   - **AES-128** This is the default algorithm and cipher length.
   - **AES-256** Same as AES-128, but with a double-sized cipher length.

- **XTS-AES-128** Provides Federal Information Processing Standard (FIPS) compliancy and additional features, but is incompatible with previous Windows Server versions.

- **XTS-AES-256** Same as XTS-AES128, but with a double-size cipher length.

The trade-off with encryption algorithms is the inversely proportional relationship between cipher strength and performance.

In the BitLocker Drive Encryption Control Panel interface, you're asked to choose either New Encryption mode (which uses XTS-AES-128) or Compatible mode (which uses XTS-AES-128).

8. Ensure that the Run BitLocker system check option is selected and click Continue to proceed. After being prompted to restart, BitLocker Drive Encryption proceeds to encrypt the operating system volume.

You can see the BitLocker Drive Encryption startup password prompt in Figure 1-4.

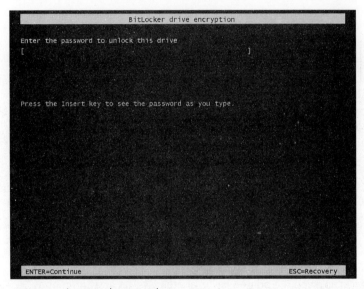

FIGURE 1-4 An example screen shot

NOTE **ALTERNATE METHODS FOR ENCRYPTING THE OPERATING SYSTEM VOLUME WITH BITLOCKER**

Windows Server 2016 loads the BitLocker Windows PowerShell cmdlets when you install the BitLocker Drive Encryption feature. To that point, use the EnableBitLocker cmdlet to encrypt a specified local or remote drive by using PowerShell. The following example encrypts the C drive by specifying the TPM and PIN protectors:

```
$SecureString = ConvertTo-SecureString '$tr0ngP@$$w0rd!!' -AsPlainText -Force
Enable-BitLocker -MountPoint 'C:' -EncryptionMethod Aes256 -UsedSpaceOnly
-Pin $SecureString -TPMandPinProtector
```

Alternatively, you can run the legacy manage-bde command line executable to encrypt, manage, and decrypt BitLocker on operating system and data volumes.

Implement BitLocker on Hyper-V virtual machines

Hyper-V in Windows Server 2016 allows both Secure Boot and virtualized TPM (vTPM) for virtual machine (VM) guests. As you can see in Figure 1-5, these capabilities are now "baked into" the Hyper-V VM properties sheet.

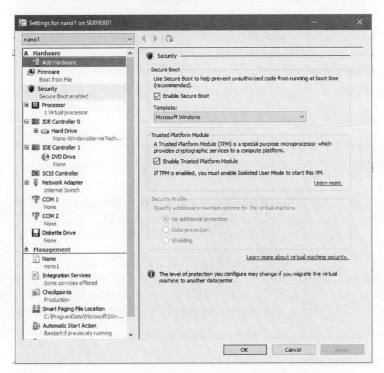

FIGURE 1-5 Enabling both Secure Boot and vTPM in a Hyper-V VM

Of course, this now means that you can deploy BitLocker Drive Encryption in local VMs the very same way you do in host hardware, including requiring TPM!

Implement BitLocker on CSVs and SANs

Windows Server 2012 introduced the ability to apply BitLocker Drive Encryption on cluster shared volumes (CSVs) based in storage area network (SAN) shared storage; this capability is known as CSV v2. Volumes can be encrypted either before you add them to a cluster or afterward. Use either Windows PowerShell or managzbde.exe to perform the task.

Configure Network Unlock

Windows Server 2016 supports the BitLocker Network Unlock feature that was introduced in Windows Server 2012. Network Unlock allows automatic access to BitLocker decryption keys, which means that you can start, restart, or remotely manage (perhaps via Wake on LAN) your Windows Server 2016 servers without the manual intervention required by the PIN protector method.

Besides having servers that use UEFI firmware and have TPM chips installed, there are a number of other infrastructure requirements for implementing Network Unlock:

- **UEFI DHCP**   This UEFI feature has historically been known as Preboot Execution Environment (PXE). In other words, the server can startup and obtain a TCP/IP configuration from a DHCP server directly from UEFI and the installed network interface card (NIC).

- **No CSM**   Your servers' UEFI firmware must have legacy mode disabled completely (that is, no Compatibility Support Modules (CSMs).

- **Separate WDS and DHCP servers**   You'll need separate servers running the Windows Deployment Service (WDS) and Dynamic Host Configuration Protocol (DHCP) server roles.

- **PKI**   You'll need a public key infrastructure (PKI) in order to generate the X.509 digital certificates required for Network Unlock. Active Directory Certificate Services (AD CS) works perfectly fine for this purpose.

- **Network Unlock Group Policy settings**   You'll configure the previously mentioned Group Policy settings to specify the TPM+PIN protectors. For the Network Unlock certificate policy, navigate to Computer Configuration\Policies\Windows Settings\Security Settings\Public Key Policies\BitLocker Drive Encryption Network Unlock Certificate and upload the .cer file.

The Network Unlock sequence

Let's walk through how BitLocker Network Unlock works from a bird's eye perspective.

1. Upon server startup, the Windows boot manager detects the presence of the Network Unlock protector. This protector is realized by the Allow Network Unlock At Startup Group Policy setting.

2. The server uses its UEFI DHCP driver to obtain a valid IPv4 address from a DHCP server.

3. The server broadcasts a vendor-specific DHCP request that's encrypted with the WDS server's Network Unlock certificate (which the local server has thanks to Group Policy configuration).

4. The WDS provider processes the request and produces an AES-256 key that unlocks the local server's operating system volume.

5. The server continues the boot process with no administrator intervention required.

Implement the BitLocker Recovery Process

What if you can't unlock a BitLocker-protected operating system drive normally? The reasons why this might happen aren't necessarily nefarious, but abjectly human: you may simply forget your PIN or unlock password. This is especially easy to do if you manage several servers and each has its own passwords and PINs.

Recovery password

Perhaps the most straightforward way to recover from a BitLocker unlock failure is to provide the 48-digit unlock key that BitLocker generated during the encryption process. Remember that? Take a look at Figure 1-6, which shows the contents of test recovery key files.

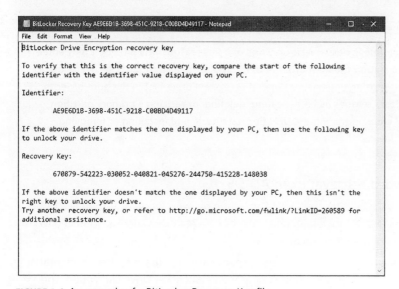

FIGURE 1-6 An example of a BitLocker Recovery Key file

You press ESC at the BitLocker Drive Encryption unlock screen to enter Recovery mode manually. As shown in Figure 1-7, this is where you type the recovery key to unlock the drive.

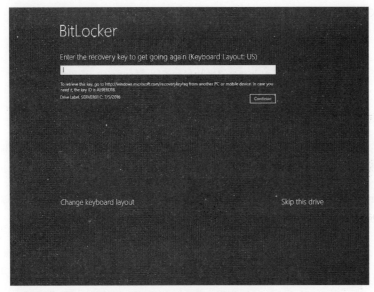

FIGURE 1-7 BitLocker Drive Encryption Recovery mode

Recovery password retrieval from AD DS

It's been possible to back up BitLocker Drive Encryption recovery passwords to Active Directory Domain Services (AD DS) for a long time. For your 70-744 exam success, you need to understand the basics of how this process works.

The configuration setting lies in Group Policy, specifically in path Computer Configuration\Policies\Administrative Templates\Windows Components\BitLocker Drive Encryption. The Group Policy setting in question is Store BitLocker recovery information in Active Directory Domain Services.

This policy gives you the choice of storing only BitLocker Recovery passwords in AD DS, or both the passwords as well as the underlying encryption keys.

You'll also need to enable the policy Choose How BitLocker-Protected Operating System Drives Can Be Recovered from the Operating System Drives subfolder in Group Policy Editor. Specifically, make sure you enable the option Save BitLocker Recovery Information To AD DS for operating system drives.

Next, run the InvokeGPUpdate cmdlet against the relevant servers. For example, the following PowerShell pipeline forces a remote refresh of every Windows server in my servers.txt data file:

```
Invoke-GPUpdate -Computer (Get-Content -Path .\servers.txt) -Force
```

From now on, any server on which you enable BitLocker stores its recovery password and possibly its encryption keys in Active Directory. One gotcha: this Group Policy change doesn't affect servers that already use BitLocker. On these machines, run the following managebde command to obtain your system's numerical password iD:

```
manage-bde -protectors -get c:
```

And then run this command to force the key/password archival, substituting your appropriate drive letter and password ID (make sure to include the braces surrounding the ID):

```
manage-bde -protectors -adbackup c: -id {password id}
```

If or when you need to access the recovery password, open Active Directory Users and Computers, locate the target server, open its Properties sheet, and navigate to the BitLocker Recovery tab. You'll see the recovery password as shown in Figure 1-8. By the way, this Active Directory Users and Computers integration happens by virtue of the BitLocker Recovery Password Viewer that's included in the BitLocker Drive Encryption server feature.

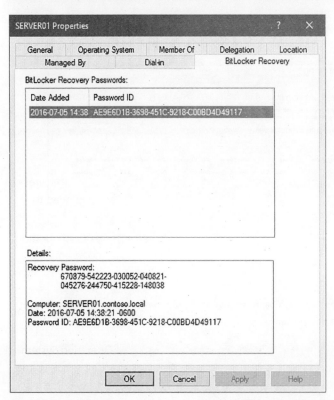

FIGURE 1-8 Retrieving a BitLocker recovery password from Active Directory Users and Computers

Self-service recovery

Another BitLocker recovery key management option, especially for larger enterprises, is the Microsoft BitLocker Administration and Monitoring (MBAM) toolset. MBAM v2.5 SP1 is part of the Microsoft Desktop Optimization Pack (MDOP) 2015 add-on package. Be warned that MBAM is quite a complex installation because it's a full-fledged multi-tier application that can be deployed either stand-alone or integrated with System Center Configuration Manager 2012 R2.

The good news for Windows systems administrators is that MBAM provides end-to-end automation for BitLocker: self-service key retrieval, agent-based user guidance, and so forth. For reference, Figure 1-9 shows a screen shot of the MBAM self-service portal. Notice that the portal allows us to not only manage BitLocker keys and recovery, but also to perform status monitoring and auditing.

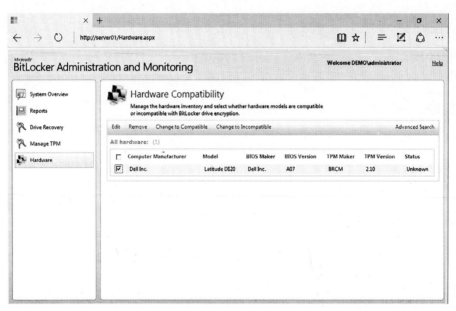

FIGURE 1-9 The MBAM self-service web portal

Manage Encrypting File System (EFS)

BitLocker Drive Encryption functions at the volume level. It's certainly true that you can use BitLocker to encrypt removable media, but for most production servers, we're encrypting entire, fixed hard disk volumes.

We can use BitLocker to create encrypted container files, but these too are treated by Windows Server 2016 as virtual hard drive (VHD) images.

Encrypting File System (EFS) presents a more granular solution to data encryption. We can leverage EFS to protect individual folders and files.

Data recovery agents

By default, EFS generates self-signed certificates and stores them in each user or administrator's profile folder. This is a bad idea in production because:

- The EFS encryption keys can be stolen or damaged
- There's no trust chain with self-signed certificates

Therefore, if you plan to implement EFS in your enterprise, you should have a "true blue" public key infrastructure (PKI) established, preferably with Active Directory Certificate Services (AD CS) so you can fully manage EFS certificates. After all, AD CS includes Basic EFS and EFS Recovery Agent certificate templates out of the box.

The data recovery agent (DRA) is a privileged user account who can decrypt other domain users' EFS certificates. By default, the domain Administrator account is the domain's *de facto* DRA, but we can certainly include other administrative accounts.

Follow these steps to define the current administrator a new EFS DRA in a Windows Server 2016 Active Directory domain that has an online enterprise root certification authority:

1. Request an EFS Recovery Agent certificate from your AD CS certification authority. From the Certificates Microsoft Management Console (MMC) snap-in, this is done by right-clicking the Personal certificate store and clicking All Tasks | Request New Certificate.

2. From the Certificates snap-in, we can easily back up our EFS, BitLocker, or any other digital certificate by right-clicking the certificate and clicking All Tasks | Export. To restore a backed-up certificate, right-click the Personal store and click All Tasks | Import. This can all be seen in Figure 1-10. In the screenshot, note that the user account has both the Basic EFS and EFS Recovery Agent certificates; that's important.

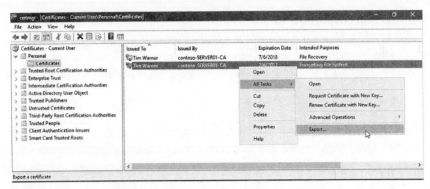

FIGURE 1-10 Managing EFS certificates

3. To assign DRAs at the domain level, open an appropriate Group Policy Object (GPO) and navigate to the path Computer Configuration\Windows Settings\Security Settings\ Public Key Policies. You'll see two subfolders: Encryption File System and BitLocker Drive Encryption. As it happens, you can nominate DRAs for both technologies.

4. Right-click the Encrypting File System policy folder and select Add Data Recovery Agent from the context menu. You have two options in the Add Recovery Agent Wizard for locating the appropriate users:

   - Browse Directory   Locate the user by searching Active Directory directly. To use this option, the certificate(s) must be published to AD.

   - Browse Folders   Locate the .cer exported EFS Recovery Agent certificate in a local or remote file system.

5. Refresh Group Policy, and now your new DRAs have privilege to decrypt all domain users' EFS-encrypted files. This comes in handy during emergency access situations like user profile corruption, lost certificates, employee termination, and so forth.

Skill 1.2: Implement server patching and updating solutions

Next on the agenda is server patching and updating. This subject ordinarily brings out a sigh from most experienced Windows systems administrators. Have you ever been "bitten" by deploying a server update that crippled services instead of strengthening them?

A core IT security principle is ensuring that all infrastructure servers are patched against known exploits and vulnerabilities. WSUS can help us to accomplish this security goal with fewer mistakes.

To these points, for our 70-744 exam success we need to have a well-rounded understanding of Windows Server Update Services (WSUS) and how we can use it to protect our Windows Server 2016 servers while simultaneously reducing the likelihood of an update-related service failure.

Most Windows systems administrator know that Microsoft releases security patches and software updates on the second Tuesday of every month; this is known informally as "Patch Tuesday." Of course, as Microsoft addresses zero-day exploits, they also release these patches on a priority basis.

Install and configure WSUS

In a nutshell, Windows Server Update Services (WSUS, typically pronounced either *WUH-sus* or *double-yew-sus*), is a longstanding Windows Server client/server web application that gives administrators full control over the Windows Update process. WSUS can be deployed in many different ways, including as an integrated component of System Center Configuration Manager.

As far as refreshing your knowledge of WSUS topology is concerned, take a look at Figure 1-11 and I'll walk you through each major component.

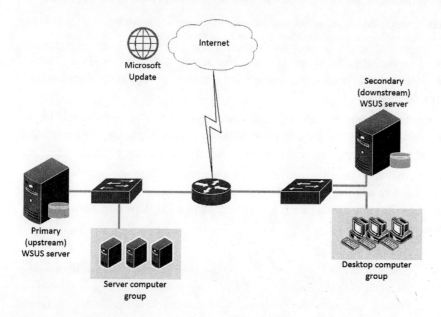

FIGURE 1-11 WSUS topology

- WSUS can be deployed either as a single-server standalone solution or as a replicated server farm. Secondary (downstream) servers pull their updates from the upstream (master) WSUS server; the master server downloads updates from Microsoft Update over the Internet.

- Computer groups help make testing and deploying Windows Updates and hotfixes easier. For instance, you may have a group of development servers that you use as "guinea pigs" to ensure that updates won't affect production services before releasing the updates to your production computer.

The primary benefits of WSUS can be summed up this way:

- You save bandwidth because local servers and client computers download updates at LAN speeds from local WSUS points of presence.

- You improve the stability of your network because you have a chance to test, approve, and blacklist updates before the computers you support receive them.

- You control how and when approved updates are installed by client machines in your environment.

Next, consider how to install and configure WSUS in Windows Server 2016.

Install WSUS

Follow these steps to install WSUS on a Windows Server 2016 member server in a domain:

1. Install the Windows Server Update Services (WSUS) server role by using Server Manager or by using Windows PowerShell. For example, here's a PowerShell "one liner" that installs WSUS and specifies the Windows Internal Database (WID) as the data store:

```
Install-WindowsFeature -Name UpdateServices, UpdateServices-WiDB,
UpdateServices-Services, UpdateServices-API, UpdateServices-UI
```

Windows Server 2016 allows you to use a full installation of SQL Server as well. That's a good idea for larger organizations who place emphasis on regular database backups and optimization.

2. After installation completes, open the Windows Server Update Services console from Server Manager. This starts the Complete WSUS Installation Wizard. You're asked for an update storage location; type your desired path and press Run to continue.

3. The post-installation tasks normally take a few minutes to complete, after which you're taken into a second wizard. Rather than describe each step in excruciating detail, I'll provide you with a punch list of the configuration steps with a few words concerning each:

- **Before You Begin** Verification step that asks you if your WSUS server's firewall rules are configured appropriately and you're logged on with proper credentials.

- **Microsoft Update Improvement Program** Opt-in or opt-out, it's your choice.

- **Choose Upstream Server** Synchronize updates either with Microsoft Update directly or with an upstream WSUS server available in your environment.

- **Specify Proxy Server** Use one or not, depending on your network rules. You'll be forced to apply your changes and create an initial connection with your upstream serve; this takes several minutes to complete.

- **Choose Languages** Be careful here and select only those languages that you actually support. Otherwise the WSUS server downloads far more content than you need.

- **Choose Products** Again, you want to download updates only for the operating system platforms and Microsoft software that you actually support.

- **Choose Classifications** By default, only Critical Updates, Windows Defender malware definition updates, and Security Updates are selected. Make additional selections here as appropriate.

- **Configure Sync Schedule** Specify manual synchronization with your upstream partner or put it on a schedule. Choose also when to perform an initial synchronization (understand this takes a long time depending upon your previous choices).

4. After your initial synchronization completes, you're ready to define computer groups, apply approval policies, and configure Automatic Update. You can do all of this from the Update Services MMC console, shown in Figure 1-12.

NEED MORE REVIEW? **DIGGING DEEPER WITH WSUS**

If you'd like more planning/architectural details on WSUS, as well as a step-by-step installation and configuration tutorial, consider reading the TechNet whitepaper series "Deploy Windows Server Update Services in Your Organization" at *https://technet.microsoft.com/ en-us/library/hh852340%28v=ws.11%29.aspx?f=255&MSPPError=-2147217396*.

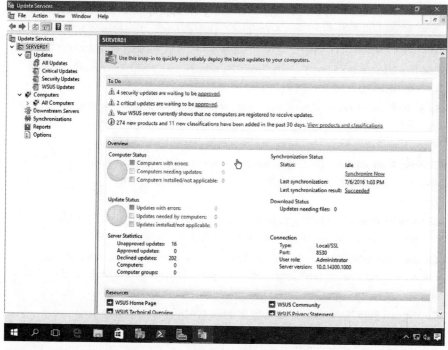

FIGURE 1-12 The Update Services administration console

Create computer groups and configure Automatic Updates

By default, WSUS creates (but does not populate) a single computer group called, appropriately enough, Unassigned Computers. Some Windows administrators create computer groups based on geographical location, other admins use departments, and the list goes on. In this example, follow these steps to define a new computer group to contain our infrastructure servers.

1. In the Update Services console, right-click the Computers | All Computers node and select Add Computer Group from the shortcut menu.

2. Give the new group a descriptive name (Infrastructure Servers, for example) and then click Add.

You might find it unintuitive that the Update Services console has no control for, say, adding one or more domain servers to your new computer group. That actually isn't how WSUS works at all; rather, we must use Group Policy to point our client servers and desktop computers at a given WSUS server.

However, once a client has been associated with a given computer group, you can reassign the host from within the Update Services console by right-clicking the host and selecting Change Membership from the shortcut menu.

Complete these steps to define the configuration using the appropriate Active Directory GPO:

1. Navigate to Computer Configuration\Policies\Administrative Templates\Windows Components\Windows Update and open the policy Specify Intranet Microsoft Update Service Location. You'll need to provide two URLs:

   - **Intranet update service**   HTTP(s) address of your WSUS server. Make sure to check Internet Information Services (IIS) Manager to see which port WSUS is using. By default, WSUS uses TCP 8530 for HTTP, so the URL is *http://server01.contoso.local:8530.*

   - **Intranet statistics server**   HTTP(S) address of your WSUS server.

   This policy ensures that any computers targeted by this GPO look to your WSUS server for updates instead of Windows Update.

2. In the same GPO path, open the Configure Automatic Updates policy. This is where you control how often targeted hosts query the WSUS server for updates. The options here are the same as found in the Update & Security Control Panel item in Windows Server 2016 and Windows 10.

3. As a convenience to non-administrative users, you may want to enable the policy Allow non-administrators to receive update notifications as well.

4. Finally, link your new computer group. Open the Enable Client-Side Targeting policy and type the name of your previously-created WSUS computer group. Note the following:

   - The spelling and spacing of the computer name must match precisely what's in WSUS.

   - You'll need to deploy a separate GPO for each computer group (bad news!).

5. After a Group Policy refresh, you should see two things: (a) the targeted server's Update & Security Control Panel shows a management banner as shown in Figure 1-13; and (b) your targeted nodes appear in their assigned computer group in the Update Services console. You may need to run wuauclt /reportnow from an elevated PowerShell console and refresh the display to move things along. Incidentally, wuauclt.exe is the Windows Update Client, and is a useful tool for troubleshooting (more on that later).

NOTE **MANAGING WSUS BY USING WINDOWS POWERSHELL**

You can manage most WSUS actions, at least from a basic level, by using the UpdateServices PowerShell module. Run this command to get a listing of available cmdlets:

```
Get-Command -Module UpdateServices
```

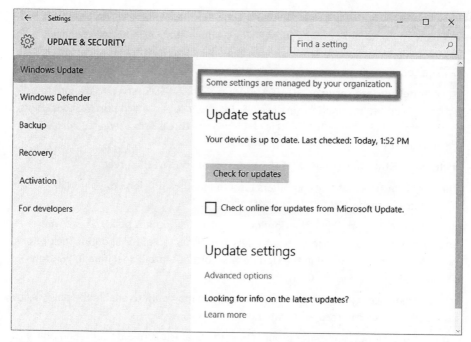

FIGURE 1-13 This Windows Server 2016 computer is configured as a WSUS client, as shown by the management banner text

Manage updates using WSUS

We manage Windows update approvals and deployments from the Updates node in the Update Services MMC console. This node is divided into four separate views:

- **All Updates**   Unfiltered list of all downloaded updates
- **Critical Updates**   Widely-released fixes for specific problems
- **Security Updates**   Malware definition updates and widely released fixes for security-related vulnerabilities
- **WSUS Updates**   Updates to the WSUS server role itself

The update approval process has three general steps, as annotated in the composite screenshot in Figure 1-14:

1. Locate an update from one of the previously-listed views.
2. Right-click the update and select Approve from the shortcut menu.
3. In the Approve Updates dialog box, select the appropriate computer group, open the menu, and select Approved For Install.

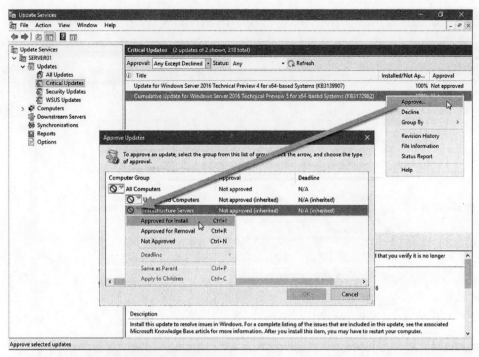

FIGURE 1-14 The WSUS update approval process

Configure WSUS reporting

Being able to control which updates are applied to which network hosts is only half the Windows Update battle. You may be asked to account for this data, quantitatively, to fulfill compliance audits, or if something goes terribly wrong after an update.

The Reports node in the Update Services console has a number of pre-built reports. These are depicted in Figure 1-15.

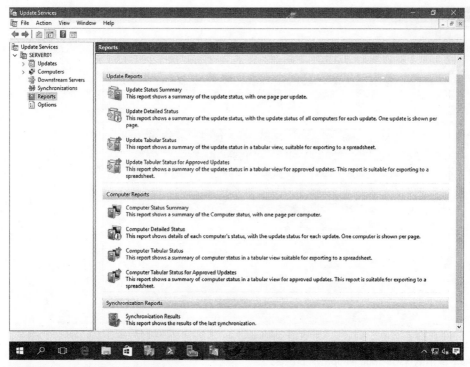

FIGURE 1-15 The WSUS reports gallery

The "gotcha" regarding WSUS reports is that you need to install the Microsoft Report Viewer 2012 Runtime and the system CLR types from the SQL Server 2012 SP1 Feature Pack before you can actually view these reports. This actually makes sense because WSUS uses either WID or full SQL Server database to run appropriate T-SQL queries and to generate the reports.

After you install the necessary components (which may already be installed if your run a full SQL Server instance) and re-open the Update Services console, you can click any report to run it. Before the console generates the report, you can include one or more of the following filters:

- Classifications
- Product
- Computer(s)
- Computer status
- Whether to include status from replica downstream WSUS servers

You can use the Print button in the Report Viewer tool to generate a hard copy version, or the Export button to to create Excel, PDF, or Word versions. Figure 1-16 shows you what the tool looks like after running the Synchronization Report.

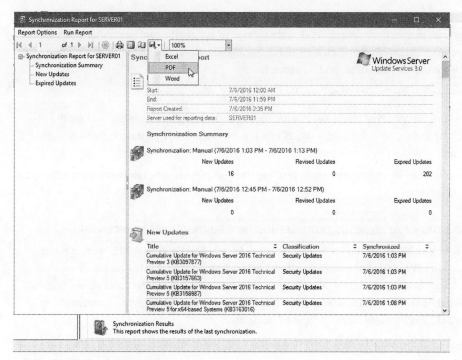

FIGURE 1-16 A typical WSUS report

Troubleshoot WSUS configuration and deployment

Most WSUS configuration and deployment troubles come from the client side rather than from the server. We close this section by reviewing some "quick fix" approaches to solving WSUS client agent woes.

- **Verify that the client has proper WSUS settings**   In other words, you need to verify that the target node is in fact configured for WSUS client-side targeting in Group Policy. Generate a Resultant Set of Policy (RSoP) report and view it in Notepad by running the following two commands from an administrative PowerShell console:

```
gpresult /V > gpresult.txt
notepad gpresult.txt
```

- **Check for BITS-related issues**   Windows uses the Background Intelligent Transfer Service (BITS) to download updates from your WSUS server or Microsoft Update. We can use Windows PowerShell to query BITS service status, start it, or restart it:

```
Get-Service -Name BITS
Start-Service -Name BITS
Restart-Service -Name BITS -Force
```

While we're on the subject of BITS, make sure that the service is configured to run under the Local System user account.

- **Issues with the WSUS agent service** Once again, we can leverage Windows PowerShell to check the Windows Update service to ensure it's running. What's especially powerful about PowerShell is its remote administration capabilities. In this example, we check the service status on two servers:

```
Get-Service -ComputerName server01, server02 -Name wuauserv
```

Make sure the WSUS server is reachable from the client. Open a web browser on the affected client and try to download a WSUS test file: *http://server01.contoso.local/Selfupdate/iuident.cab.*

If the client can download the small test file, then you've validated network connectivity to the WSUS server.

> ***NEED MORE REVIEW?*** **WSUS TROUBLESHOOTING GUIDANCE FROM MICROSOFT**
>
> Given how much TechNet documentation exists for troubleshooting WSUS, I would guess that Microsoft has fielded quite a few WSUS-related support incidents over the years. Perhaps the most comprehensive guide for you to start with is the TechNet wiki library "WSUS Troubleshooting Survival Guide" at *http://social.technet.microsoft.com/wiki/contents/articles/2491.wsus-troubleshooting-survival-guide.aspx.*

Skill 1.3: Implement malware protection

In BitLocker Drive Encryption we saw remediation against rootkits and sundry boot-time (kernel-mode) malware. Now we need to take a closer look at some first-party methods for preventing user-mode malicious software of all types: viruses, worms, spyware, and so on. We'll also review how AppLocker protects our environment against potentially dangerous applications, and how Control Flow Guard and Device Guard protect your servers and client system at a much lower level in the operating system.

> **This section covers how to:**
> - Implement an antimalware solution with Windows Defender
> - Integrate Windows Defender with WSUS and Windows Update
> - Implement AppLocker rules
> - Implement Control Flow Guard
> - Implement Device Guard policies

Implement an antimalware solution with Windows Defender

Malware is a portmanteau of malicious and software. The 70-744 exam assumes that you already understand the basics of IT security, so we'll skip preliminary definitions and jump to the heart of the matter; namely, remediating malware with Windows Defender.

Windows Defender is Microsoft's free antimalware application, and it's included by default in Windows Server 2016. As you can see in Figure 1-17, the server-based Windows Defender application looks exactly like the client version you see in Windows 10—it's the same app.

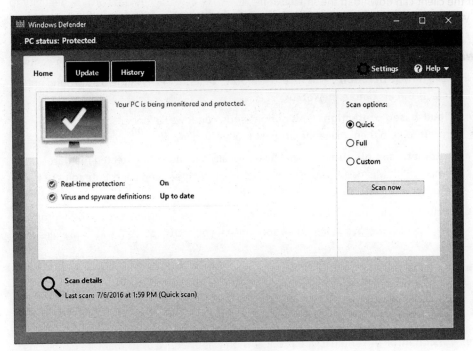

FIGURE 1-17 Windows Defender in Windows Server 2016

Managing Windows Defender in Windows Server 2016

One thing that's great about the Windows Defender server version is that the scanning engine is decoupled from the graphical user interface (GUI). Check out this Windows PowerShell code:

```
Get-WindowsFeature -Name *defend* | Format-Table -AutoSize

Display Name                    Name                         Install State
------------                    ----                         -------------
[X] Windows Defender Features   Windows-Defender-Features        Installed
[X] Windows Defender            Windows-Defender                 Installed
[X] GUI for Windows Defender    Windows-Defender-Gui             Installed
```

In Windows Server 2016, Windows Defender behavior is configurable through the Update & Security pane in Settings, as shown in Figure 1-18. Specifically, here's what you can control:

- **Real-time protection**   This means Windows Defender runs in the background and detects threats before they occur.

- **Cloud-based protection**   This option sends Windows Defender scan results to Microsoft to help them make the product more effective.

- **Automatic sample submission**   By optionally sharing your detected malware samples with Microsoft, you improve Windows Defender and contribute to better security worldwide.

- **Exclusions**   Instructing Windows Defender *not* to scan certain files is a risky proposition, but can improve scanning performance if you're 100 percent sure those files are safe.

- **Windows Defender Offline**   Some malware creates file handles and locks that make removal impossible without restarting the computer and scanning the system from an alternative startup volume. You need to download and install Windows Defender Offline to use this feature.

- **Version Info**   An antimalware product is only as effective as its malware definitions are recent. Be sure update the definitions often, preferably daily.

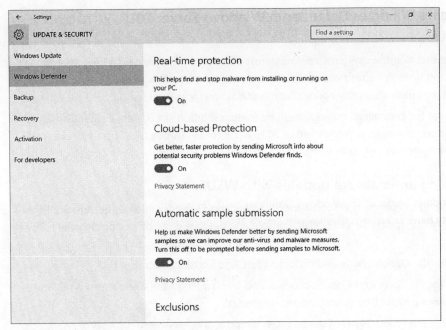

FIGURE 1-18 Configuring Windows Defender through the Settings app

Running Windows Defender scans by using Windows PowerShell

Let's have a look at the contents of the Defender PowerShell module in Windows Server 2016:

```
Get-Command -Module Defender | Select-Object -Property Name | Format-Wide -Column 2
```

```
Add-MpPreference          Get-MpComputerStatus
Get-MpPreference          Get-MpThreat
Get-MpThreatCatalog       Get-MpThreatDetection
Remove-MpPreference       Remove-MpThreat
Set-MpPreference          Start-MpScan
Start-MpWDOScan           Update-MpSignature
```

These functions are quite simple: use StartMpScan to run a real-time scan, and StartMpW-DOScan to initiate an offline scan, assuming you've created Windows Defender Offline boot media.

Better understand these and other Windows PowerShell cmdlets by updating your server's local help repository:

```
Update-Help -Force
```

Then, view the command's full help file in a separate window (this is especially useful for administrators who use multiple monitors):

```
Get-Help -Name Start-MpScan -ShowWindow
```

Integrate Windows Defender with WSUS and Windows Update

It's crucial that Windows systems administrators do everything they can to keep their server and desktop systems current with their antimalware definition files. Going further, your department may have a security policy that mandates weekly system scans.

You'll get full centralized management by using a solution like System Center Configuration Manager. However, Windows Server 2016 has a couple in-box tricks up its sleeve. We'll begin with Windows Defender integration with WSUS.

Approving antimalware updates with WSUS

You may want to configure WSUS to approve Windows Defender updates automatically. Let's open the WSUS Update Services MMC console and get that done by performing the following steps:

1. Click the Options node and click Products And Classifications.

2. In the Products And Classifications dialog box, switch to the Classifications tab and make sure that Definition Updates is selected.

3. Close the Products And Classifications dialog and open Automatic Approvals.

4. In the Automatic Approvals dialog box, select the Default Automatic Approval Rule (or click New Rule to define a new rule). Next, click Edit.

5. In the Edit Rule dialog box, for Step 1, ensure that When An Update Is In A Specific Classification is selected. In Step 2, click When An Update Is In: hyperlink and select Definition Updates.

Once you complete the previous steps, your WSUS server automatically approves any downloaded Windows Defender malware definition updates.

> **NOTE WINDOWS DEFENDER VS. MICROSOFT SECURITY ESSENTIALS**
>
> In your Windows Server 2016 WSUS console, don't be surprised if you see some of your Windows Defender definition updates listed as *Definition Update for Microsoft Security Essentials*. Microsoft Security Essentials (MSE) is the older (Windows 7-compatible) version of today's Windows Defender antimalware engine. Both applications use the same definition update files.

Configuring Windows Defender through Group Policy

Windows Server 2016 Group Policy gives administrators wide-spectrum control over Windows Defender behavior. The Group Policy settings are located in the path Computer Configuration\Policies\Administrative Templates\Windows Components\Windows Defender.

You can ensure that Windows Defender can't be turned off on target systems by disabling (not enabling, if you're following) the policy Turn Off Windows Defender.

Navigate to the Scan folder to configure Group Policy settings that govern all aspects of system scanning. Here are some goodies:

- Check For The Latest Virus And Spyware Definitions Before Running A Scheduled Scan
- Specify The Time Of Day To Run A Scheduled Scan
- Allow Users To Pause Scan

Implement AppLocker rules

The "blacklisting" approach to malware infections is what lies behind Windows Defender. That's all well and good, but is ultimately a losing battle when you consider just how many new malware signatures appear in the world every single day.

The idea behind AppLocker is just the opposite: "Whitelist" authorized applications, and any application execution attempt on a protected system fails unless that application is part of the whitelist.

AppLocker is the successor to the old Software Restriction Policies introduced in Windows Server 2003. AppLocker, like BitLocker or any security application, presupposes the principle of least privilege. After all, administrators can launch whatever applications they want on a system.

The whitelist approach to application security takes a lot more testing and overall administration, but is bulletproof once the solution is implemented.

> **NOTE LEAST PRIVILEGE AND STANDARD USER ACCOUNTS**
>
> An easier (but not easy) way to limit the introduction of installed malware on your network is to ensure that all users and admins operate their computers under standard user identities. Thus, any software installer that requires administrative elevation simply fails.
> Two issues with this approach are (a) some software installers allow standard users to install their product in, say, the user's profile folder; and (b) you have to be an administrator to log onto a Windows Server computer.

AppLocker rule types

In Windows Server 2016 we defined AppLocker rules in (surprise surprise) Group Policy. As shown in Figure 1-19, The AppLocker management interface is, well, substantial.

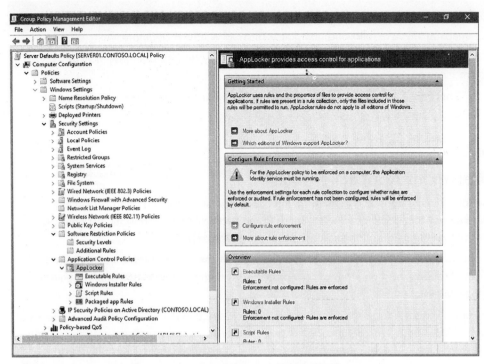

FIGURE 1-19 Configuring AppLocker in Windows Server 2016 Group Policy

You'll need to make sure that the Application Identity service (AppIDSvc) is running on all protected servers and desktop systems to use AppLocker. Of course, Group Policy can be used to force-enable this service.

Let's define each of the five AppLocker rule types:

- **Executable rules**   Applies to executable code with the .exe and .com file types
- **Windows Installer rules**   Applies to .msi and .msp installation packages
- **Script rules**   Applies to scripts with the extensions .ps1, .bat, .cmd, .vbs, and .js
- **Packaged app rules**   Applies to Universal (formerly called "Metro") Windows apps
- **DLL rules**   Applies to dynamic link library (DLL) binaries. Not recommended to use because of the adverse overhead these rules incur on system performance

For each rule we have a choice of one of three conditions:

- **Publisher**   This is the preferred condition type due to its high flexibility. You can allow or block applications based on Publisher, Product name, File name, or file version
- **Path**   You can allow or block apps according to local or remote paths (for instance, C:\ Program Files*)
- **File hash**   This is a frustrating condition type because if a whitelisted or blacklisted app receives an update, its hash totally changes, rendering the condition null and void

Implement an AppLocker policy

In this example we'll configure our AppLocker GPO along the following lines:

- Apply an automatically-generated rule to whitelist the standard application locations
- Block installation of the Firefox browser executable. We're not picking on Mozilla here, it's just a good example because Firefox allows standard users to install the software by default

Use this procedure to configure our AppLocker rules from an Active Directory-based Group Policy Object on a Windows Server 2016 domain controller:

1. Make sure the Application Identity service is running on all systems that are in scope for the Group Policy:

```
if ((Get-Service -Name AppIDSvc).Status -eq 'Stopped') {
    Start-Service -Name AppIDSvc
    }
else {
    Write-Output -InputObject 'The AppID service is running.'
    }
```

2. In Group Policy Editor, navigate to Computer Configuration\Policies\Windows Settings\Security Settings\Application Control Policies\AppLocker. In this simple example we'll create a rule that blocks the execution of the Service Control Manager (services.msc) console. This is an admittedly contrived example, but it works for learning purposes.

3. Right click the Executable Rules node and select Automatically Generate Rules. These are "failsafe" rules that prevent the system from being totally inaccessible. The default executables allow:

   - Everyone to run all files located in the Program Files folder
   - Everyone to run all files located in the Windows folder
   - Local administrators to run all files, period

4. Right-click Executable Rules again and select Create New Rule from the menu. Click Next on the welcome page.

5. On the Permissions page, select the Deny action, and change the User or group scope to Authenticated Users.

6. On the Conditions page, select File Hash. In practice, file hash rules are largely ineffective because they invalidate whenever the executables in question are updated. For our purposes, though, that's fine.

7. On the File Hash page, click Browse Files to locate C:\Windows\System32\calc.exe.

8. Click Create to finish rule creation.

9. Use Windows PowerShell to force a domain-wide Group Policy update starting from the server's organizational unit (OU):

```
Get-ADComputer –Filter * -Searchbase "cn=servers, dc=contoso,dc=local" | foreach{
Invoke-GPUpdate –Computer $_.name -Force}
```

Testing and monitoring AppLocker policies

Log onto a system that is in scope for your newly created GPO and attempt to open Service Control Manager. My favorite way to do this is type Windows key + R, services.msc, and Enter. When the AppLocker policy goes through, you see an Access Denied message as shown in Figure 1-20.

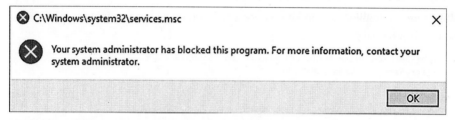

FIGURE 1-20 What a user sees when they trigger an AppLocker restriction

You can use the trusty Event Viewer to view and analyze AppLocker policy events. The insights you glean here are excellent for auditing and troubleshooting purposes.

Use the eventvwr.msc command from an elevated PowerShell session. Next, navigate in the console tree to Application And Services Logs\AppLocker. You'll have the following four logs available to you:

- EXE and DLL
- MSI and Script
- Packaged app-Deployment
- Packaged app-Execution

The two "Packaged app" logs are for universal Windows apps, which are also known as Windows Store apps. They are also known as Metro apps. Which are, well, you get the idea.

You can also monitor AppLocker events by using Windows PowerShell. For instance, the following one-liner retrieves all EXE and DLL-related AppLocker audit events:

```
Get-AppLockerFileInformation -EventLog -LogPath "Microsoft-Windows-AppLocker/EXE and
DLL" -EventType Audited
```

This one-liner gathers AppLocker file information against the Windows\System32 path:

```
Get-AppLockerFileInformation -Directory C:\Windows\System32\ -Recurse -FileType Exe,
Script
```

Implement Control Flow Guard

Control Flow Guard (CFG) is a developer-focused feature which remediates against memory corruption vulnerabilities. If application data in server RAM were to break, a vulnerability could be exposed that makes it possible for an attacker to steal sensitive data from memory.

Windows has long supported Data Execution Prevention, or DEP. When enabled, DEP protects operating system RAM as non-executable. The idea is that rogue software that tries to overwrite system memory fails in its attempt. On the other hand, during the first few years of its presence, some administrators found they had to disable DEP in order to maintain system stability.

Another Windows feature that protects system memory is Address Space Layout Randomization (ASLR.) With ASLR, Windows loads operating system data into different (pseudo-randomized) memory areas upon each system startup. This prevents attackers from relying upon default memory addresses when attempting to inject malicious code into target RAM.

EXAM TIP

Microsoft has a free tool called Enhanced Mitigation Experience Toolkit (EMET) that allows administrators to tweak DEP and ASLR settings. EMET also includes built-in application profiles that remediate against low-level vulnerabilities in certain software applications such as Adobe Acrobat and the Internet Explorer browser.

Enabling Control Flow Guard

To repeat, Control Flow Guard is not a tool within the reach of Windows systems administrators or even security consultants. Instead, this is a feature that .NET software developers enable in their applications.

For example, in Visual Studio 2015 you can enable Control Flow Guard by right-clicking your project in the Project Explorer and selecting Properties from the shortcut menu. In the Code Generation configuration element, you can set the Control Flow Guard property to Yes, as shown in Figure 1-21.

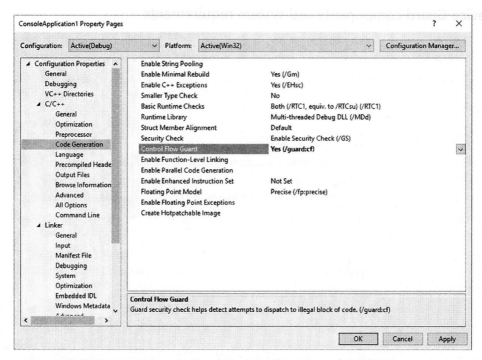

FIGURE 1-21 Enabling Control Flow Guard in a Visual Studio 2015 console application

Implement Device Guard policies

The first thing you should understand about Device Guard is that it isn't a single Microsoft product. Instead, Device Guard is a collection of security-related hardware and software features that, when implemented together, fully protects the server's executable environment.

Device Guard is the ultimate extension of application whitelisting. If any component of a system firmware, installed operating system, device drivers, or application does not exist on the system's code integrity policy whitelist, then the system won't start or the application won't run, period.

The paradigm shift for us Windows administrators is to think of all applications and services as existing inside or outside a "circle of trust;" the trustworthiness of a software component relies upon digital code signing. After all, how many piece of malware have you seen that are digitally signed?

Device Guard is aimed only at mission-critical servers with stable workloads. Also, as of this writing Device Guard is extremely difficult to manage because every change requires a reboot and Microsoft hasn't yet released user-friendly tooling.

Device Guard components and system requirements

Code Integrity Policies form the actual whitelist of software that's allowed to run on a given Windows system. This feature protects against exposure to new ("zero day") malware, for which the signature is not yet known and addressed. No security-related hardware features are required to implement this feature. Code integrity policies also protect against unsigned code.

Virtualization-Based Security (VBS) employs the Hyper-V hypervisor to protect the operating system kernel and other potentially vulnerable components. This feature protects the core operating system files as well as device drivers from being overwritten by malicious, trojan horse variants.

VBS does have hardware requirements, particularly 64-bit processors with CPU virtualization extensions and Second-Level Address Translation (SLAT) support. Your system firmware, as I'm sure you'd expect by now, must use UEFI v2.3.1c or higher with UEFI Secure Boot enabled.

VBS Input/Output Memory Management Units (IOMMUs) protect server memory against Direct Memory Access (DMA) attacks. DMA is a hardware bus architecture that has historically been vulnerable to attacks and corresponding data theft. IOMMU is a hardware feature, so you need to ensure your system motherboards support it prior to Device Guard deployment.

From a software perspective, Device Guard works with both Windows Server 2016 editions, and Windows 10 Enterprise and Education stock-keeping units (SKUs).

You can manage Device Guard by using any combination of the following tools:

- **Group Policy** Use the Device Guard GPO administrative template to deploy catalogs and code integrity policies
- **System Center Configuration Manager (SCCM)** Provides centralized management of Device Guard
- **Microsoft Intune** This product puts Device Guard within reach of consumers and smaller business owners
- **Windows PowerShell** The ConfigCI PowerShell module contains cmdlets to view, create, and edit Device Guard code integrity policies

> **NOTE DEVICE GUARD INTEGRATION**
>
> Device Guard is one of several technologies that rely upon the Hyper-V hypervisor to virtualize and protect critical system files and volatile memory. Later in the chapter you'll find out about Credential Guard; Credential Guard virtualizes Local Security Authority (LSA) memory to protect cached credentials against theft.
>
> At first blush, Device Guard may remind you of AppLocker, at least in terms of its focus on application whitelisting. The Microsoft best practices are in flux on this subject, but as of this writing they suggest using Device Guard for your most restrictive application whitelisting, and consider AppLocker for fine-tuning code execution/application restrictions in your organization.

Creating code integrity policy rules

Code integrity policies define the actual application whitelist that is enforced on the target node. Microsoft' suggested workflow involves creating "golden" server and desktop workstation images that contain all the signed software and components that are allowed by the policy.

Note that a Windows Server 2016 or Windows 10 computer can have only one code integrity policy at a time; this means that you'll be spending perhaps the majority of your time testing and tweaking your code integrity policies to get them right at deployment time. The default directory path and filename of a code integrity policy is C:\Windows\System32\CodeIntegrity\SIPolicy.p7b.

Code integrity policies include one or more policy rules that specify "meta" code integrity policy options such as audit mode or whether you need User-Mode Code Integrity (UMCI) enabled.

For instance, you can run the following PowerShell one-liner to enable UMCI to an existing code integrity policy:

```
Set-RuleOption -FilePath 'D:\cipolicies\testpolicy.xml' -Option 0
```

By contrast, code integrity file rules specify the level at which applications are identified and trusted by Device Guard. The following code integrity file rule levels should largely be familiar to you if you've already studied AppLocker from earlier in the chapter.

- **Hash**   Version-specific, so you'll need to update the policy for every new app version
- **FileName**   Matches on the binary executable's file name
- **SignedVersion**   Allows any app from the specified publisher to run
- **Publisher**   Whitelists apps that are signed from a given certificate authority (CA)
- **FilePublisher**   Trusts specific files from an approved publisher
- **WHQL**   Used to trust Windows kernel binaries
- **WHQLFilePublisher**   Specifies that binary code must be certified by Windows Hardware Quality Labs (WHQL); this rule pertains to device drivers

As you can see, Device Guard offers far more flexibility over application whitelisting rules than do AppLocker policies.

From a "bird's eye" perspective, let's run through the highest-level steps for deploying code integrity policies:

1. Prepare a "golden" computer. Make sure that your reference server and workstation computers have been scanned for malware prior to defining the code integrity policy. Code integrity use XML as its source, but are converted to a binary format upon creation.

2. From an elevated PowerShell session, run NewCIPolicy To Create A New Code Integrity Policy whose file rules are picked up by a thorough system scan.

3. Use the ConvertFromCIPolicy cmdlet to convert the code integrity policy from plain-text to binary format. Microsoft best practice suggests that you use a public or Active Directory Certificate Services (AD CS) code-signing certificate to sign your code integrity policies.

4. Audit the code integrity policy thoroughly before applying the policy in production. For instance, you can use local Group Policy on a testing computer and enable the Deploy Code Integrity Policy Group Policy setting from the path Computer Configuration\Policies\Administrative Templates\System\Device Guard. The policy requires that you enter the path to your Code Integrity policy file as shown in Figure 1-29.

5. Restart the target system and check the event log for results. Specifically, code integrity policy events are written to the Applications and Services Logs\Microsoft\Windows\CodeIntegrity\Operational event log.

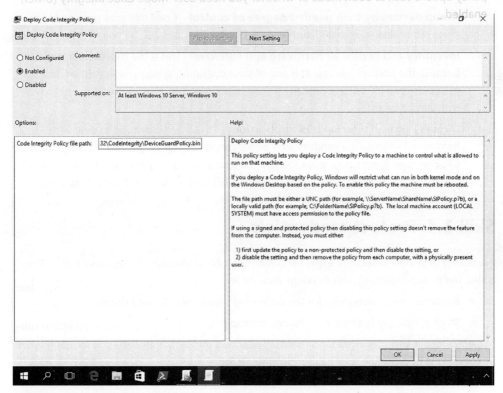

FIGURE 1-22 As you'd expect, we use Group Policy to deploy a Device Guard code integrity policy

Catalog files

The truth of the matter is that it's likely that not all your system hardware and software components are digitally signed. Catalog files serve an important function in this regard. Specifically, you can store your application whitelisting exceptions in catalog files and Device Guard whitelists the catalog entries the same way it does with ordinary signed code.

Of course the preferred option is to have 100 percent of your supported software signed, but again, we're living in the real world here.

You use the PackageInspector.exe command-line tool, which is included by default in Windows Server 2016, to create catalog files for your unsigned apps.

High-level overview of the Device Guard deployment workflow

Device Guard is far too complex a technology to cover in just a few Exam Ref pages. To make sure you have the big picture and are equipped to answer associated questions on your 70-744 exam, let's walk through the Device Guard process:

1. **Make sure the system meets all Device Guard requirements**   As has become a theme for this chapter, server hardening begins with qualified hardware. Specifically, we need a system that can perform virtualization-based security (VBS).

2. **Group devices by their needed degree of control**   Code integrity policies are anything but a "one size fits all" solution.

3. **Inventory and review all hardware and software**   This is the most important step because the bottom line is that if any of your operating system, device driver, or application components aren't digitally signed by a CA you trust, they aren't going to work with Device Guard.

4. **Digitally sign all internal LOB applications**   It can be frustrating to deal with hardware and software vendors who either cannot digitally sign their code by a trusted CA. However, there's no excuse for your company to digitally sign all "homegrown" applications and services, even with an internal AD CS public key infrastructure (PKI).

Skill 1.4: Protect credentials

According to Windows security expert and Microsoft Most Valuable Professional (MVP) Sami Laiho, the two immutable laws of system security are:

- BitLocker Drive encryption for the operating system and all data drives
- Strict adherence to the least privilege principle

Sami's idea is that if you grant administrative access unnecessarily, then you defeat the first BitLocker rule because the user can simply disable the feature.

The least privilege rule, which centers on users and administrators logging onto their workstations with standard user privileges instead of administrative credentials, is perhaps more important in Windows Client than on Windows Server. After all, default user rights policy on any Windows Server computer prohibits all but administrators from interactive logon anyway.

Nonetheless, systems administrators should consider features such as Credential Guard for our servers because under normal circumstances Windows stores credentials in user-mode Local Security Authority Subsystem Service (LSASS) process memory.

Unfortunately, community tools such as Mimikatz can attack LSASS memory and steal NTLM hashes and/or Kerberos tickets; these are known as "pass the hash" or "pass the ticket" attacks, respectively.

Credential Guard is a Windows Server 2016 feature that is actually a subset of the Device Guard feature we examined earlier in the chapter. We cover how to use Credential Guard to make pass-the-hash attacks nearly impossible for an attacker on our infrastructure servers.

This section covers how to:

- Determine requirements for Credential Guard
- Configure Credential Guard using Group Policy, WMI, and the Command Prompt
- Implement NTLM blocking

Determine requirements for Credential Guard

You may be aware that there's been User Account Control (UAC) and file/folder virtualization since Windows Server 2008. This type of virtualization protects key areas of the Windows file system and registry against unauthorized access.

Credential guard uses what Microsoft calls "virtualization-based security" to store NTLM and Kerberos secrets in an isolated Local Security Authority (LSA) process. Take a look at Figure 1-23.

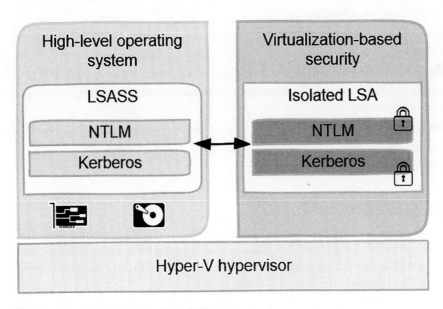

FIGURE 1-23 Credential Guard conceptual diagram

In Figure 1-23 we see a Windows computer on which Credential Guard is not configured. Notice that the NTLM and Kerberos secrets are stored in user-mode memory inside the LSASS process. This makes the credentials accessible to attackers seeking to elevate their privilege with hacking tools such as Mimikatz.

On the right we see the same Windows system, this time with Credential Guard enabled. Thanks to the underlying Hyper-V hypervisor, the NTLM and Kerberos secrets are stored in an isolated, protected LSA process.

> ***NOTE* DERIVED CREDENTIALS**
>
> If you check the Microsoft TechNet literature, you'll see references to "derived credentials," and an explanation of how Credential Guard protects them. According to the National Institute of Standards and Technology (NIST), derived credentials refers to cryptographic identities (usernames and password hashes, most commonly) that are cached on a mobile device. For our purposes, we can consider domain derived credentials as the NTLM hashes and/or Kerberos tickets that Windows caches by default in the user-mode LSASS process.

Credential Guard system requirements

It's interesting because the system requirements for Credential Guard actually harken back to some of the features we discussed earlier in this chapter:

- **64-bit operating system**   This isn't a problem for Windows Server, but could be an issue for Windows Client devices.

- **UEFI firmware, v2.3.1 or higher**   UEFI is necessary when relying upon Secure Boot for Credential Guard.

- **CPU virtualization extensions**   For Intel processors, this is VT-x. For AMD processors, it's AMD-V. Either way, the extensions must support Second Level Address Translation (SLAT) as well.

- **TPM v1.2 or 2.0**   The TPM is required to store the Credential Guard encryption keys.

Also, you need to run Windows 10 Enterprise Edition if you plan to enable Credential Guard on Windows Client systems.

Configure Credential Guard

Assuming your server supports the technology, you're ready to deploy Credential Guard. Do this by enabling the Turn On Virtualization Based Security Group Policy settings in the path Computer Configuration\Policies\Administrative Templates\System\Device Guard. A screen shot of the policy is shown in Figure 1-24.

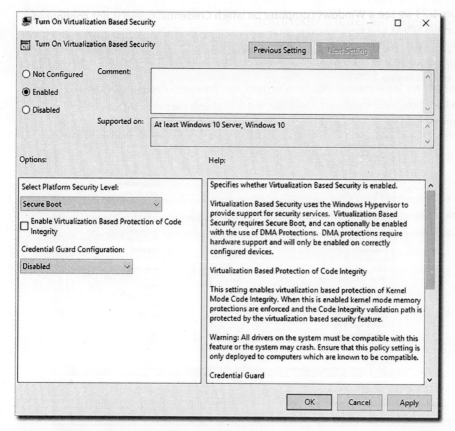

FIGURE 1-24 We enable Credential Guard in Group Policy

The following options are available in this Group Policy setting:

- **Platform Security Level** Remember that Credential Guard relies partially on hardware (TPM) and firmware (UEFI) security. You can use "only" Secure Boot with Credential Guard, or you can optionally enable Direct Memory Access (DMA) protection. DMA protection provides a countermeasure against side channel attacks against the system's DMA bus.

- **Virtualization Based Protection of Code Integrity** This option is related to Device Guard, discussed earlier in this chapter.

- **Credential Guard Configuration** If you choose Enabled Without Lock, then Credential Guard can be disabled remotely via Group Policy. If you choose Enabled With UEFI Lock, then Credential Guard can be disabled only via interactive logon and never remotely.

Verifying Credential Guard operation

Credential Guard is largely a "set it and forget it," proactive security solution. One easy way to verify its presence on a Windows Server or Client system is to open the System Information tool, as shown in Figure 1-25.

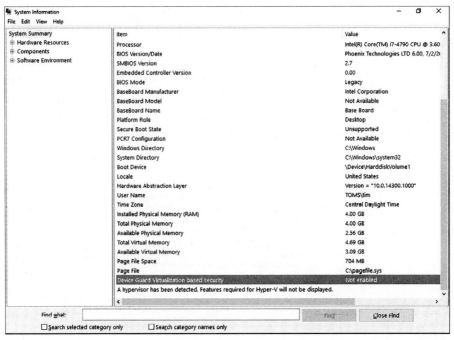

FIGURE 1-25 The System Information tool verifies whether Credential Guard is active on the system

In System Information, The Device Guard Virtualization Based Security item shows as Running, and the Device Guard Security Services Running item lists Credential Guard on a fully enabled system.

> **NOTE MICROSOFT SYSTEM INFORMATION POWER USER TIPS**
>
> In my experience, the fastest way to open the System Information tool is to press **Windows key + R** to open the Run dialog, type **msinfo32**, and press Enter.
>
> As you would expect, the System Information tool displays local system data by default. Connect to a remote system by open the View menu and selecting Remote Computer.

Credential Guard via WMI and Command Prompt

Windows Management Instrumentation (WMI) is Microsoft's implementation of the Distributed Management Task Force (DMTF) Common Information Model (CIM) system configuration standard. That's a mouthful of acronyms for sure!

You can run a WMI/CIM query to verify whether Credential Guard is enabled on a target system. Open an elevated Windows PowerShell session and run the following command:

```
Get-CimInstance -Namespace root/Microsoft/Windows/DeviceGuard -ClassName Win32_
DeviceGuard
```

Specifically, in the above output look for the `VirtualizationBasedSecurityStatus` property; a value of 0 means Credential Guard is disabled, and a value of 1 signifies the feature is enabled.

Microsoft Learning's inclusion of "command prompt" to this 70-744 exam objective refers to Windows PowerShell. Speaking of which, remember that in a domain environment you can run the above (or any) PowerShell command on any number of remote systems.

For example, the following PowerShell "one-liner" prompts the administrator for credentials and runs the previously-given WMI/CIM query against five remote servers simultaneously. Now that's administrative power!

```
Invoke-Command -ComputerName server1, server2, server3, server4, server5 -ScriptBlock
{ Get-CimInstance -Namespace root/Microsoft/Windows/DeviceGuard -ClassName Win32_
DeviceGuard } -Credential (Get-Credential)
```

Credential Guard - Areas of Weakness

Credential Guard provides an additional layer of security to our Windows Server 2016 systems, particularly in protecting derived domain credentials against memory attacks, but no security solution is infallible. For your 70-744 exam success and beyond, you need to know which scenarios are not protected by Credential Guard. Here's the list of stored credentials and attack types that are unaffected by Credential Guard status:

- Local accounts and Microsoft accounts (Credential Guard pertains to on-premises Active Directory domain credentials only)
- Third-party credential management software
- Key loggers
- Physical attacks
- Malware that leverages the currently logged on user's credentials (another argument in favor of implementing least privilege always)
- Digest and CredSSP credentials

Implement NTLM blocking

Many Windows systems administrators (maybe even you) have allowed the antiquated NT LAN Manager (NTLM) authentication protocol to exist in your environment simply because it's easier that way.

After all, NTLM doesn't have the delegated credential headaches inherent in the Kerberos authentication protocol. On the other hand, we must remember that NTLM, especially NTLM vX, is an old, flawed protocol that doesn't contribute to acceptable authentication security in most 21st century IT environments.

In a nutshell, NTLM blocking is nothing more than preventing NTLM from being used for authentication in your domain, period.

The Group Policy settings you'll want to consider for your domain controllers are:

- Network Security: Restrict NTLM: NTLM Authentication In This Domain
- Network Security: Restrict NTLM: Incoming NTLM Traffic
- Network Security: Restrict NTLM: Outgoing NTLM Traffic To Remote Servers
- Network Security: Restrict NTLM: Audit NTLM Authentication In This Domain
- Network Security: Restrict NTLM: Audit Incoming NTLM Traffic

All of the previous settings are found in the Group Policy Path Computer Configuration\Policies\Windows Settings\Security Settings\Local Policies\Security Options.

Please don't simply dive into blocking NTLM authentication on your network, erroneously concluding "Active Directory uses Kerberos, so we can dump NTLM." Not so fast. Please perform due diligence and audit all of your line-of-business and network infrastructure services to find "show stopper" NTLM dependencies.

The previously-listed auditing policies represent an excellent first step in evaluating the impact of removing NTLM from your application and service authentication profiles may have on your business.

According to Microsoft documentation and best practices, it typically takes a business at least six months of testing before "pulling the trigger" on production NTLM blocking.

Skill 1.5: Create security baselines

A security baseline in Microsoft nomenclature is a standard security configuration to which you can compare with other systems and enforce compliance. Although Windows Power-Shell Desired State Configuration (DSC) is becoming an increasingly popular configuration management and enforcement technology, as of this writing Group Policy remains the gold standard for server hardening and security configuration.

Security baselines make it easier for your company not only to maintain compliance with any governmental and/or industry regulations is subject to, but also allows you to perform rich reporting and auditing.

To those points, Microsoft publishes a free tool called Security Compliance Manager (SCM). SCM is a solutions accelerator that simplifies the analysis, creation, comparison, and deployment of Group Policy-based security templates.

Install and Configure Security Compliance Manager

You'll need to download and install SCM v4.0 to configure Windows Server 2016 and Windows 10 computers. Note that you don't have to install SCM on a server; you can perform all your security baseline configuration work from your Windows 10 administrative workstation. The SCM 4.0 installation executable weighs in at approximately 130 MB.

Installing SCM v4.0

Perform a search engine query for "Download Security Compliance Manager 4" to visit the Microsoft Download Center and download the software. Then start the installer with elevated credentials and follow these steps to complete the process:

1. If your system doesn't have the Microsoft Visual C++ 2010 x86 redistributable package installed, let the SCM installer download it and apply the package for you.

2. The .NET Framework 3.5 redistributable also needs to be installed. However, the SCM installer can't automatically do that for you, so you'll have to use Server Manager or the Windows Features Control Panel as necessary to fulfill this prerequisite.

3. On the installer Welcome page, make sure to leave the option Always Check For SCM And Baseline Updates checked. The SCM product team updates Microsoft's security baseline library regularly.

4. Accept the license agreement terms.

5. The SCM tool is backed by a SQL Server database. Thus, you can either point the Microsoft Security Compliance Manager Setup wizard to an existing local or remote SQL Server instance or let the installer deploy a SQL Server 2008 Express Edition instance on the local computer.

6. After the installation completes, the SCM MMC console appears as shown in Figure 1-26.

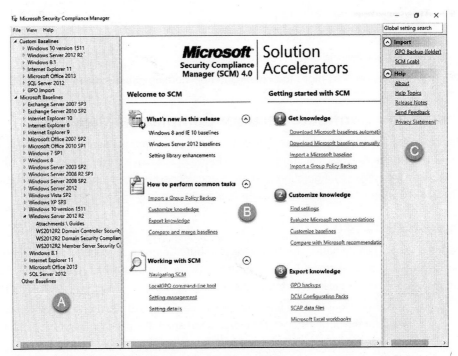

FIGURE 1-26 Security Compliance Manager (SCM) console

Take another look at Figure 1-26 and let me briefly explain the user interface:

- **A. Baseline Library Pane**   Here we have all available security baselines, both the read/only copies from Microsoft as well as our read/write copies
- **B. Details Pane**   Here you can learn how to use the tool or delve into a particular security baseline
- **C. Actions Pane**   Here we can import security baselines either in GPO Backup for Cabinet (.cab) file formats

Configuring SCM 4.0 and Viewing Baselines

Now that we have SCM installed on our administrative workstation or infrastructure server, our first order of business is to download the latest security template versions from the SCM development team at Microsoft.

Click File | Check For Updates and review any available security templates. As of this writing, the Windows Server 2016 templates are in draft mode. However, several Windows Server 2012 R2 and Windows 10 templates exist and are available for download.

From the SCM Baseline Library pane, go ahead and double-click one of the available baselines. In Figure 1-27 you can see the contents of the Windows Server 2012 R2 Domain Controller Security Compliance baseline.

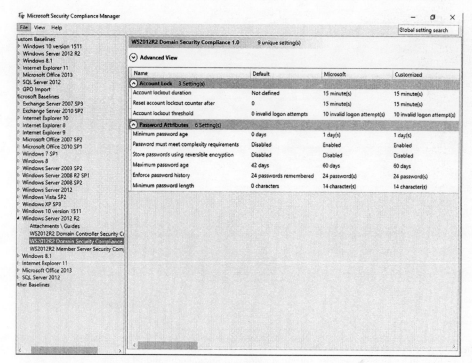

FIGURE 1-27 Viewing the contents of a security baseline

Once again, have a closer look at Figure 1-34, paying attention to the three columns in the Details pane. For each Group Policy setting, three states exist:

- **Default** These are the settings that ship with Windows Server out of the proverbial box.
- **Microsoft** These are the Microsoft-recommended settings as defined in the current template.
- **Customized** These are the settings contained in your customized version of the template, if you have one.

The SCM user interface is cluttered, to put it kindly. You'll find a wealth of security guidance and additional details concerning the GPO security settings surfaced in each baseline.

For example, click to select a GPO policy setting. As shown in Figure 1-28, we expanded the Minimum password age policy, and then clicked Setting Details to expose additional information. What we love about this is that (a) you see vulnerability and potential impact insights; and (b) you can view which underlying registry value is being modified. That's useful!

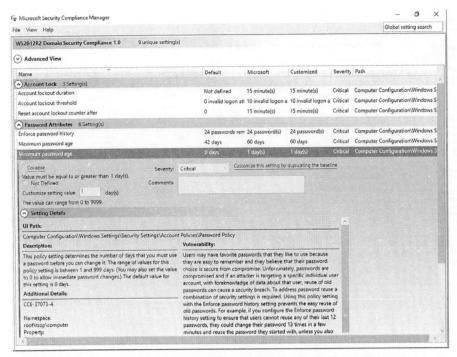

FIGURE 1-28 Examining a baseline policy setting provides additional educational details

You can use the arrow buttons to collapse policy settings. Observe that you cannot actually change baseline security settings in this view; we'll cover how to create your own baselines in the next section.

Create and import security baselines

In order to develop your own security baselines, you must duplicate one of the Microsoft read-only baselines. One easy way to do this is to expose a security setting and click the Customize this setting by duplicating the baseline hyperlink.

You now have full read-write access to all policy settings contained within the baseline. In Figure 1-29, you can see that your own baselines show up in SCM under the appropriately named Custom Baselines category (annotation A), and that all baseline security settings are unlocked for editing (annotation B).

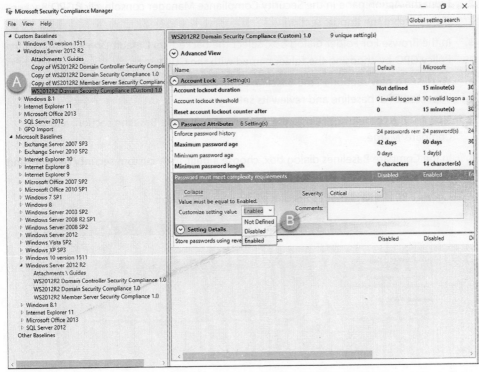

FIGURE 1-29 You can modify your custom security baselines to your heart's content

In case you're wondering, the "big picture" here is that we can use the Microsoft-provided security baselines as starting points for developing our own baselines. Next, we'll want to consider how to compare the security settings in an already-deployed GPO with one of the built-in or one of our custom baselines.

Import and compare security baselines

In the following procedure we'll export our domain's Default Domain Controllers GPO by using Windows PowerShell, import the settings into SCM, and then compare the deployed GPO's security settings with that of a stored baseline.

1. Open an elevated PowerShell console and run the following command. Of course, you need to customize the commands I provide to suit your environment:

   ```
   Backup-GPO -Guid 6ac1786c-016f-11d2-945f-00c04fb984f9 -Path c:\backups
   ```

   By the way, you can run the following command to retrieve a list of all domain GPOs and fetch the appropriate globally unique identifiers (GUIDs):

   ```
   Get-GPO -All -Domain contoso.local
   ```

2. From the Action pane in the Security Compliance Manager console, click GPO Backup (Folder) from the Import section.

3. In the Browse For Folder dialog box, select the backed-up Default Domain Controllers Policy GPO by choosing the folder named with the GUID.

4. You'll see a new section in the Baseline Library tree called GPO Import; find your newly imported GPO baseline and review its settings.

5. Now for the comparison: Go to the Action pane, find the Baseline section, and click Compare/Merge.

6. In the Compare Baselines dialog box, choose a built-in or custom security baseline and click OK.

7. Figure 1-30 displays the results of a particular comparison.

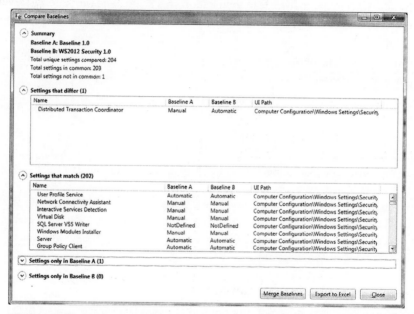

FIGURE 1-30 Here we compare the security settings in a deployed domain GPO with settings stored in a Microsoft-provided security baseline

8. If you have Microsoft Excel available, click the Export To Excel button to send all the comparison findings to a spreadsheet for offline analysis.

Remember that the built-in baselines are read-only; in order to perform a merge operation, you first need to select a custom baseline, and then use the Compare/Merge command to point to your imported GPO or another custom baseline. In this case you'll see an additional Merge Baselines button in the Compare Baselines dialog. The merged baseline is stored in the Custom Baselines section of the baseline library under a new name.

To recap, we now understand how to import an existing GPO into SCM and store it as a baseline. We also know how to perform a comparison and potentially a merge between two read-write baselines, and how to export that comparison to an Excel workbook.

Our final order of business is deploying custom security baselines to both domain-joined and workgroup servers.

Deploy configurations to domain and non-domain-joined servers

The most common method to deploy a custom security baseline is to export that baseline as a GPO backup folder. Select the appropriate baseline in the SCM baseline library, navigate to the Action pane, and click GPO Backup (Folder) under the Export section.

You'll have a GUID folder that you can then import to a standalone (workgroup) server or a domain-joined computer by using either Windows PowerShell or the Group Policy Management Console (GPMC).

For instance, use the following procedure to import settings from an exported SCM baseline into a Windows Server 2016 domain controller's GPO store:

1. Open the Group Policy Management Console and create a new GPO to hold the baseline settings

2. Right-click the new GPO and select Import Settings from the shortcut menu. This opens the Import Settings Wizard.

3. In the Backup Location screen, click Browse to locate the GPO backup folder you created in the Security Compliance Manager tool. If the target folder has multiple GPO backups, then select the proper baseline from the list.

4. On the Migrating References screen, you'll have a chance either to import the baseline settings as-is or use a migration table to customize references to security principals or specific file paths in the target GPO.

5. Click Finish to complete the import.

In the Export section you'll also see references to SCCM, DCM, SCM and SCAP. What do these acronyms mean?

- **SCCM**   Microsoft System Center Configuration Manager. This is Microsoft's enterprise configuration management platform.

- **DCM**   Desired Configuration Management. This package format is easily consumable by SCCM 2012 R2.

- **SCM**   Security Compliance Manager. Here you can back a baseline up in a format that is natively understandable by an instance of SCM running on another computer in your environment.

- **SCAP**   Security Content Automation Protocol. This is an Extensible Markup Language (XML)-based data stream that is managed by the US National Institute of Standards and Technology (NIST).

LocalGPO

LocalGPO.wsf is a Windows Script File that is a useful "Swiss Army Knife" for deploying SCM-created security baselines, especially to non-domain-joined servers.

The first order of business is to actually find the tool. Microsoft deprecated the LocalGPO.wsf that so many admins know and love in favor of the LGPO.exe executable. You can download LGPO.exe from the Microsoft Security Guidance blog: *http://timw.info/lgpo*.

> **NOTE ADD LGPO.EXE TO YOUR SEARCH PATH**
>
> To make it as easy as possible to access the LGPO.exe executable from wherever you are in a command-prompt session, you should edit your system's PATH environment variable to include the path to the script.
>
> To add the path value persistently by using the built-in SetX utility, open an administrative PowerShell console run the following statement, editing the path as appropriate on your system:
>
> ```
> setx PATH "$env:path;e:\lgpo" -m
> ```
>
> Assuming you've created a GPO backup folder from the SCM console, you're ready to import the baseline settings into the local security settings of a workgroup server. The tool is portable, so you can simply copy over the tool along with the GPO backup to the target server.

Next, fire up an administrative PowerShell console and run the following command:

```
.\LGPO.exe /g '<GPO_backup_folder_path>'
```

There's a lot more you can do with LGPO.exe; run the command .\LGPO.exe /? to get on-screen help.

Chapter summary

- It's true that BitLocker Drive Encryption as well as Encrypting File System have a strong use case in protecting corporate laptops. After all, seemingly countless laptop computers are stolen from airports around the world. Nonetheless, in this chapter we made the case that implementing BitLocker and EFS on our servers strongly improves the security posture of those machines, so long as these controls are added in addition to physical security and least privilege.

- The baseline server configuration for BitLocker involves an up-to-date UEFI firmware as well as an on-board TPM chip. These features support Secure Boot, which protects the server's startup environment against the insertion of unauthorized code.

- BitLocker is deployed largely through Group Policy, and can be implemented in the absence of the TPM chip to support legacy, down level hardware and Windows Server versions.

- Microsoft offers administrators many options for recovering a lost BitLocker unlock password. These options include key/password escrow in Active Directory and self-service key retrieval by using the Microsoft BitLocker Administration and Monitoring (MBAM) toolset.

- While BitLocker encrypts entire disk volumes, EFS provides a granular method for encrypting files and folders.

- Because EFS is accessible to standard users and uses self-signed encryption/decryption certificates by default, it's important that an internal PKI be brought online to help centralize and orchestrate EFS key distribution and management.

- Data recovery agents (DRAs) can be nominated in Active Directory to give administrators the ability to decrypt user files in emergency situations.

- Windows Server Update Services (WSUS) behaves the same way in Windows Server 2016 as it did in Windows Server 2012 R2 (and Windows Server 2008 R2, for that matter).

- WSUS can be deployed in myriad ways, including as part of a System Center Configuration Manager solution, stand-alone server, or as part of an upstream/downstream replicated partnership.

- WSUS installation involves one key choice (whether to use WID or full SQL Server) and several options, including upstream partners, update languages, and update product classifications.

- Day-to-day WSUS administration involves creating and managing computer groups and approving updates. The configuration is split between Group Policy and work in the Update Services console.

- The WSUS console includes several pre-built reports to give administrators insight into WSUS operations.

- Microsoft offers plenty of free WSUS troubleshooting guidance online.

- Windows Defender is Microsoft's free and eminently capable antimalware client. You can manage Windows Defender by using Group Policy or System Center, and its use is encouraged even if you choose to implement Device Guard or Credential Guard.

- Windows Update Server Services (WSUS) is a Windows Server 2016 server role that makes it easier to screen, test, stage, and deploy Windows Updates and security updates.

- AppLocker was Microsoft's first foray into application whitelisting. To remind you, whitelisting is the exact opposite of application blacklisting, which was the method used by Group Policy software restriction policies.

- Device Guard is a combination of hardware and software features that completely lock down the executable code that is allowed to run on a server or client system.

- Code integrity policies form the application whitelisting rulesets used with Device Guard. Catalog files allow you to trust drivers, applications, or services that are unsigned but still approved by your organization.

- Control Flow Guard is a .NET Framework development feature that strengthens a Windows desktop application's relationship with system memory.

- Credential Guard relies upon the Hyper-V hypervisor to store sensitive credentials in a secure LSASS process and thereby prevent credential theft.

- Although ordinary domain users cannot log onto Windows Server 2016 interactively, the possibility still exists that administrative credentials can be captured via network attacks against in-memory LSASS credentials.

- Credential Guard is a subset of Device Guard that focuses on the protection of cached domain credentials.

- You configure Credential Guard through Group Policy, and can verify its status via Windows PowerShell, WMI queries, and the Microsoft System Information tool.

- Because NTLM is an old and largely unsecure authentication protocol, Microsoft makes it possible for administrators to block NTLM traffic in a workgroup or domain.

- NTLM blocking is configured via Group Policy.

- The best practice suggestion is to use the NTLM auditing Group Policy settings first to ensure that blocking NTLM entirely won't break any of your applications and services.

- Security Compliance Manager (SCM) is a database-backed desktop application the aim of which is to simplify the generation, comparison, deployment, and reporting of Group Policy security settings.

- SCM includes a vast library of Microsoft-provided security baselines; you must duplicate them before you can make changes.

- You can import GPO backups into SCM and create new security baselines from them.

- You can export a security baseline in a number of different formats, including Microsoft Excel, GPO backup, or SCCM DCM.

- Baseline deployment to domain servers is accomplished most easily by (a) exporting the baseline from SCM as a GPO backup folder; and (b) importing the settings into a new or existing GPO in the domain Group Policy Management Console (GPMC).

- Baseline deployment to workgroup servers is accomplished most easily by using the LGPO.exe command-line utility. LGPO is the successor to the deprecated LocalGPO.wsf script that many administrators found so useful in previous Windows Server versions.

Thought Experiment

In this thought experiment, demonstrate your skills and knowledge of the topics covered in this chapter. You can find answers in the next section.

You are a security architect for Tailspin Toys, a children's toy manufacturer based in Nashville, TN. The corporate network is organized as a single Active Directory domain in which 60 percent of its infrastructure servers run Windows Server 2012 R2, and 40 percent run Windows Server 2016.

You have been asked by the operations team to help them choose a new hardware server that runs Windows Server 2016 Datacenter Edition and serves as a Hyper-V host. The VMs hosted on this server contains sensitive data that must be protected in memory, at rest, and in transit to comply with government regulation and SLAs.

The operations team members have three specific questions for you:

1. What specific hardware features should we look for in a secure hardware host?

2. How can we integrate this new server, which exists on an isolated subnet, into our existing WSUS infrastructure?

3. What are the mitigating factors in choosing Device Guard above AppLocker?

Thought experiment answers

This section contains the solution to the thought experiment. Each answer explains why the answer choice is correct.

1. Above all else, you should ensure that the hardware host is current enough to run UEFI in native mode, and that the motherboard has a TPM 2.0 microchip. You can then take advantage of Secure Boot and lay the groundwork for BitLocker Drive Encryption, Device Guard, and Credential Guard.

2. WSUS allows you to transfer approved updates to removable media. You can then install the updates on a second WSUS located on an isolated subnet, and then deploy on any hosts on that subnet. Of course, this solution requires at least WSUS servers.

3. AppLocker and Device Guard are both application whitelisting technologies. As such, both require a great deal of pre-planning to make sure you don't inadvertently block applications from users who should be able to run them. That said, AppLocker presents a more flexible and easy-to-use solution than Device Guard, at least as of this writing. Recall that Windows PowerShell is the only way to create Device Guard policies, and those policies can be created only by scanning a "golden" system that is set up the way you want other compliant systems to be. Device Guard has the additional complexity that all applications in the policy scope must be digitally signed, which isn't always possible for all your drivers and applications. The catalog file is a workaround to handle unsigned apps, however. As stated earlier in the chapter, both Device Guard and AppLocker can be deployed together. In this architecture, you rely upon Device Guard principally, and then use AppLocker to customize application access.

## CHAPTER 2

Secure a Virtualization Infrastructure

Matt works as a datacenter fabric engineer for Contoso, a premier datacenter service provider located in the southeast United States. Matt is a disgruntled employee who plans to resign from his position next week after performing some activities he's planned for the past several months.

First, Matt logs into a rack-mounted Hyper-V host that contains virtual machines owned by a local health care firm. He targets a virtual domain controller, stops the VM, and copies its VHD to Matt's trusty USB thumb drive. He figures, correctly, that the health care firm has several domain controllers and won't notice this virtual DC being offline for one hour.

Second, Matt copies the VHD to his personal laptop, where he uses community hacking software to launch an offline attack on the client's Active Directory database.

Third, Matt logs into one of the client's file server VMs and injects some malware that scans the server's file system for sensitive data and transmits it to Matt's offshore FTP account.

After all is said and done, Matt "owns" sensitive data from one of Contoso's most important clients, and he has a back door to their information systems, available for Matt's use whenever he wishes.

This is a nightmarish scenario, isn't it? The sad fact is that it reflects reality. In this chapter we examine new Windows Server 2016 features that remediate the problem of separation of duties between fabric and workload administrators. Specifically, we dive into Microsoft's Guarded Fabric solution, which protects Hyper-V VM workloads against virtualization host administrators. The days of the hardware host having full, "keys to the kingdom" access to all guest VMS are rapidly coming to an end.

Skills in this chapter:

- Implement a Guarded Fabric solution
- Implement shielded and encryption-supported VMs

Skill 2.1: Implement a Guarded Fabric solution

In Microsoft nomenclature, a Guarded Fabric is a Hyper-V virtualization infrastructure that provides granular, delegated access to all guest virtual machines (VMs). The key to understanding Microsoft's vision of the Guarded Fabric is to grasp the separation of concerns between fabric and workload administrators.

In information technology nomenclature, *fabric* refers not to cloth, but to computing hardware that functions together in order to accomplish a business goal. For example, a stack of Hyper-V hosts mounted in a datacenter server rack is a good example of a fabric.

More to that point, a fabric administrator is a systems administrator who is charged with the maintenance of the fabric's constituent hardware and system software. In a Hyper-V context, this normally allows the fabric administrator to perform actions like:

- Start, restart, and service the host hardware
- Start and stop the host's virtual machines (VMs)

Notice that a fabric administrator can very well have no right to actually logging into those hosted VMs. That job role is normally reserved for the workload administrator. In IT, a *workload* refers to the type of work a computer is given to do. For instance, a Hyper-V server is called a virtualization host. You have other physical or virtual servers that run Active Directory, SQL Server, SharePoint Server, and so forth.

It's true that in some businesses the fabric administrators and the workload administrators are the same people. Guarded Fabric isn't appropriate for those scenarios. Instead, let's examine how to create a hard security boundary line between those administrative roles to help your business remain in compliance with any governmental and/or industry regulations and SLAs you could be subject to.

> **This section covers how to:**
> - Install and configure the Host Guardian Service
> - Configure admin- and TPM-trusted attestation
> - Configure Key Protection Service using HGS
> - Migrate shielded VMs to other guarded hosts
> - Troubleshoot guarded hosts

Install and configure the Host Guardian Service

Building a trusted fabric for Hyper-V services involves deploying a Host Guardian Service (HGS) cluster. HGS is a new server role in Windows Server 2016. Figure 2-1 demonstrates its general workflow.

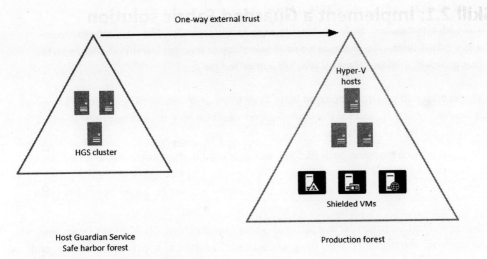

FIGURE 2-1 Guarded Fabric conceptual diagram

In Figure 2-1, observe the following points:

- The Host Guardian Service (HGS) cluster exists in a separate Active Directory forest called a *safe harbor* forest. This creates a strong security and isolation boundary between the HGS cluster and your production forest.

- You need to manually create a one-way external trust between the HGS forest and the production forest. The "resources trust accounts" directionality of the trust signifies that the HGS forest is at least theoretically willing to trust user and computer accounts from the production forest (more on that later).

Preparing your HGS nodes

Technically, the HGS server role provides two services that enable guarded hosts (also known as HGS clients) to run shielded virtual machines. For now, consider a shielded VM to be a protected VM; we'll formally delve into shielded VMs specifically later in the chapter.

What are the two services?

- **Attestation** The Host Guardian Service unlocks a shielded VM only if the identity and integrity of the VM has been verified.

- **Key protection** These are the encryption keys that enable the shielded VM to transition between the encrypted and unencrypted states.

We recommend that you deploy at least three physical or virtual HGS servers to provide high availability. The reason for this is simple: you won't be able to work with any shielded VMs unless the HGS cluster is available.

As you'll see in a moment, each HGS server becomes a domain controller in a new, separate, "safe harbor" Active Directory Domain Services (AD DS) forest. For this reason, your hosts need to be configured for workgroup networking and not be a member of any other AD domain.

We do all Host Guardian Service setup and configuration through Windows PowerShell, so make sure that you're logged onto the prospective HGS server as a local administrator; and that you've started an elevated Windows PowerShell console session.

Installing the HGS server role

You need only a single line of PowerShell to install the Host Guardian Service server role:

```
Install-WindowsFeature -Name HostGuardianServiceRole -IncludeManagementTools -Restart
```

When using the Restart switch parameter, you definitely need to restart the server after running InstallWindowsFeature. You'll also observe that PowerShell installs the Active Directory Domain Services, Failover Clustering, Web Server, and BitLocker Drive Encryption server roles or features in the bargain.

Configuring the HGS server

After you verify that the new HGS node isn't already a member of an AD domain, you're ready to set up the safe harbor forest:

```
$pw = ConvertTo-SecureString -String 'P@$$word!' -AsPlainText
Install-HgsServer -HgsDomainName 'safe.local' -SafeModeAdministratorPassword $pw
-Restart
```

When the server is back from its second reboot, you'll have a brand-new domain controller in a brand-new forest. Make sure you log into the HGS server by using the new credentials (in our case, the username is safe\administrator) and not local creds.

Configure admin and TPM-trusted attestation

Recall that the Host Guardian Service involves two services: attestation and encryption key transport. Take a close look at Figure 2-2, in which we explain in further detail how the Guarded Fabric solution works in practice.

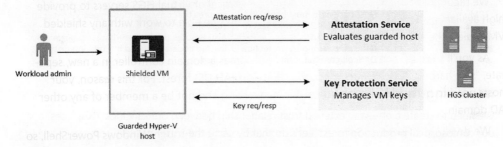

FIGURE 2-2 Guarded Fabric workflow

In Figure 2-2 you see the following:

- A workload administrator attempts to access a shielded VM, typically by using a Remote Desktop Protocol (RDP) Remote Desktop connection
- Because the VM is shielded and resides on a guarded host, the guarded Hyper-V host requests (a) host attestation; and (b) decryption keys from the HGS cluster
- Depending on how attestation is configured, the guarded host is either allowed or not allowed to unlock the shielded VM
- If the shielded VM is approved for unlock, the HGS transmits the decryption keys
- The workload administrator continues his or her work as necessary

Meanwhile, the fabric (Hyper-V host) administrator is limited only to turning on or turning off the shielded VMs. In a Guarded Fabric environment, fabric administrators cannot use tools like the Virtual Machine Connection or the PowerShell Direct to interact with shielded VMs. The shielded VMs, including their BitLocker-encrypted VHD files, are strictly off-limits to fabric administrators.

Choosing an attestation method

The guarded host attestation method you choose depends upon how current your HGS hardware is, as well as your need for high security. In Table 2-1 we compare the admin-trusted attestation and TPM-trusted attestation options.

TABLE 2-1 Comparison of HGS attestation modes

Attestation mode	Properties	Host assurances
Admin-trusted	Appropriate for commodity server hardware Simpler configuration	Ensures that only Hyper-V hosts that are designated as guarded hosts can start shielded VMs Guarded hosts are placed in a special AD security group
TPM	Host hardware must have TPM v2.0 and UEFI 2.3.1 with Secure Boot enabled Offers the strongest protection Difficult configuration	Ensures that only guarded Hyper-V hosts can start shielded VMs Also ensures that guarded hosts can run only trusted code as defined in Code Integrity policies

Initializing the HGS server

We need to create a one-way external trust relationship between our safe.local HGS forest and our contoso.local production forest. Let's do that by using the trusty netdom command-line tool:

```
netdom trust safe.local /domain:contoso.local /userD:contoso\Administrator /
passwordD:P@$$w0rd /add
```

Although netdom is considered by many Windows systems administrators to be a legacy tool and you can perform the previous action by using PowerShell, I personally adhere to the mantra "Whatever works best." If you saw the cumbersome, non-intuitive PowerShell that's required to create that trust relationship, you'd understand.

We also need to ensure DNS name resolution between the production and HGS forests. Run the following PowerShell command on a DNS server in your production forest:

```
Add-DnsServerConditionalForwarderZone -Name 'safe.local' -ReplicationScope 'Forest'
-MasterServers 10.0.0.2
```

Okay, let's go back to our elevated Windows PowerShell session. We need to generate signing and encryption digital certificates for the cluster. In production you'd most likely using an Active Directory Certificate Services (AD CS) public key infrastructure (PKI). However, for test/dev/study purposes, self-signed certificates are just fine.

```
$certificatePassword = ConvertTo-SecureString -AsPlainText 'P@$$w0rd' -Force

$signingCert = New-SelfSignedCertificate -DnsName 'signing.safe.local'
Export-PfxCertificate -Cert $signingCert -Password $certificatePassword -FilePath 'C:\
signingCert.pfx'

$encryptionCert = New-SelfSignedCertificate -DnsName 'encryption.safe.local'

Export-PfxCertificate -Cert $encryptionCert -Password $certificatePassword -FilePath
'C:\encryptionCert.pfx'
```

Now, initialize the HGS server:

```
Initialize-HgsServer -LogDirectory C:\ -HgsServiceName 'HGS' -Http -TrustActiveDirectory
-SigningCertificatePath 'C:\signingCert.pfx' -SigningCertificatePassword
$certificatePassword -EncryptionCertificatePath 'C:\encryptionCert.pfx'
-EncryptionCertificatePassword $certificatePassword
```

That's a lot of code. Here are the main takeaways:

- The HgsServiceName is the host name of the Host Guardian Service cluster. Therefore, my safe.local DNS includes an entry for hgs.safe.local that refers to the cluster itself

- The TrustActiveDirectory switch signifies admin-trusted attestation; the TrustTPM switch signifies TPM-trusted attestation

- The pfx files contain the private and public keys for the certificates the cluster uses to encrypt and decrypt shielded VMs

We're using admin-trusted attestation in our test lab. Therefore, we need to work with Active Directory global security groups in both forests.

- **Production forest** We created a global security group called GuardedHostGroup that contains the hostname of our hyperv1.contoso.local Hyper-V server.

- **HGS forest** We ran the following PowerShell command to include the GuardedHost-Group to the HGS cluster's attestation group. This means that only Hyper-V hosts that reside in this group is allowed to work with shielded VMs.

```
Add-HgsAttestationHostGroup -Name 'GuardedHostGroup' -Identifier S-1-5-21-2964496017-
1673051062-3633127581-1603
```

You can obtain the security identifier (SID) of the group by running GetADGroup on one of your fabric domain controllers. Finally, you can run the following command to verify that your first HGS host is correctly set up:

```
Get-HgsTrace -RunDiagnostics
```

A result of "Pass" is what you want to see. We'll cover troubleshooting in the "Troubleshoot guarded hosts" section later in this section. For reference, Figure 2-3 shows you an example forest trust and AD security group setup.

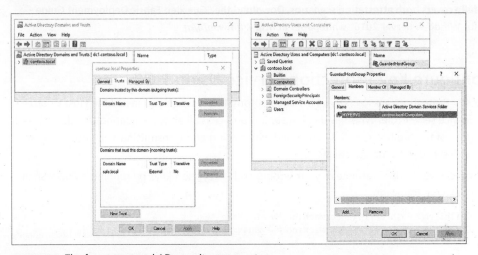

FIGURE 2-3 The forest trust and AD security group setup

A word about TPM-trusted attestation

As we've seen, in admin-trusted attestation we verify only that the guarded Hyper-V host belongs to the appropriate Active Directory security group.

TPM-trusted attestation kicks Guarded Fabric security up several notches. Specifically, we take advantage of hardware TPM, UEFI, and Secure Boot to ensure that your guarded hosts are in a "healthy" state and they run only trusted code.

The TPM-trusted attestation setup process actually involves Device Guard, which we covered in Chapter 1. Specifically, you need to capture the following information from each guarded host:

- **TPM identifier** This is an endorsement key (EK) that uniquely identifies each Hyper-V guarded host.

- **TPM baseline** Measurements of boot environment. If a single bit falls out of compliance, the guarded host is not able to start shielded VMs.

- **Code integrity policies** This is Device Guard, where we whitelist digitally signed software that the Hyper-V guarded host can run. Any software not in the whitelist simply cannot be performed.

As you'd expect, we use Windows PowerShell to capture guarded host state and transfer this data to the HGS cluster.

> **NEED MORE REVIEW? SET UP HGS IN YOUR TEST LAB**
>
> The purpose of this book is certification exam prep, not comprehensive lab procedures. To that point, the procedures given here should be considered as overviews rather than comprehensive step-by-steps.
>
> Microsoft has published an exhaustive step-by step Guarded Fabric deployment guide that fully covers both attestation scenarios. Download the "Guarded Fabric Deployment Guide for Windows Server 2016" whitepaper at *http://timw.info/gf*.

Configure Key Protection Service Using HGS

The Key Protection Service (KPS) is installed automatically when you install the Host Guardian Service server role. Whereas the Attestation service is all about validating the identity and integrity of trusted hosts, KPS is concerned with storing and transmitting encryption keys for use with shielded virtual machines.

You can verify the presence of your signing and encryption keys by running a PowerShell query like the following:

```
Get-ChildItem -Path Cert:\LocalMachine\My -DnsName *enc*
Get-ChildItem -Path Cert:\LocalMachine\My -DnsName *sign*
```

The preceding statements work fine in our environment because the DNS names of our two certs are encryption.safe.local and signing.safe.local, respectively.

Hardware Security Module (HSM)

We've seen a trend thus far that if your server hardware fabric is more capable (if you've invested capital in the latest and greatest tech), then you can step up your security benefits tremendously.

Take the hardware security module (HSM), for example. Like the TPM, this is a dedicated hardware cryptoprocessor. Unlike the TPM, however, the HSM is typically an aftermarket purchase and installation rather than a native enhancement to the system motherboard.

Let's assume you installed an HSM on an HGS host—how can you migrate your existing certificates to the HSM? You can just use the Add-HgsKeyProtectionCertificate cmdlet. You then use Set-HgsKeyProtectionCertificate to make your HSM-backed keys the default ones to be used by each node in the cluster.

Configuring the guarded host

You may be thinking that "we showed you the basics of setting up an Host Guardian Service cluster, but are you going to teach me how to set up the HGS clients?"

Yes, indeed! Let's move over to my HYPERV1.contoso.local member server. Recall that in our lab we're using admin-trusted attestation, and that our HYPERV1 host exists in a special security group considered to be trusted by the HGS cluster.

Begin by installing the Hyper-V server and Host Guardian Client server roles and rebooting the server.

```
Install-WindowsFeature -Name Hyper-V, HostGuardian -IncludeManagementTools -Restart
```

HGS makes use of Representational State Transfer (REST) application programming interfaces (APIs) to perform the attestation and key transfer operations. That's why the IIS Web Server was installed when you set up your HGS cluster.

You can retrieve your HGS cluster's attestation and key protection URLs by running Get-HgsServer on any of your HGS cluster nodes.

On the guarded host, run the following PowerShell command from an elevated console:

```
Set-HgsClientConfiguration -AttestationServerUrl 'http://hgs.safe.local/Attestation'
-KeyProtectionServerUrl 'http://hgs.safe.local/KeyProtection'
```

In the previous example, recall that hgs.safe.local is the cluster's fully qualified domain name (FQDN). Just because we have only one HGS host in our fabric doesn't mean you should do the same. According to Microsoft best practices, your HGS cluster should include at least three hosts.

To initiate an attestation attempt on the guarded host, run the following PowerShell command and take note of the output:

```
PS C:\> Get-HgsClientConfiguration
IsHostGuarded                : True
Mode                         : HostGuardianService
KeyProtectionServerUrl       : http://hgs.safe.local/KeyProtection
AttestationServerUrl         : http://hgs.safe.local/Attestation
AttestationOperationMode     : ActiveDirectory
AttestationStatus            : Passed
AttestationSubstatus         : NoInformation
```

Migrate shielded VMs to other guarded hosts

Have you ever heard the age-old expression, "You have to learn how to crawl before you can walk?" That's kind of how we feel about this particular exam objective. Why cover how to migrate shielded VMs to other guarded hosts when you haven't formally been introduced to shielded VM setup yet?

At any rate, here we go. We'll actually start from an exceedingly common scenario in which we have an unshielded Generation 2 VM running on a Hyper-V host that is presently not a guarded host, and we want the VM to move to the guarded host; and take on shielding. The process of shielding an existing VM is called grandfathering by Microsoft.

Here's the high-level procedure; again, we're taking these steps on a Hyper-V host that is not part of our Guarded Fabric. The VM in question is a Generation 2 Windows Server 2016 system named vs1.contoso.local:

1. Retrieve the HGS guardian metadata from the HGS server. The output, which allows us to create a key protector for the VM, is an extensible markup language (XML) file that needs to be copied to the non-guarded Hyper-V host. The command to do this is as follows:

    ```
    Invoke-WebRequest http://hgs.safe.local/KeyProtection/service/metadata/2014-07/
    metadata.xml -OutFile C:\HGSGuardian.xml
    ```

2. The following PowerShell command sequence, which is annotated with in-line comments, performs the shielding operation on the vs1 VM. The Key Protector that is

created contains one owner guardian, and one or more HGS guardians (thanks to the Microsoft Datacenter and Private Cloud Security team for authoring this script).

```
# vs1 is the VM name to be shielded
$VMName = 'vs1.contoso.local'

# Turn off the VM first. You can only shield a VM when it is powered off
Stop-VM -VMName $VMName

# Create an owner self-signed certificate
$Owner = New-HgsGuardian -Name 'Owner' -GenerateCertificates

# Import the HGS guardian
$Guardian = Import-HgsGuardian -Path 'C:\HGSGuardian.xml' -Name 'TestFabric' -
AllowUntrustedRoot

# Create a Key Protector, which defines the fabric that's allowed to run this
shielded VM
$KP = New-HgsKeyProtector -Owner $Owner -Guardian $Guardian -AllowUntrustedRoot

# Enable shielding on the VM
Set-VMKeyProtector -VMName $VMName -KeyProtector $KP.RawData

# Set the security policy of the VM to be shielded
Set-VMSecurityPolicy -VMName $VMName -Shielded $true

# Enable vTPM on the VM
Enable-VMTPM -VMName $VMName
```

> **NOTE GENERATION 1 NEED NOT APPLY**
>
> The Host Guardian Service can work with only Generation 2 virtual machines that use the .VHDX virtual hard disk file format. Generation 2 VMs are required to support UEFI firmware and virtual TPM, among other features.
> Because Microsoft Azure supports only Generation 1 .VHD VMs, Host Guardian Service does not work in Azure. This is likely to change, given that the Azure development team ships several new features every single business day.

3. Because you won't get console access to the VM once it becomes shielded, it's crucial that you prepare the unshielded VM beforehand. This involves setting appropriate rules in Windows Firewall, configuring WSMan remote management, and (most importantly) enabling BitLocker Drive Encryption on the VM's virtual hard drive.

4. Export the VM from the tenant host, and import it on a guarded Hyper-V host.

The VM is now shielded and thereby protected against fabric administrators. Let's test that so we can get the full experience!

Testing a guarded host

Let's pretend that we're a fabric administrator and we're poking around the host operating system on a guarded Hyper-V host. As you can see in Figure 2-4:

- Shielded VMs don't display a live thumbnail preview in Hyper-V Manager. Instead, you see a pale grey rectangle.

- Shielded VMs don't allow direct connection via the Hyper-V Virtual Machine Connection tool.

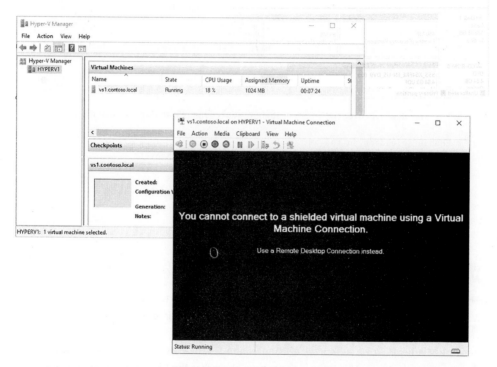

FIGURE 2-4 Here we see that Hyper-V Manager doesn't display a thumbnail preview of a shielded VM, and you also receive an error message when you attempt to start a local connection to the VM

Likewise, you'll receive an "access denied" error if you shut down the shielded VM, open Disk Management on the guarded host and attempt to mount a shielded VM's virtual hard drive. This is BitLocker Drive Encryption at work, and the error is shown in Figure 2-5.

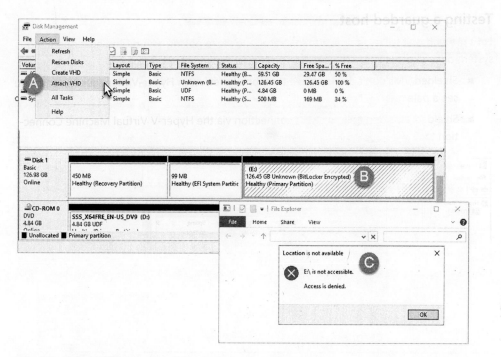

FIGURE 2-5 Shielded VMs rely upon BitLocker Drive Encryption to prevent rogue administrators from mounting the VM's virtual disks

Here are the details that explain the annotations in Figure 2-5:

- **A** As long as the shielded VM is powered off and the VHDX is thereby unlocked (figuratively speaking), you can attach it to your host system.
- **B** The shielded VM disk volumes actually are listed, but notice the BitLocker Drive Encryption label.
- **C** Sure enough, BitLocker isn't going to allow any type of offline attack.

We'll have much more to say about virtual TPM in the next section, but for now you should be able to view a shielded VM's TPM data by opening the TPM Management console from within the shielded VM. As you can see in Figure 2-6, the TPM shows Microsoft as the manufacturer, and 2.0 as the specification version.

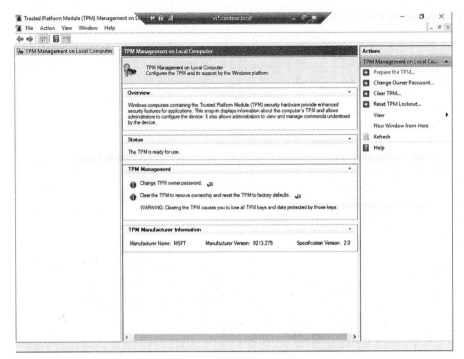

FIGURE 2-6 A view of the virtual TPM from within a shielded virtual machine

Migrating a shielded VM to another guarded host

The great beauty of Guarded Fabric is that as long as you want to migrate a shielded VM from one guarded host to another within a single HGS cluster, you can use any of the standard VM migration methods, including:

- Live migration (with or without shared storage)
- Hyper-V replica
- VM checkpoints
- Hyper-V export/import

Troubleshoot guarded hosts

Let's get some of the preliminary queries out of the way first. You can determine whether a VM is shielded by running the GetVMSecurity command on the guarded host:

```
PS C:\> Get-VMSecurity -VMName 'vs1.contoso.local'
TpmEnabled                        : True
Shielded                          : True
EncryptStateAndVmMigrationTraffic : True
CimSession                        : CimSession: .
ComputerName                      : HYPERV1
IsDeleted                         : False
```

You can also verify the VM's status by examining the VM's properties in Hyper-V Manager, as shown in Figure 2-7. Notice that the fabric administrator cannot disable shielding; all options on the page are unavailable.

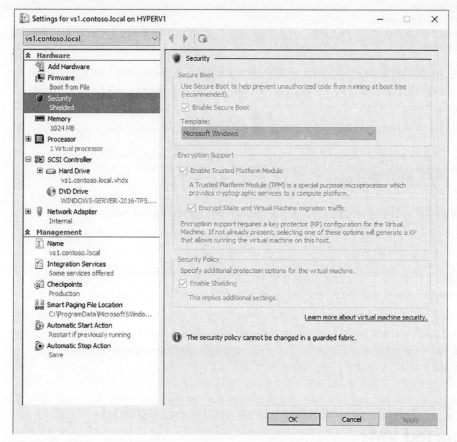

FIGURE 2-7 This is a shielded VM, and the fabric administrator cannot disable the protection

You can determine whether a host is guarded by verifying that the Host Guardian Hyper-V Support feature is enabled on the system. Here's the PowerShell and resulting output:

```
PS C:\> Get-WindowsFeature -Name HostGuardian
Display Name                          Name             Install State
------------                          ----             -------------
[X] Host Guardian Hyper-V Support     HostGuardian     Installed
```

Next, perform the final confirmation by inspecting the host's HGS client configuration, paying particular attention to the IsHostGuarded property:

```
PS C:\> Get-HgsClientConfiguration
IsHostGuarded           : True
Mode                    : HostGuardianService
KeyProtectionServerUrl  : http://hgs1.safe.local/KeyProtection
AttestationServerUrl    : http://hgs1.safe.local/Attestation
AttestationOperationMode : ActiveDirectory
AttestationStatus       : Passed
AttestationSubstatus    : NoInformation
```

Finally, we have the sticky situation of RDP sessions failing to a shielded VM and all local console access blocked. Add BitLocker to the equation, and you might think both the workload and fabric admins are hosed.

Not so fast. Shielded VM recovery is possible. Try to remove shielding from the VM on the guarded host:

```
Set-VMSecurityPolicy -VMName 'vs1.contoso.local' -Shielded $false
```

That's going to fail, for obvious reasons. According to Microsoft's "Guarded Fabric and Shielded VMs Troubleshooting Guide" white paper, you can try the following:

1. Export the shielded VM from the guarded host and import it on a host along with the owner's guardian key.

2. On the second host, run the previous PowerShell command to disable shielding.

3. Make whatever modifications you need to repair the VM's configuration.

Obviously, shielded VM recovery is a proverbial "sticky wicket" because any backdoors to defeat a security system can obviously be abused by bad actors. Later in the chapter we cover how you can use encryption-supported VMs to make troubleshooting and recovery a bit more flexible.

Skill 2.2: Implement shielded and encryption-supported VMs

In covering the Host Guardian Service, we laid the groundwork for a trusted computing platform with Hyper-V shielded virtual machines. Now let's turn our attention formally to this subject.

This section covers how to:

- Determine requirements and scenarios for implementing shielded VMs
- Create a shielded VM using the Hyper-V environment
- Enable and configure vTPM to allow operating system and data disk encryption within a VM
- Determine requirements and scenarios for implementing encryption-supported VMs
- Shielded VM connections and recovery

Determine requirements and scenarios for implementing shielded VMs

First of all, we probably ought to formally define a shielded VM. A shielded virtual machine is a Generation 2 Hyper-V virtual machine running Windows Server 2012 R2, Windows Server 2016, or Linux that uses a variety of current-generation technologies, including virtualization based security (VBS) and BitLocker Drive Encryption, to protect its contents from fabric administrators. Workload administrators use RDP and PowerShell remoting to access the VM as they normally would.

> **NOTE DID YOU SAY WINDOWS SERVER 2012R2? AND LINUX?**
>
> Windows Server 2012 R2 supports Generation 2 VMs, so you can deploy Windows Server 2012 R2–based shielded virtual machines on Windows Server 2016 Hyper-V hosts. Although the documentation is sketchy as of this writing, Windows Server 2016 supports Linux-based Hyper-V shielded VMs as well. Linux supports TPM, UEFI, and Secure Boot, but not BitLocker Drive Encryption. To that end, Microsoft plans to employ the dm-crypt disk encryption subsystem to provide whole-disk encryption for Linux-based shielded VMs.

We need to be clear here in stating that the problem of the untrusted fabric admin is in no way unique to Microsoft Hyper-V scenarios. Wherever we have a hypervisor, be it VMware, Citrix Xen, KVM, whatever, this issue exists. The difference is that the Host Guardian Service represents a Microsoft-and-Hyper-V-centric solution to the problem.

Moreover, remember that Microsoft's current and future security focus is on embracing an "assume breach" posture. For example, let's imagine that our Hyper-V hardware hosts have been compromised by malware. Let's go further and conceive that the malware has elevated permissions to that of fabric administrator. Those virtual machines suddenly become pretty darned vulnerable, don't they?

So what we're saying is that the need for shielded virtual machines is just as much about protecting our VMs from the host itself as it is about protecting those resources from rogue fabric administrators.

Virtualization-based security

The fact that Windows Server 2016 supports nested virtualization is a big deal. Recall that nested virtualization allows you to set up a Hyper-V VM as a virtualized Hyper-V host itself. That might seem like simply an intellectual exercise or a parlor trick, but not so fast.

Remember in the previous chapter when we discussed Credential Guard? That's VBS, and it's the technology behind virtual TPM (vTPM). We can take advantage of this Virtual Secure Mode (VSM, and yes, we're dealing with far too many three-letter acronyms (TLAs)) both at the host and guest operating system level. At the guest level, VBS protects Windows Server 2016 VMs against "pass the hash" or "pass the ticket" memory attacks.

Workload administrator access

The purpose of shielded VMs is to ensure that their VHDX virtual hard disk files as well as their configuration data are protected (shielded) from fabric administrators. Fabric administrators fail at any of the following attempts to access a shielded VM from the host:

- VM Connect console access
- RDP access (unless they have guest operating system credentials)
- PowerShell Direct

The guarded hosts are part of an HGS guarded fabric; Windows PowerShell Just Enough Administration (JEA) protects the endpoints on guarded hosts. But what about the workload administrators?

The good news is that workload administrators can use their standard methods for interacting with the shielded VMs to which they legitimately have access:

- RDP
- PowerShell remoting
- Remote Server Administration Tools (RSAT)
- Browser-based connectivity

The worst case scenario for a workload administrator is deploying a shielded VM without first ensuring that remote management is enabled and working on those VMs. We'll cover options for remediating this very real problem later in this section.

Create a shielded VM using Hyper-V

As of this writing, fabric administrators have two methods for creating shielded VMs:

- **Converting an existing, non-shielded VM** This process is called "grandfathering," and we covered it earlier in the chapter
- **Using a template VHDX** This is the preferred way to deploy shielded virtual machines because it subscribes to the "clean source" security principle and the VM is protected over its entire lifecycle

Benefits of a fabric manager

Let's face it: manually performing any manual task is a pain in the neck, and prone to costly human error. If your company is on-board with virtualization, then adding administrative automation and orchestration to the mix is a no-brainer.

System Center 2016 Virtual Machine Manager is Microsoft's primary tool for fabric administrators to centrally manage Hyper-V hosts and VM templates. As you can see in Figure 2-8, SCVMM 2016 is fully enlightened with regard to shielded VMs, and enables you to store pre-shielded templates for rapid deployment.

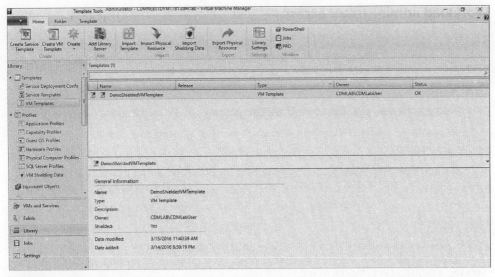

FIGURE 2-8 System Center 2016 Virtual Machine Manager can work natively with shielded virtual machines

Azure Stack is a forthcoming Microsoft solution that packages the Azure public cloud services (mainly infrastructure-as-a-service (IaaS), but also some platform-as-a-service (PaaS)) for use on-premises. Once again, Azure Pack, whose release date is scheduled for late 2017 as of this writing, are fully shielded VM-aware and allow you to deploy and manage shielded VMs.

Creating a new shielded VM without SCVMM

Let's work through how we can deploy a new VM with shielding in the absence of a fabric-management tool such as SCVMM or Azure Stack.

We'll work from a hyperv1.contoso.local guarded Hyper-V host; we can (and should) run Get-HgsClientConfiguration to make sure our link to the Host Guardian Service cluster is still active and problem-free.

Specifically, we're going to deploy a new shielded VM by creating the following artifacts on our host:

- signed template VHDX
- shielding data file
- Unattend.xml answer file

Don't worry, you'll understand those previous three items momentarily. The first thing we need to do on our Hyper-V host is to install the Shielded VM Tools server feature. As usual, we'll use Windows PowerShell exclusively:

```
Install-WindowsFeature -Name RSAT-Shielded-VM-Tools
```

You'll need to have a new Generation 2 VM ready to rock; the virtual hard disk file in our example is named template.vhdx.

You should perform the following actions in the guest VM in order to prepare it for shielding:

- Enable and configure RDP and PowerShell remoting
- Configure Windows Firewall in correspondence with network security policies
- Encrypt the disk with BitLocker Drive Encryption

If you plan to reuse the VHDX template, you'll want to sysprep and shut down the VM before proceeding.

Digital certificates remain the primary method for providing authentication, integrity, and confidentiality. To that end, we need to digitally sign our unshielded template disk. In production you'd use a valid certificate that's trusted throughout your organization; here we'll create a self-signed cert:

```
$cert = New-SelfSignedCertificate -DnsName 'signing.contoso.com'
Protect-ServerVHDX -Path 'C:\vms\template.vhdx' -TemplateName 'ServerOSTemplate'
-Version 1.0.0.1 -Certificate $cert
```

> **NOTE THE EVER-VOLATILE NATURE OF WINDOWS**
>
> Don't be surprised if you try the Protect-ServerVHDX command on your Windows Server 2016 server and receive an error from the PowerShell engine. This cmdlet could very well be renamed to Protect-TemplateDisk.
>
> You could see a similar shift from the Protect-ShieldingDataFile cmdlet to its supposed, eventual New-ShieldingDataFile replacement.
>
> We need to keep in mind that today's rapid development/continuous delivery IT service model means that what's true today with Microsoft technology can be renamed (at the least), or removed or replaced (at the worst), with minimal advance notice from the Microsoft development teams.

Create the shielding data (PDK) file

Now we get to the heart of the matter. If the (untrusted) fabric administrator is tasked with deploying a shielded VM for his or her client, then how can we prevent that fabric administrator from viewing VM-specific secrets such as the guest operating system administrator password? This seems like a "chicken vs. egg" proposition at first.

The PDK file is essentially an encrypted collection of secrets that allows you to shield the VM, link the VM to your HGS cluster, and keep sensitive data out of the reach of the fabric admin who is provisioning the VM in the first place.

The idea is that it is the workload administrators who create the shielding data; these admins can then hand off the encrypted PDK file to the fabric admins who actually provision the shielded VM.

The following is a sample annotated PowerShell to give you the shielding data creation workflow. Thanks to the Microsoft Datacenter and Private Cloud Security team for providing the code for us to adapt:

```
#Create a volume signature catalog file for the template disk; this ensures the template
disk is not being tampered with at deployment time
Save-VolumeSignatureCatalog -TemplateDiskPath '.\template.contoso.local.vhdx' -
VolumeSignatureCatalogPath '.\ServerOSTemplate.vsc'

# Create an owner certificate
$Owner = New-HgsGuardian -Name 'Owner' -GenerateCertificates

# Import the HGS guardian
$Guardian = Import-HgsGuardian -Path '.\HGSGuardian.xml' -Name 'TestFabric' -
AllowUntrustedRoot

# Create the PDK file on the tenant host server
Protect-ShieldingDataFile -ShieldingDataFilePath "template.contoso.local.
pdk" -Owner $Owner -Guardian $guardian -VolumeIDQualifier (New-VolumeIDQualifier
-VolumeSignatureCatalogFilePath '.\ServerOSTemplate.vsc' -VersionRule Equals)
-WindowsUnattendFile '.\unattend.xml' -Policy Shielded
```

We want you to understand the PowerShell command workflow, but don't expect that the code always runs exactly as recorded in this book. Instead, use the Microsoft TechNet documentation because the product teams regularly update it as technology evolves.

In the Protect-ShieldingDataFile statement you saw a WindowsUnattendFile parameter; this answer file contains important secrets that pertain to the new VM, including:

- local administrator password
- time zone
- AD DS domain join metadata
- RDP certificate thumbprint and .pfx password

If you're not yet up-to-speed with Windows PowerShell (although you certainly must be if you're to pass the 70-744 certification exam), the Shielded VM Tools feature does have a graphical Shielding Data File Wizard located at C:\Windows\System32\ShieldingDataFileWizard.exe. Figure 2-9 depicts the user interface.

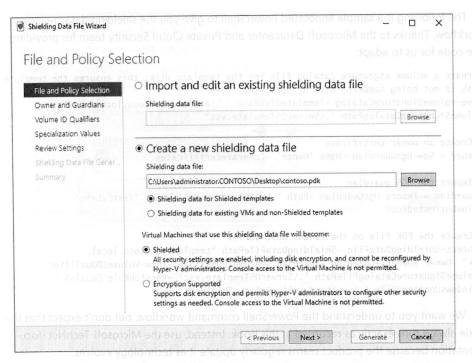

FIGURE 2-9 The Shielding Data File Wizard makes it easier for workload admins to create shielding data files for new shielded or encryption-supported VMs

Provision the shielded VM on a guarded host

At this point the fabric administrator completes the process by placing the signed and encrypted template VHDX file and encrypted shielding data PDK file on a guarded Hyper-V host, and then initializing the shielded VM by using the shielding data file.

Enable and configure vTPM

What's so cool about virtual Trusted Platform Module (vTPM) is that we can use TPM technology on our Hyper-V VMs even if the hardware host doesn't have a physical TPM. Of course, the best-case scenario is that your Hyper-V hosts all have on-board TPMs and potential hardware security modules (HSMs) as well.

Isolated User Mode

The "secret sauce" behind vTPM is what Microsoft calls Isolated User Mode (IUM). Take a look at Figure 2-10, and we'll expand upon what we covered about IUM.

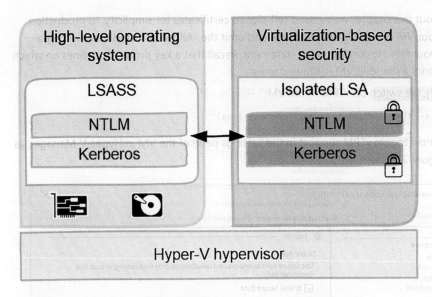

High-level operating system

LSASS

NTLM

Kerberos

Virtualization-based security

Isolated LSA

NTLM 🔒

Kerberos 🔒

Hyper-V hypervisor

FIGURE 2-10 vTPM and Credential Guard both rely upon Isolated User Mode

Notice in Figure 2-10 that historically the LSASS process stores credentials in unprotected memory space. This, of course, opens the system to memory attacks and credential theft. As long as you have Hyper-V running on your Windows Server 2016 servers, the operating system can store secrets in strongly-isolated memory space.

EXAM TIP

Microsoft is infamous for spontaneously and repeatedly changing product and technology names. On the 70-744 exam you could see references to Virtual Secure Mode (VSM), Isolated User Mode (IUM), or Virtualization-Based Security (VBS). These acronyms all mean the same thing.

Enable vTPM in a Hyper-V VM

Use the following procedure to enable vTPM on a new unshielded Hyper-V VM.

1. Recall that the "guardian" in a Host Guardian Service context refers to the HGS cluster; specifically, its certificate-based key. We'll assign a variable named owner to our guardian (which is unfortunately named Owner).

```
$owner = Get-HgsGuardian -Name Owner
```

2. Next we'll generate a key protector and then associate it with our VM:

```
$kp = New-HgsKeyProtector -Owner $owner -AllowUntrustedRoot
Set-VMKeyProtector -VMName 'server02.contoso.local' -KeyProtector $kp.RawData
```

Throughout this chapter we've used self-signed certificates for simplicity. In production you'd use your VM owner digital certificate and omit the -AllowUntrustedRoot switch parameter in your NewHgsKeyProtector statement. Recall that a key protector defines on which guarded fabrics a shielded VM is allowed to run.

1. Finally, we switch on vTPM in the VM:

```
Enable-VMTPM -VMName 'server02.contoso.local'
```

You can now toggle vTPM support in the Settings page of the VM in Hyper-V Manager, as shown in Figure 2-11.

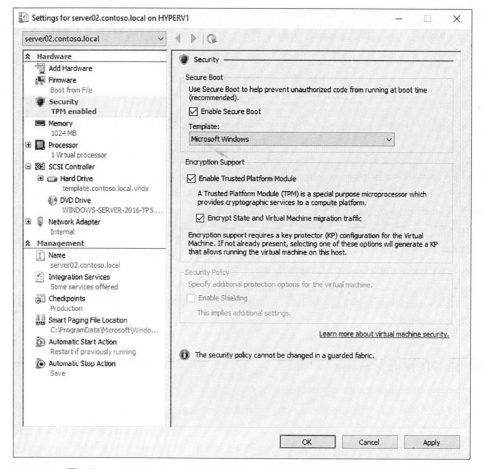

FIGURE 2-11 The Hyper-V VM can benefit from TPM services even if the hardware host does not have a physical TPM installed

Encryption at rest and in-flight

BitLocker Drive Encryption ensures that your shielded VM's VHDX files are secure when at rest. The shielding data file that contains VM-specific secrets is encrypted as well.

But what about when shielded VMs (including their memory state, configuration, as well as virtual hard disks) are in transit, for example during a live migration?

The good news is that the VM's vTPM is as portable as the rest of the VM. This means that your shielded VMs remain protected even when their data is transmitted over the network.

Recall that VM live migration can take place both in failover clusters as well as in standalone scenarios, and shielded VMs work perfectly fine in either one. However, the source and destination hosts need to be valid members of your guarded fabric.

While we're on the subject, each Hyper-V VM runs as a worker process named vmwp.exe on the host. Shielded VMs have "hardened" VM worker processes that prevent illicit tampering from fabric administrators; for instance, attaching a debugger to the process.

Determine requirements and scenarios for implementing encryption-supported VMs

Everything we've done thus far in this module pertains to "classic" shielded VMs. We also noticed an Achilles Heel to the technology: that there is no built-in recovery method to provide console VM access in the event that workload administrators forgot to configure remote management in the virtual machine prior to its shielding.

Microsoft offers the encryption-supported VM option for businesses who:

- trust their fabric administrators
- require console access to Hyper-V VMs
- can meet their compliance requirements without full VM shielding

Let's compare shielded vs. encryption-supported virtual machines with respect to how the relate to core Windows Server 2016 security features. Check out Table 2-2:

TABLE 2-2 Comparison between encryption-supported and shielded Hyper-V VMs

Feature	Encryption-supported	Shielded
vTPM	Required but configurable	Required and enforced
Secure Boot	Required but configurable	Required and enforced
Encrypted VM state and live migration traffic	Required but configurable	Required and enforced
VM console connection	Enabled and cannot be disabled	Disabled and cannot be enabled
Attach debugger to VM worker process	Enabled	Disabled

Deploying an encryption-supported VM

The anticlimax here is that the process of creating an encryption-supported VM is nearly identical to that of creating a shielded VM. Let's run through the procedure of "grandfathering" an existing unshielded VM named server10.contoso.local on our guarded host named hyperv1.contoso.local.

1. First, we pull down the HGS guardian metadata to our workload (tenant) server. Recall that this is the HGSGuardian.xml file we worked with earlier.
2. We make sure the VM to be shielded is stopped.
3. We create a variable to hold our owner (workload administrator) certificate.
4. We import the HGS guardian metadata from the previously downloaded
5. We create the key protector, which links the owner and the guardian together
6. We run SetVMKeyProtector to enable shielding
7. Finally, we set the security policy (this is where the difference comes in):

```
Set-VMSecurityPolicy -VMName 'server01.contoso.local' -Shielded $false
```

Although this is in no way obvious or intuitive, it all comes down to the value of the Shielded parameter. If $true, then the VM is shielded. If $false, then the VM is encryption-supported.

Shielded VM recovery

As of this writing, Microsoft doesn't have a solid story on recovering from an inaccessible shielded virtual machine. Perhaps a workload administrator accidentally disabled remote connections. Perhaps the firewall was misconfigured--the reasons stack up as to why a particular VM is no longer accessible. Of course, if this is an encryption-supported VM, a fabric administrator can gain host-level access to the VM as previously described. But fully shielded VMs are another story.

The Microsoft Datacenter and Private Cloud Security team put up a blog post called "Step by Step - Shielded VM Recovery (*http://timw.info/svm*) that cleverly takes advantage of the nested virtualization feature of Windows Server 2016 Hyper-V to get around the console access problem.

Have a look at the illustration in Figure 2-12 and let's make sense of the recovery approach.

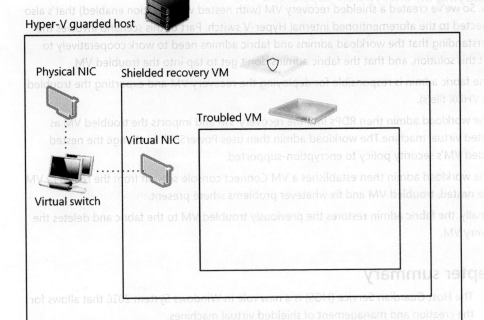

Hyper-V guarded host

Physical NIC   Shielded recovery VM

Troubled VM

Virtual NIC

Virtual switch

FIGURE 2-12 Conceptual diagram of shielded VM recovery

In Figure 2-12, we start from the perspective of a Hyper-V hardware host that's connected to an Internal Hyper-V switch. We create a dedicated, shielded recovery VM that has nested virtualization enabled. Incidentally, you can enable nested virtualization on a VM by running the following PowerShell command from the host:

```
Set-VMProcessor -VMName <VMName> -ExposeVirtualizationExtensions $true
```

It's important for you to know that you must disable dynamic memory on the virtual machine, and that you need to allocate enough host RAM to cover any nested VMs you plan to run on the virtual Hyper-V host.

> **NOTE OTHER USES FOR NESTED VIRTUALIZATION**
>
> Nested virtualization refers to the capacity of a virtual machine to become a virtualization host itself. This is a feature that customers asked Microsoft about for many years, and it's great that we finally have it in Windows Server 2016.
>
> With host hardware being so powerful nowadays, it makes sense to deploy virtualized Hyper-V hosts Going further, shared storage has become much more affordable in Windows Server 2016, so it's almost trivial to deploy highly available virtual machines that themselves spring from the nested virtualization scenario. Finally, in today's age of rapid application development and continuous integration, developers appreciate being able to deploy "second level" VM pods from "first level" VMs to which they have access.

The recovery process

Okay. So we've created a shielded recovery VM (with nested virtualization enabled) that's also connected to the aforementioned internal Hyper-V switch. Part of this scenario involves the understanding that the workload admins and fabric admins need to work cooperatively to enact this solution, and that the fabric admins don't get to tap into the troubled VM.

The fabric admin is responsible for deploying the recovery VM and exporting the troubled VM's VHDX file(s).

The workload admin then RDPs into the recovery VM and imports the troubled VM as a nested virtual machine.The workload admin then uses PowerShell to change the nested shielded VM's security policy to encryption-supported.

The workload admin then establishes a VM Connect console session from the recovery VM to the nested, troubled VM and fix whatever problems where present.

Finally, the fabric admin restores the previously troubled VM to the fabric and deletes the recovery VM.

Chapter summary

- The Host Guardian Service (HGS) is a new role in Windows System 2016 that allows for the creation and management of shielded virtual machines.

- The need for HGS and shielded VMs is based in the separation of duties between workload (VM) administrators and fabric (Hyper-V host) administrators and least-privilege security.

- HGS is deployed exclusively with PowerShell; Microsoft recommends at least three nodes per HGS cluster to support high availability.

- HGS and shielded VMs rely upon various hardware and software features (physical and virtual TPM, UEFI, Secure Boot, Hardware Security Module (HSM), and more.

- HGS has two main functions: attestation that a guarded host is healthy, and key transfer to lock and unlock shielded virtual machines.

- Local console access is blocked for shielded virtual machines, making pre-shielding VM configuration crucial to allow for remote management.

- Shielded VMs offer strong protection against fabric (host) administrators as well as compromised Hyper-V host servers themselves.

- Shielded VM deployment is inextricably tied to the presence and availability of a Host Guardian Service (HGS) cluster.

- The strong protections offered by shielded VMs have one potential downfall—no host console access could lead to connectivity and availability problems if the shielded VM isn't correctly configured.

- Encryption-supported VMs represent an approach that combines some of the shielded VM protections but preserves console access. However, this protection method involves trusting your fabric admins.

Thought experiment

In this thought experiment, demonstrate your skills and knowledge of the topics covered in this chapter. You can find answer to this thought experiment in the next section.

You are a datacenter administrator for Contoso Solutions, a managed service provider (MSP) located in Buffalo, NY. Your newest client, Woodgrove Bank, has strict regulatory requirements that limit access to their servers only to their own full-time information technology staff.

You installed four hardware Hyper-V hosts in a secure server rack for Woodgrove Bank; each host contains five virtual machines. All server hardware includes a TPM v2.0 chip and UEFI firmware and runs Windows Server 2016 Datacenter Edition with the full GUI.

You've outlined the new Hyper-V security features offered by Windows Server 2016. In reply, Woodgrove IT personnel have the following questions for you:

1. If we accidentally mess up RDP or WinRM access to our workload VMs, we need another way to access them. How can we accomplish this goal?

2. Woodgrove plans to virtualize more of its infrastructure over the coming years, and we need a way to automate (or at least make easier) shielded VM deployment. What's possible?

3. What are the pros and cons of TPM-trusted vs. admin-trusted attestation?

Thought experiment answers

This section contains the solution to the thought experiment.

1. Shielded VM recovery is very much a "version 1.0" technology as of this writing. We really have only one solution: to implement the "repair garage" scheme as we discussed earlier in the chapter. By this method, fabric admins would be allowed temporary access to the VMs to unlock them. Then, presumably Woodgrove staff would connect to the workload VMs, reconfigure, and then allow the fabric admin to re-lock the shielded VMs.

   Configuring the VMs as encryption-supported would enable console access, but this option gives fabric administrators the ability to access the workload VM data permanently.

2. Microsoft discourages the approach of "grandfathering" existing, unshielded VMs into shielded state because this is a violation of the "clean source" principal. In other words, the best practice is to deploy new VMs in a guarded state to ensure integrity throughout the VM's lifetime.

3. That said, both System Center 2016 Virtual Machine Manager and Azure Stack both include in-box features that make it easier to store shielded VM templates. The big question for Woodgrove is who does the shielded VM deployment work; remember

that SCVMM and Azure Stack are fabric management tools, and would be more suited for Contoso Solutions' use rather than for Woodgrove workload administrators.

TPM-trusted attestation provides a much stronger set of protections for virtual machines running in a guarded fabric. Technically, we can use virtual TPM functionality in Hyper-V virtual machines even in the absence of a server physical TPM, but Woodgrove is fortunate enough to have host hardware that allows for TPM-trusted attestation.

Recall that in the TPM-trusted attestation scenario, we capture the startup and runtime environment of each guarded host. This means we need to perform the extra work of capturing a "golden image" of each host's state and deploying a Code Integrity (CI) policy that whitelists the code that can run.

If Woodgrove's security requirements are this strict, then AD-trusted attestation is a much easier implementation approach. However, the only thing we're attesting in this scenario is that a guarded host belongs to the appropriate AD security group. If the HGS cluster domain were to be compromised, then this defeats the entire attestation method and trust path.

## CHAPTER 3

Secure a network infrastructure

K arl is the IT director of a local law firm. He doesn't believe in enabling Windows Firewall on any of his infrastructure servers. "It's just too much hassle," Karl explained. "We have a strong hardware firewall at our network perimeter. Inside the firewall we believe we have a trusted fabric, so we turn off the Windows Firewall on all server and desktop systems to facilitate remote management."

Don't be like Karl. Windows Firewall is a software, host-based firewall that is every bit as present in Windows Server 2016 as it is in every previous server operating system since Windows Server 2003.

By restricting the network traffic that is allowed to reach your servers, you reduce those servers' attack surface. Ideally, your servers should never even respond to port or service probes. In other words, your servers should be "ghosts" on your network and respond only to legitimate connection requests by authorized parties.

In this chapter, we explain how to configure Windows Firewall in Windows Server 2016. We also cover Microsoft's vision to bring Azure's software-defined networking (SDN) stack to your on-premises network. Finally, we dig into Server Message Block (SMB) and Internet Protocol Security (IPSec) and discover how to provide confidentiality, integrity, and authentication to selected network traffic flows.

Skills in this chapter:

- Configure Windows Firewall
- Implement a Software Defined Distributed Firewall
- Secure network traffic

Skill 3.1: Configure Windows Firewall

A firewall is hardware or software that protects a host by screening inbound (and, potentially, outbound) network traffic. Windows Firewall is the host-based software firewall that's been part of Windows Server since Windows Server 2003.

Configure Windows Firewall with Advanced Security

Although this 70-744 exam topic gets directly to the "meat and potatoes" by indicating the Windows Firewall with Advanced Security MMC console, we think it's appropriate for us to review all the ways we can interact with Windows Firewall on Windows Server 2016 systems.

From an elevated Windows PowerShell console, try the following commands:

- **firewall.cpl**   This opens the Windows Firewall Control Panel
- **wf.msc**   This command opens the Windows Firewall with Advanced Security MMC console.
- **netsh advfirewall firewall**   This command employs the legacy netsh command-line program to allow you to manage Windows Firewall programmatically
- **ShowControlPanelItem -Name 'Windows Firewall'**   This PowerShell statement opens the Windows Firewall Control Panel

The Windows Firewall Control Panel

Open the "standard" Windows Firewall Control Panel either by using the Control Panel interface or by invoking one of the previously listed commands. Figure 3-1 showcases the interface.

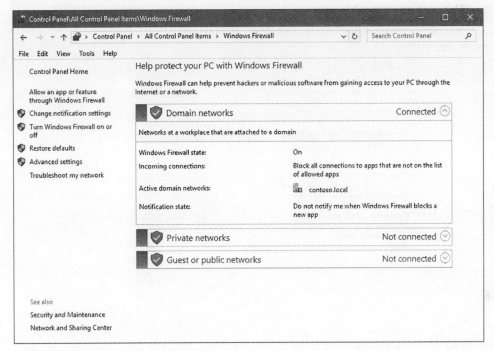

FIGURE 3-1 The "standard" Windows Firewall

The following are important Windows Firewall Control Panel elements:

- **Allow an app or feature through Windows Firewall**   This option, shown in Figure 3-2, gives you control over basic firewall rules for installed services and applications.

- **Turn Windows Firewall on or off**   This option allows you to enable or disable Windows Firewall for each network location profile.

- **Advanced settings**   This option opens the Windows Firewall with Advanced Security console.

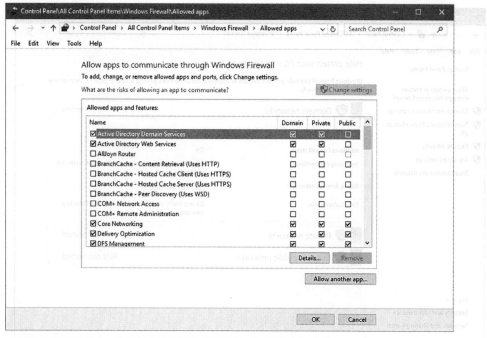

FIGURE 3-2 Allow or block app traffic in Windows Firewall

These Windows Firewall rules can embrace several different layers of the Open Systems Interconnection (OSI) reference model. For instance, the applications and services listed in Figure 3-2 require no knowledge of the underlying IP addresses, protocols and port numbers involved. This is Layer 7 (Application layer) firewall filtering.

On the other hand, some line-of-business applications require much more granular firewall rules. That's what the Windows Firewall with Advanced Security console is all about.

The Windows Firewall with Advanced Security console

At first blush, the Windows Firewall with Advanced Security Microsoft Management Console (MMC) looks pretty complicated. Take a look at Figure 3-3 where we walk you through it.

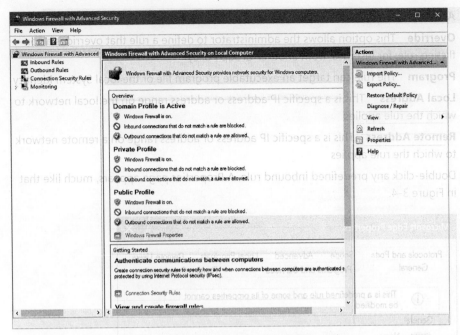

FIGURE 3-3 The Windows Firewall with Advanced Security MMC console

- **Inbound Rules** Firewall rules that pertain to incoming network traffic
- **Outbound Rules** Firewall rules that apply to outgoing network traffic
- **Connection Security Rules** Network policies that employ IPSec to control host-to-host authentication, encryption, and data integrity
- **Monitoring** Interface to audit the behavior of the firewall and connection security rules and IPSec security associations (SAs)

Examine a default inbound rule

Follow these steps to take a deep-dive tour of the building blocks of a Windows Firewall with Advanced Security console. Know that this process applies identically to outbound rules.

1. In the Windows Firewall with Advanced Security console, select the Inbound Rules node. Each rule has the following properties:

- **Name** You can't change the name of predefined rules, but you certainly can name your own custom rules to meet your business requirements
- **Group** Several firewall rules can be logically associated with a name (typically a service or application name)
- **Profile** The rule can apply to the Domain, Public, or Private network location profiles
- **Enabled** You often need to disable firewall rules temporarily while troubleshooting connectivity problems

- **Action**   The firewall either allows or block the connection
- **Override**   This option allows the administrator to define a rule that overrides a conflicting rule; for instance, from another Group Policy
- **Program**   The rule can target an executable program file or the local System identity
- **Local Address**   This is a specific IP address or address range on the local network to which the rule applies
- **Remote Address**   This is a specific IP address or address range on a remote network to which the rule applies

2. Double-click any predefined inbound rule. A Properties page appears, much like that in Figure 3-4.

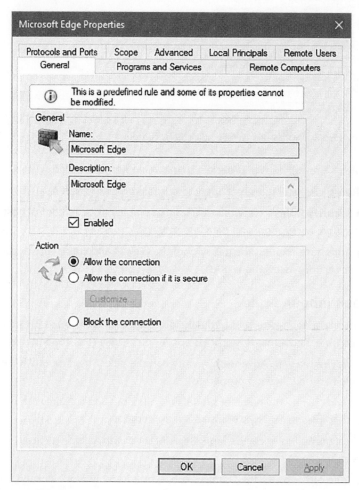

FIGURE 3-4 Each Windows Firewall rule has its own Properties sheet in which you can customize the behavior of the rule

The Properties sheet has quite a few tabs which we explain shortly.

3. Finally, right-click the Inbound Rules node and observe the options available in the context menu:

- **New Rule**   Self-explanatory

- **Filter by Profile**   This option is great for a domain administrator who needs to see only Domain-linked firewall rules

- **Filter by State**   **This option quickly reveals disabled rules**

- **Filter by Group**   This option rounds up all rules associated with a particular logical group (service or application)

Create a new inbound rule

Follow these steps to define a new inbound rule. Let's imagine that our task is to create an inbound rule that allows traffic on TCP 1433 from all hosts on the 192.168.1.0/24 subnet to the local host.

1. Right-click the Inbound Rules node in the Windows Firewall with Advanced Security console and select New Rule from the shortcut menu.

2. You have the following rule types to choose from in Rule Type page in the New Inbound Rule Wizard:

   - **Program**   You can match all programs or a selected path

   - **Port**   A given Transmission Control Protocol (TCP) or User Datagram Protocol (UDP) port or port range

   - **Predefined**   Here you can create a new rule that uses a predefined rule as a template. Popular options here include File and Printer Sharing, Windows Management Instrumentation (WMI), and Windows Remote Management

   - **Custom**   Create your own rule that combines any of program, protocol, or port combination

   In this example, select Port and then click Next to continue.

3. In the Protocol And Ports dialog box, select TCP for the Does This Rule Apply To TCP Or UDP? options, and type **1433** in the Specific local ports text box.

4. In the Action dialog box, you can choose what Windows Firewall should do in the event that the local host receives an incoming connection request on TCP 1433. The options are:

   - Allow The Connection

   - Allow The Connection If It Is Secure

   - Block The Connection

   The second Allow The Connection If It Is Secure means that you need IPSec-encrypted traffic to allow this traffic flow. We cover IPSec in much greater depth as we move through the remainder of the chapter.

In this case, of course, we should choose Block the connection and then click Next to continue.

> **NOTE** **TCP 1433**
>
> In our first exercise we define a Windows Firewall exception for TCP 1433 network traffic. Database administrators recognize this as the default communications port for SQL Server, Microsoft's flagship relational database management system (RDBMS).
>
> As a general security best practice, you should change as many default port assignments as possible to improve your servers' security posture. If you do this with SQL Server, however, you need to define SQL Server aliases to reflect the non-standard port assignment.

5. In the Profile page, we decide which network location profiles should be linked to this inbound rule. Options include:

   - Domain
   - Private
   - Public

   For now, let's select the Private profile and click Next to continue. This New Inbound Rule Wizard configuration page is shown in Figure 3-5.

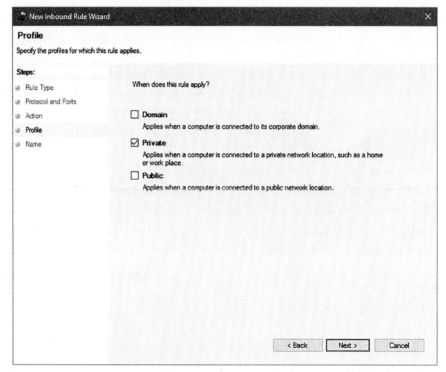

FIGURE 3-5 Assigning a new Windows Firewall rule to a network location profile

6. In the final Name dialog, type a meaningful name for the new rule (SQL Server Default Port-Allow might work well), and then click Finish to complete the rule creation process.

You should find that you're able to fully modify, or even delete, your new rule from within the Windows Firewall with Advanced Security console.

Exporting a firewall configuration

Here's an excellent time-saving tip for you: spend the time to define your relevant Windows Firewall rules from a "golden" or "reference" Windows Server 2016 computer, and then *export the settings for easy import into Group Policy*. Yes, it's that simple!

It's true that you can copy individual rule definitions between servers and/or Group Policies, but for now let's imagine you've set up a baseline server firewall policy, and you want to retain that policy for deployment of your infrastructure servers.

From the Windows Firewall with Advanced Security console, right-click the root node in the console tree and then choose Export Policy from the shortcut menu. Choose a file name and save location for the resulting .wfw file, and you're all set.

The exported file is in binary format, so don't expect to open and analyze the file in, say, Windows Notepad or Microsoft Excel.

Listing and exporting rules with Windows PowerShell and netsh

From an elevated PowerShell console, you can list some or all Windows Firewall rules by employing the logically named GetNetFirewallRule cmdlet:

```
PS C:\> Get-NetFirewallRule -DisplayName *SQL*
```

```
Name                 : {92F47B33-9064-4A43-945C-0777BBB6D21F}
DisplayName          : SQL Server Default Port Allow
Description          :
DisplayGroup         :
Group                :
Enabled              : True
Profile              : Private
Platform             : {}
Direction            : Inbound
Action               : Block
EdgeTraversalPolicy  : Block
LooseSourceMapping   : False
LocalOnlyMapping     : False

Owner                :
PrimaryStatus        : OK
Status               : The rule was parsed successfully from the store. (65536)
EnforcementStatus    : NotApplicable
PolicyStoreSource    : PersistentStore

PolicyStoreSourceType : Local
```

Employ the age-old netsh command-line executable to perform a Windows Firewall policy export like so:

```
netsh advfirewall export 'C:\advfirewallpolicy.wfw'
```

Next up we explain the purpose of network location profiles and how to deploy firewall rules by using Group Policy.

Configure network location profiles and deploy profile rules using Group Policy

The Network Location Awareness (NlaSvc) service runs on Windows Server and Windows Client systems and is used to configure Windows Firewall. We have three default location profiles:

- **Public** This is the default network location profile, provides the strongest default firewall security, and is recommended for untrusted network connections.

- **Private** This connection type provides some isolation for systems on trusted networks. For instance, internal business networks that employ Network Address Translation (NAT).

- **Domain** This network connection is automatically assigned when an Active Directory connection is detected by Windows.

For Exam 70-744 purposes, we're concerned with Windows Server computers. More to the point, we assume Active Directory membership, so we constrain our discussions to the Domain profile. Specifically, Windows selects the Domain profile when an Active Directory domain controller is detected on that connection.

Sometimes after a server restart, you find the server's network connection (or connections) revert from "Domain" to "Private." You can correct this problem and force the domain profile with three lines of Windows PowerShell:

```
$profile = Get-NetConnectionProfile -InterfaceAlias 'Ethernet0'
$profile.NetworkCategory = 'DomainAuthenticated'
Set-NetConnectionProfile -InputObject $profile
```

Deploying Windows Firewall rules by using Group Policy is essentially the same as configuring rules with the server's local Windows Firewall with Advanced Security MMC console. Follow this procedure and see for yourself:

1. On a domain controller, start Group Policy Management Console and open the desired Group Policy Object (GPO).

2. Navigate to the following Group Policy path:

   ```
   Computer Configuration\Policies\Windows Settings\Security Settings\Windows
   Firewall with Advanced Security\Windows Firewall with Advanced Security\Inbound
   Rules.
   ```

3. Work your way through the New Inbound Rule Wizard as we did earlier in the chapter. The actual rule definitions function precisely as they do in the standalone console. In Figure 3-6 you see we can associate the new Windows Firewall rule with the Domain profile.

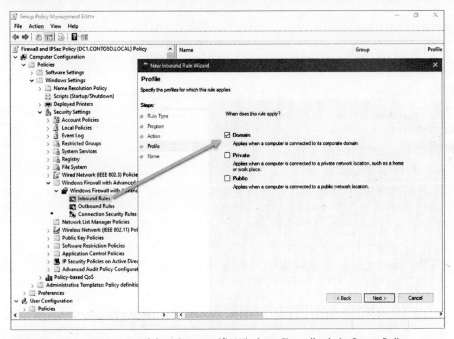

FIGURE 3-6 Creating a network location-specific Windows Firewall rule in Group Policy

Importing policy settings

Remember when we covered how to export reference Windows Firewall settings from a local Windows Firewall with Advanced Security session? Well, Group Policy is where you can bring those baseline firewall rules to bear.

From within the Group Policy Editor, right-click the Windows Firewall with Advanced Security node and select Import Policy from the shortcut menu. Browse to your handy-dandy .wfw policy file and click OK to perform the import.

> **NOTE** **BE CAREFUL WITH WINDOWS FIREWALL RULES IMPORT**
>
> When you import a .wfw file into Group Policy, any rule configuration you might have performed to that point is completely overwritten. You've been warned!

Configure connection security rules using Group Policy, the GUI console, or Windows PowerShell

Windows Firewall rules, as we've seen, provide server security by screening the types of traffic that are allowed to reach the server. Connection security rules are concerned with different types of security; namely confidentiality, integrity, and authentication. The so-called "CIA" rule of information security works like this:

- **Confidentiality**   Data is encrypted such that only authorized parties can decrypt and examine it

- **Integrity**   Data is guaranteed to be consistent from sender to receiver

- **Authentication**   The identity of each communicating party is verified

IPSec and server security

Internet Protocol Security (IPSec) is sometimes mistakenly referred to as a protocol. In fact, IPSec is an industry standard protocol suite that provides various protections for IP traffic. When you think of it, IPv4 traffic was never designed to provide CIA. We do have IPSec built into IPv6, but how many businesses have shifted to IPv6 exclusively?

The two IPSec protocols we're concerned with today are:

- **Authentication Header (AH)**   Provides authentication, anti-replay, and integrity, but no encryption

- **Encapsulating Security Payload (ESP)**   Provides data encrypting on the IP packet's payload without offering authentication

Although many systems administrators configure IPSec only in the context of virtual private network (VPN) tunnels, Group Policy-based connection security rules give us the ability to protect IPv4 traffic on our local internetworks.

> **NOTE** **IPSEC AND NETWORK OVERHEAD**
>
> Some administrators won't consider implementing IPSec policies on their LANs due to the mistaken assumption that IPSec slows down network performance with all its security overhead.
>
> While it's true that ESP adds minimal overhead to LAN traffic, you need to ask yourself if data encryption between internal hosts is truly what you need. If authenticated communication is your goal, then you can simply enable AH and experience no additional overhead at all.

IPSec connection security rule types

Creating an IPSec connection security rule in your environment involves understanding the various rule types. Here they are:

- **Isolation**   Restricts connections based on authentication criteria
- **Authentication exemption**   Blocks authentication request from specified nodes
- **Server-to-server**   Authenticates connections between two specific nodes
- **Tunnel**   Authenticates connections between two VPN gateway nodes

In the following sections we work through a simple, fictional example. Let's say we have a Windows Server 2016 server named hyperv1 that requires encrypted and authenticated communications between itself and any other node on the corporate network.

Defining a connection security rule in Group Policy

Follow this procedure to create a connection security rule from a new GPO:

1. Navigate to the following Group Policy path in Group Policy Editor:

   ```
   Computer Configuration\Policies\Windows Settings\Security Settings\Windows
   Firewall with Advanced Security\Connection Security Rules
   ```

2. Right-click the Connection Security Rules node and select New Rule from the shortcut menu.

3. Select Isolation from the available connection security rules and then click Next.

4. Choose an authentication option. Your choices are:

   - Request authentication for inbound and outbound connections
   - Require authentication for inbound connections and request authentication for outbound connections
   - Require authentication for inbound and outbound connections

   As you can see, these three options determine how important mutual authentication is to you. For our purposes, select the second option; this means that the server can communicate with any node, but only accepts incoming connections only from authenticated nodes. Click Next to continue.

5. Select an authentication method. You can choose computer and/or user authentication. Here let's select Computer and user (Kerberos V5) and then click Next. In an Active Directory domain, it's convenient and secure to rely upon the default Kerberos authentication protocol.

6. Bind the rule only to the Domain network location profile and then click Next.

7. Give the rule a name, and you're done!

As you can see in Figure 3-7, we can examine the properties of an already defined connection security rule to edit any of its attributes.

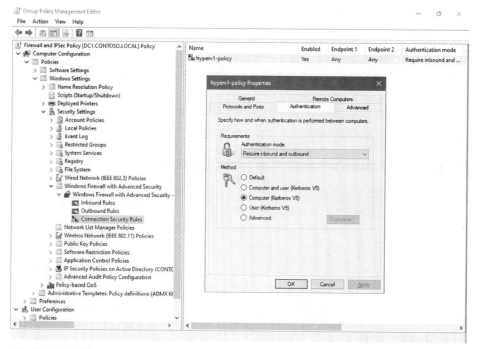

FIGURE 3-7 Modifying an IPSec connection security rule in Group Policy

In our example, the communication between hyperv1 and any other system on the network proceeds only if they authenticate to each other successfully using Kerberos V5 and Active Directory.

Defining a connection security rule in the IPSec Console

Windows Server has supported IPSec connection policies for many years. Specifically, you can load two IPSec-specific MMC snap-ins into a new MMC console:

- **IP Security Policy Management**   Create new IPSec policies
- **IP Security Monitor**   View and troubleshoot IPSec policy configuration and communications

We cover this exam topic lightly, because the Microsoft documentation states explicitly that we should always use the Windows Firewall with Advanced Security connection security rules instead of these. Why? We should because the legacy IP Security Policies console hasn't been updated to current-generation security algorithms and features. For instance, you can configure IPSec policy to use the deprecated (and cryptographically weak) MD5 and DES security protocols.

For an illustration of this concept, check out Figure 3-8, which shows you an IP Security Policy Wizard screen that references Windows Server 2003 and Windows XP, neither of which is any longer supported by Microsoft at all.

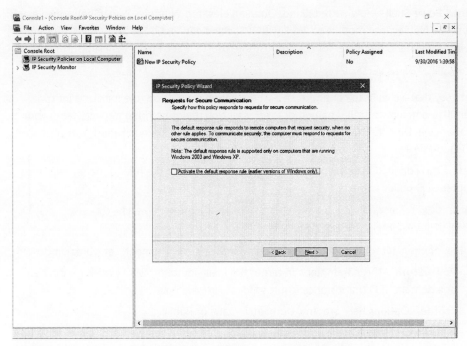

FIGURE 3-8 Note that the legacy IP Security Policies console references Windows Server 2003 and Windows XP, which are both "dead" operating systems; not a good sign

Microsoft continues to include the IP Security Policies MMC snap-in in Windows Server 2016 to provide backward compatibility for customers who use IPSec with antiquated Windows Server and Windows Client versions.

Nonetheless, you can find the IP Security Policies node in Group Policy under the following Group Policy path:

```
Computer Configuration\Policies\Windows Settings\Security Settings\IP Security Policies
on Active Directory
```

The three default policies are as follows:

- **Client (Respond Only)** The configured computer responds to requests for IPSec communications by other systems. It's important to understand that 'client' in this context could be a server or a client role.

- **Secure Server (Require Security)**: The configured computer requires that all inbound and outbound communications employ IPSec.

- **Server (Request Security)**: The configured computer requests IPSec security but not require it for communications.

Defining a connection security rule in Windows PowerShell

Windows PowerShell—now we're talking. Open an elevated Windows PowerShell console and let's use the NetSecurity module to work with IPSec and connection security rules. Run the following pipeline to get a feel for how robust Microsoft's IPSec PowerShell support is:

```
Get-Command -Module NetSecurity | Where-Object { $_.Name -like '*ipsec*' }
```

Let's say that we want to configure an authentication exemption rule for our Windows Server 2016 domain controller named dc1. After all, you're not going to get very far in your network Active Directory communications if IPSec rules block communication with your authentication server.

Define this connection security rule directly on dc1 and bind the rule to the server's local computer GPO policy store:

```
New-NetIPSecRule -DisplayName 'dc1exempt' -PolicyStore 'dc1' -Profile 'Domain'
-InboundSecurity 'None' -OutboundSecurity 'None'
```

There is quite a bit to unpack in the preceding PowerShell statement. Let's break it down:

- **PolicyStore**   This parameter can target the local computer GPO (which we did here) or a domain GPO (for instance, contoso.local\FirewallPolicy).
- **Profile**   Options here are Any, Domain, Private, or Public.
- **InboundSecurity**, **OutboundSecurity**   None is used when we want to exclude a server from IPSec communications as we do in this case. The other options are Require and Request.

Windows PowerShell is known for its consistent command syntax. We can leverage related PowerShell cmdlets to modify connection security rules programmatically:

- **SetNetIPSecRule**   Edit an existing connection security rule
- **CopyNetIPSecRule**   Copy an existing IPSec rule to the same or different policy store
- **DisableNetIPSecRule**   This command, as well as Enable-NetIPSecRule, is useful when troubleshooting secure communications
- **GetNetIPSecRule**, **ShowNetIPSecRule**   The Get cmdlet gives you a concise list, and the Show cmdlet provides an expanded rule
- **RemoveNetIPSecRule**   Deletes one or more rules from a given policy store

> **NOTE**   **EMBRACING THE POWER OF POWERSHELL**
>
> At first glance, configuring IPSec connection security rules with Windows PowerShell might appear awkward and unnecessarily slow.
>
> Please remember that a 'clean' Windows PowerShell script can replicate a desired configuration as many times as you need with zero human error. Moreover, Windows PowerShell was developed to perform remote administration, so you can deploy and manage IPSec policies across your entire domain with only a few lines of code. That's true administrative power!

Configuring IPSec defaults

In Group Policy, right-click the Windows Firewall with Advanced Security node and select Properties from the shortcut menu. On the IPsec Settings tab we have a number of configuration policies specific to, well, IPSec protocols. Let's have a quick look at those, using Figure 3-9 as reference.

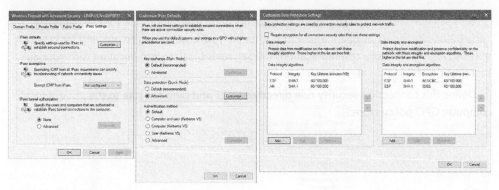

FIGURE 3-9 Configuring IPSec in Windows Server 2016

Under IPsec defaults, we click Customize to reach the Customize IPsec Defaults dialog box. Here we can set protocol defaults for both data protection (encryption) as well as authentication. Under Data protection (Quick Mode), we click Customize to visit the Customize Data Protection Settings dialog.

You are likely fine with the defaults and never need to get to this level of granular detail. This is only to show you that it is possible to specify, for example, which encryption algorithms should be used in your domain for IPSec-secured data exchange.

Configure Windows Firewall to allow or deny applications

Windows Firewall is a host-based software firewall that provides stateful packet inspection (SPI) for inbound and outbound traffic flows. To that point, we can create Windows Firewall rules that operate at higher OSI layers than you might originally think.

Recall that traditional IP address and TCP/UDP port firewall rules operate at OSI layers 3 and 4, respectively. But what about creating firewall rules that target applications using several different ports and protocols? This is why OSI layer 7 (application layer) is so important for us to understand.

Application-level rule presets

The first step in defining a Windows Firewall with Advanced Security rule is to choose what type of rule you want. As shown in Figure 3-10, Windows Server 2016 includes a large number of application and/or service-specific rules.

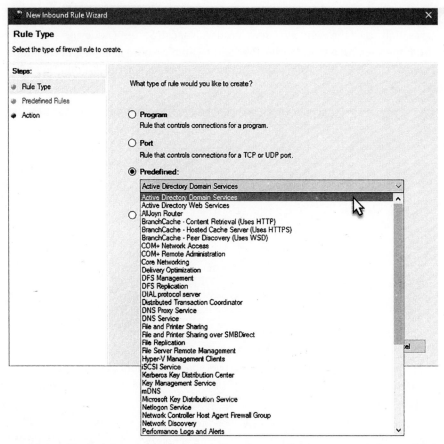

FIGURE 3-10 We don't have to worry about ports and protocols when we can define application-specific firewall rules

Some of these presets are very useful in day-to-day Windows Server administration. We have entries for DNS, BranchCache, DFS, File and Printer Sharing, and remote management.

Alternatively, you can go down the "Program" path in the Inbound or Outbound Rule Wizards, respectively, and simply browse to find an executable program file to which you want to scope a firewall rule. Figure 3-11 depicts the interface.

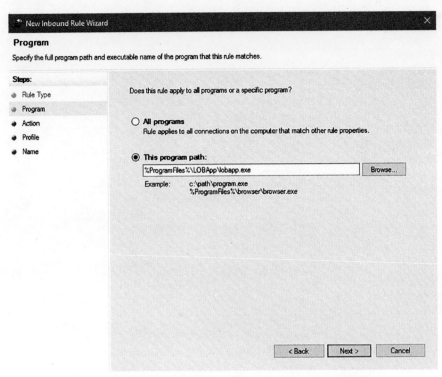

FIGURE 3-11 Specifying a program path when defining a Windows Firewall rule

Other than specifying an executable file name as opposed to discrete IP addresses and/or port numbers, application firewall policy configuration is exactly the same as we've covered earlier in the chapter.

Configure authenticated firewall exceptions

The use case here is straightforward: we want strict Windows Firewall rules protecting our domain servers, but we also use enterprise configuration and security management tools that need to scan and update those same servers.

Authenticated firewall bypass works by specifying that all authenticated IP traffic from approved computers bypasses Windows Firewall. We customize Windows Firewall traffic exceptions in (you guessed it) Group Policy, under the following path:

```
Computer Configuration\Policies\Administrative Templates\Network\Network Connections\
Windows Firewall
```

Specifically, look at the policy Windows Firewall: Allow Authenticated IPsec Bypass, shown in Figure 3-12.

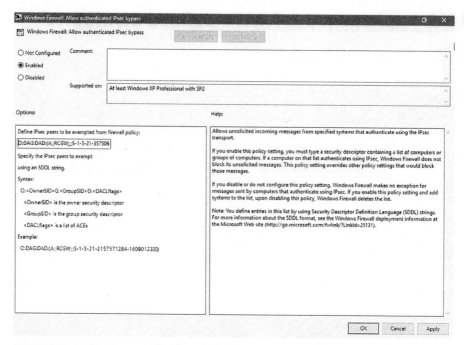

FIGURE 3-12 Configuring an authenticated Windows Firewall exception in Group Policy

We enable the policy and then craft a Security Descriptor Definition Language (SDDL) string that defines the computers or computer groups whose network traffic should be allowed to bypass Windows Firewall.

For example, the following SDDL string defines an exception for a single computer group named Policy Servers:

```
O:DAG:DAD:(A;;RCGW;;;S-1-5-21-2964486071-1673034363-2324534321-1522)
```

How did we know the security identifier (SID)? Simple, we ran Get-ADGroup. Alternatively, we could have opened Active Directory Users and Computer, enabled Advanced Features, and inspected the Properties sheet of the object.

> **NOTE IPSEC EXEMPTION**
>
> We just saw a policy called Allow Authenticated IPSec Bypass that whitelists one or more domain computers with Windows Firewall. Don't get confused between this policy and the IPSec connection security rule type **Authentication exemption**. This latter policy is used to exempt servers from IPSec authentication, not Windows Firewall.

Skill 3.2: Implement a software-defined Distributed Firewall

There is some good news and bad news. The good news is that much of the Azure public cloud functionality is coming to your local data center in Windows Server 2016. The bad news is that, at least as of this recording, Microsoft hasn't given us too many details.

In this section, we pay particular attention to the new Network Controller server role and how it supports the datacenter firewall. Along the way you're bound to pick up some useful background knowledge on software-defined networking (SDN) and how Microsoft plans to give us SDN on-premises as well as in the Azure cloud.

> **This section covers how to:**
>
> - Determine requirements and scenarios for Distributed Firewall implementation with Software Defined Networking
> - Determine usage scenarios for Distributed Firewall policies and network security groups

Determine requirements and scenarios for Distributed Firewall implementation with Software Defined Networking

Our first order of business is to understand what "software defined networking" (SDN) actually is. As you know, powerful server hardware keeps getting less expensive, while its power and capabilities grow in an inversely-proportional manner.

At base, SDN refers to the separation of computing resources' data plane and control plane.

Microsoft Azure and SDN

To illustrate SDN, let's consider Microsoft Azure, which is Microsoft's quintessential SDN implementation. Figure 3-13 depicts the basic Azure Resource Manager (ARM) architecture.

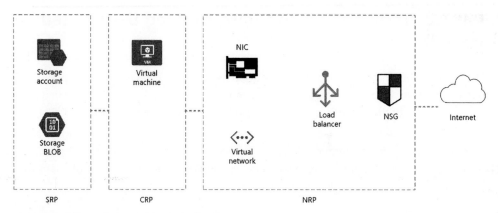

FIGURE 3-13 Microsoft Azure schematic diagram

Referring to Figure 3-13, SRP stands for Storage Resource Provider, and relates to the Azure storage account. As far as the Azure customer is concerned, he or she provisions as much storage as he or she needs to suit business requirements. We don't care specifically how the physical hard drives located in the Azure datacenters are being tended to; that's Microsoft's responsibility.

Likewise, CRP is the Compute Resource Provider, where we deploy and manage our Azure virtual machines in an infrastructure-as-a-service (IaaS) scenario. Once again, we leave the physical hardware (data plane) to Microsoft; our scope of responsibility is the control plane; namely the Azure web portal, Windows PowerShell, REST API access, and so forth.

Finally, NRP stands for the Network Resource Provider. This is where we're particularly concerned at this point in our studies. Notice the logical network interface card (NIC), and how that abstracted NIC attaches both to a virtual IP network and subnet as well as to a logical load balancer.

NSG stands for Network Security Group, and in Azure this object serves as a stateful firewall. It is through administrator-defined endpoints that the Azure virtual machine can reach the public Internet or a site-to-site VPN link.

Bringing Azure SDN on-premises

The new Network Controller server role in Windows Server 2016 is one aspect of Microsoft's plans to bring full Azure SDN to your local datacenter. The public cloud isn't for everyone; your business could be subject to governmental and/or industry compliance requirements that mandate your having full control of your intellectual property and confidential data.

Distributed Firewall, which has since been renamed in (most) Microsoft literature as Datacenter Firewall, is one aspect of the Network Resource Provider component of the Network Controller role, and it's what we need to drill into.

EXAM TIP

We see in this section a discrepancy between "Distributed firewall" and "Data center firewall." The fact that Microsoft seemingly changes its product names on a whim can be reflected in your 70-744 exam. Therefore, you should be prepared to see references to product names that have since been changed. That means the onus is on you to keep current with your Microsoft technology news to keep abreast of these many (often spontaneous) name shifts.

Getting started with the Network Controller

We can install the Network Controller role with a single line of PowerShell:

```
Install-WindowsFeature -Name NetworkController -IncludeManagementTools -Restart
```

The specifics of Network Controller are beyond our scope; however, it looks like we are limited to Windows PowerShell for Network Controller configuration in Windows Server 2016 out of the proverbial box.

But you can do a lot with only the PowerShell. Run the following one-liner to get a cmdlet count; here are 264 Network Controller cmdlets on a test server.

```
Get-Command -Module NetworkController | Measure-Object
```

The long-term plan is that Windows systems administrators should use a front-end orchestration tool like System Center 2016 Virtual Machine Manager (VMM) to "ride on top of" Network Controller and facilitate our provisioning assets like virtual networks, virtual NICs, network security groups, and so forth.

For instance, see in Figure 3-14 how straightforward VMM makes this process:

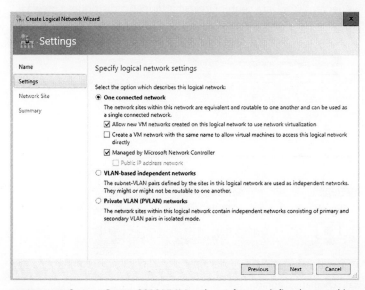

FIGURE 3-14 System Center 2016 VMM makes software-defined networking much easier

In Figure 3-14 we see a screenshot from the System Center 2016 VMM Create Logical Network Wizard. Our on-premises private cloud workflow might look something like the following:

- We start with aggregating commodity hardware into a back-end data plane fabric; this consists of compute, storage, and network resources
- Hyper-V forms the hypervisor layer and virtual machine "engine"
- Network Controller orchestrates the inter-relationship between SDN virtual networks and your organization's physical LAN/WAN topology
- System Center 2016 VMM or Azure Stack form the administrative control plan that links your storage, compute, and networking subsystems

> **NOTE   PLANNING AN SDN INFRASTRUCTURE**
>
> Planning for SDN involves purchasing hardware that is optimized not only for performance but also for the heavy abstraction and access control involved. This subject is far outside this book's scope, so we want to draw your attention to the excellent Microsoft TechNet article "Plan a Software Defined Network Infrastructure" at *http://timw.info/sdn*.

Determine usage scenarios for Distributed Firewall policies and network security groups

Now let's turn our attention to the usage scenario and basic operation of the data center firewall. We call this feature "data center firewall" instead of "distributed firewall" to reflect current Microsoft TechNet nomenclature.

Regardless, the Windows Server 2016 Data center Firewall is indeed a distributed firewall. Take a look at Figure 3-15 to see how it works.

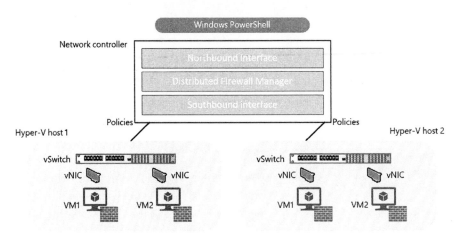

FIGURE 3-15 Datacenter Firewall schematic diagram

Figure 3-15 has quite a bit of information packed in there, so let's take this one component at a time. First, let's understand the north-south-east-west terminology as it relates to distributed firewalls:

- **Northbound interface**   This isn't an interface like an RJ-45 jack. Instead, this is the application programming interface (API) used by Network Controller to communicate with your LAN, WAN, and the Internet.

- **Southbound interface**   This is the API used by Network Controller to communicate with your SDN.

- **West- or eastbound interfaces**   These APIs allow multiple Network Controller nodes within a cluster to communicate.

Specifically, Microsoft employs Representational State Transfer (REST) APIs "wrapped" in Windows PowerShell for Network Controller and Datacenter Firewall operations.

What that means for us administrators more concretely is that the Datacenter Firewall allows us to define firewall policies centrally and distribute them to Hyper-V VMs running on separate hardware virtualization hosts.

Azure Stack and multi-tenancy

The Datacenter Firewall and Network Controller are core components of the forthcoming Azure Stack. Azure Stack gives us an on-premises private cloud experience that closely mirrors what we have now in the Azure public cloud, including use of the web portal and REST APIs.

Figure 3-15 depicted Datacenter Firewall distributing security policies to two separate Hyper-V hosts intentionally. We want to underline the concept of multi-tenancy for you because this idea permeates cloud computing.

Have you ever rented an apartment? The landlord probably owns the physical infrastructure (that is, the apartment building and its enclosed units). You, the tenant, pay the landlord a monthly fee for use of a single apartment dwelling. You're sharing the physical infrastructure with other tenants at the behest of the landlord.

As a rent-paying tenant, you can manage your bills and activities of daily life with no knowledge of or reliance on other tenants in the building. And that fundamental separation between tenants is just fine.

This balance between tenant isolation and shared back-end infrastructure is the central point of the multi-tenant cloud. For example, if you're a managed service provider, then you offer virtual networks, storage accounts, and compute resources to your customers. Even within a single organization, business units sometimes need strong isolation boundaries between their computing assets.

Datacenter Firewall access control lists (ACLs)

In Azure terminology, the Network Security Group (NSG) is a firewall that granularly allows or blocks traffic to a particular virtual machine. Windows Server 2016 Datacenter Firewall uses the older term "access control list" but for the same purpose: we apply Datacenter Firewall ACLs to individual virtual network interfaces, or to virtual networks.

Your ACL rules can enforce policies such as preventing Hyper-V VMs from specific subnets from communicating with each other.

A word about Hyper-V network virtualization

In server virtualization, we run several virtual server instances on a physical Hyper-V host. Likewise, network virtualization involves multiple virtual networks, possibly with overlapping IP addresses, running on the same physical network infrastructure. Once again, this is SDN and supports multi-tenant isolation.

Many Windows Server 2016 features undergird Hyper-V network virtualization, but we want to draw your attention specifically to the Hyper-V virtual switch. Even more specifically, take a look at Figure 3-16.

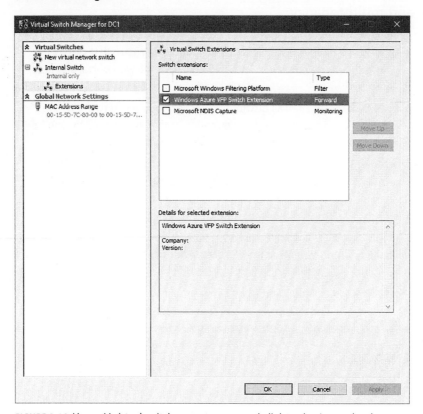

FIGURE 3-16 Hyper-V virtual switches can transparently link to the Azure cloud

Notice the new virtual switch extension called Windows Azure Virtual Filtering Platform (VFP). Now besides the reference to "Windows Azure" in Windows Server 2016 (Microsoft renamed Azure to Microsoft Azure many moons ago) and missing metadata details in the interface, our imagination should be rightly fired.

That is, according to Microsoft's preliminary literature on the subject, we can leverage this extension to link our Hyper-V virtual switches to on-premises SDN or directly to public Azure virtual networks.

Skill 3.3: Secure network traffic

In this section we turn our attention to the venerable Server Message Block (SMB) file-sharing protocol, and how Microsoft has increased its security and performance in Windows Server 2016. We also take a detour to consider industry-wide advances to DNS, and the retooled Microsoft Message Analyzer, a tool that should be in every Windows system administrator's toolbelt.

This section covers how to:

- Determine SMB 3.1.1 protocol security scenarios and implementations
- Enable SMB encryption on SMB shares
- Configure SMB signing and disable SMB 1.0
- Secure DNS traffic using DNSSEC and DNS policies
- Install and configure Microsoft Message Analyzer (MMA) to analyze network traffic

Determine SMB 3.1.1 protocol security scenarios and implementations

Server Message Block (SMB) is Window's default file-sharing protocol, and has been for a long time. Specifically, SMB is a dialect of the old Common Internet File System (CIFS) protocol, and is tied to two key Windows services:

- Server (for defining file shares)
- Workstation (for connecting to file shares)

SMB operates on OSI Layer 4 (Session layer) using TCP port 445, and when using the Net-BIOS API UDP ports 137-138 and TCP ports 137 and 139.

But first, SMB 3.0

We want to go over the excellent new functionality Microsoft added to SMB 3.0 in Windows Server 2012 R2.

- **SMB Transparent Failover**   Supports file share high availability in Windows Failover Clustering scenarios

- **SMB Direct**   Takes advantage of Remote Data Memory Access (RDMA) to transfer data with little CPU involvement. This NIC-related features drastically improves performance of Hyper-V hosts and VMs

- **SMB Multichannel**   An alternative to NIC teaming that adds redundancy to the path between, say, a Hyper-V host and SMB shares

- **SMB PowerShell**   Microsoft added a large number of Windows PowerShell cmdlets and Windows Management Instrumentation (WMI) objects to manage SMB servers, file shares, and clients

To get a feel for what's possible with SMB PowerShell, open an administrative PowerShell console session on one of your Windows Server 2016 servers and run the following pipeline:

```
Get-Command -Module SmbShare | Select-Object -Property Name | Format-Wide -Column 2
```

So yes, SMB took a giant leap forward with SMB 3.0 in Windows Server 2012 R2. Let's see what's new in SMB 3.1.1. in Windows Server 2016 by touring three features:

- Pre-authentication integrity
- Encryption performance improvements
- Cluster dialect fencing

Pre-authentication integrity

Pre-authentication integrity is an SMB 3.1.1 feature in Windows Server 2016 and Windows 10 that protects against man-in-the-middle (MITM) attacks. It does this by using cryptographic hashing to prevent tampering with SMB 2.0's Negotiate and Session Startup messages. The net effect is that the SMB client and server authenticate to each other throughout their communications.

To this point, disable SMB v1 and v2 in your environment. On your SMB servers, run the following PowerShell command to check whether legacy SMB versions are enabled:

```
Get-SmbServerConfiguration | Select-Object -Property EnableSMB1Protocol,
EnableSMB2Protocol
```

To disable SMB v1 and v2, run the following commands on the server:

```
Set-SmbServerConfiguration -EnableSMB1Protocol $false -Force
Set-SmbServerConfiguration -EnableSMB2Protocol $false -Force
```

Of course, you should perform due diligence and examine the possible side effects of disabling older SMB versions, especially if you run in a mixed environment with older Windows Server hosts. To disable SMB v1 on Windows Client devices, run the following Service Control (sc.exe) commands:

```
sc.exe config lanmanworkstation depend= bowser/mrxsmb20/nsi
sc.exe config mrxsmb10 start= disabled
```

Encryption performance improvements

The key (pun intended) to stronger encryption is longer encryption keys and more robust encryption algorithms. SMB 3.1.1 uses the AES-128-GCM algorithm by default. This is a 2x improvement over AES-128-CCM used in previous SMB versions.

What's more is that the GCM algorithm is backward-compatible with Windows Server 2012 R2 SMB encryption.

Cluster dialect fencing

Windows Server 2012 R2 gave us Cluster Rolling Upgrade (CRU). CRU is a new Windows Server 2016 feature that helps you avoid Service Level Agreement (SLA) downtime penalties when you upgrade Windows failover cluster nodes from Windows Server 2012 R2 to Windows Server 2016.

Look, SMB involves a lot of protocol and version negotiation between SMB server and clients. Hyper-V and Scale-out File Server are two popular high-availability workloads in Windows failover clustering.

Cluster Dialect Fencing, in a nutshell, makes it easier for SMB clients and servers to find a common SMB version dialect during the cluster upgrade process.

Enable SMB encryption on SMB shares

Okay, enough theory. Let's cover how to enable SMB encryption on SMB servers. We perform these configuration changes by using good old Windows PowerShell.

First of all, obtain SMB server and client configuration by running the following cmdlets:

```
GetSmbServerConfiguration
GetSmbClientConfiguration
```

To force all SMB sessions on a server to be encrypted, try this:

```
SetSmbServerConfiguration -EncryptData 1
```

To enable SMB encryption on a specific file share, run the following PowerShell command, substituting <share-name> with the name of your file share as appropriate:

```
Set-SmbShare -Name <share-name> -EncryptData 1
```

Actually, you can enable SMB encryption when you define the share instead:

```
New-SmbShare -Name ProjectDocs -Path D:\projectdata001 -EncryptData 1
```

Another SMB server configuration option you might want to consider is preventing clients that do not support SMB encryption from connecting to encrypted shares:

```
Set-SmbServerConfiguration -RejectUnencryptedAccess 1
```

As shown in Figure 3-17, we can enable or disable SMB encryption on a per-share basis by opening Server Manager, navigating to File and Storage Services | Shares, and examining the Properties sheet of an SMB share.

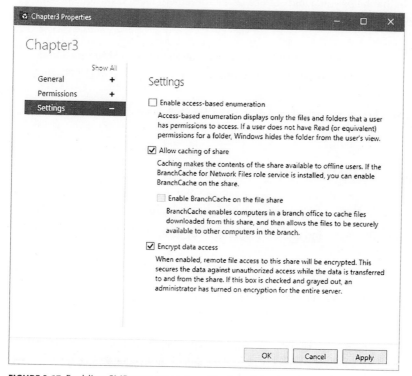

FIGURE 3-17 Enabling SMB encryption for a file share by using Server Manager

Configure SMB signing and disable SMB 1.0

Digital signatures provide a useful method to ensure data integrity and expose attempts to forge or otherwise modify packets in transit between hosts.

SMB has long supported cryptographic signing at the packet level. SMB signing should be enabled on your domain controller because it ensures that client devices receive genuine Group Policy configurations.

Configure SMB signing

There are no big surprises here, even in Windows Server 2016: We can use Group Policy to configure SMB signing for our domain controllers and domain members. Navigate to the age-old Group Policy path:

```
Computer Configuration\Policies\Windows Settings\Security Settings\Local Policies\
Security Options
```

> **NOTE SMB SIGNING AND NETWORK PERFORMANCE**
>
> According to the Microsoft TechNet library (*http://timw.info/smb*),using SMB packet sign-ing can degrade file service transaction performance by up to 15 percent. This makes sense when you remember that Windows needs to calculate hash values on every single packet in an SMB stream.

On the SMB server side, the Microsoft Network Server: Digitally Sign Communications (Al-ways) policy configures SMB servers not to communicate with SMB clients unless those clients agree to participate in SMB packet signing.

The Microsoft network server: Digitally Sign Communications (If Client Agrees) policy isn't as black-and white as the previous Group Policy setting. Here, the SMB server negotiates the highest level of SMB security with connecting clients, but does not drop the connection if the client cannot participate in SMB packet signing.

On the SMB client side we have the Microsoft Network Client: Digitally Sign Communica-tions (Always) and Microsoft Network Client: Digitally Sign Communications (If Server Agrees) policies. These behave the same way as the server-side policies, except the roles are reversed.

Secure DNS traffic using DNSSEC and DNS policies

The Domain Name System (DNS) forms the foundation of hostname-to-IP address name resolution. DNS is required by Active Directory, et cetera, et cetera. What's the big deal about DNS?

Well, actually, DNS's importance and age both result in its vulnerability to abuse. Attackers can poison DNS server cache data to redirect clients to illegitimate hosts and sites. Malicious parties can 'squat' on hostnames to, again, hijack legitimate DNS name resolution traffic for illegitimate means.

Let's have a look at one new and one newer DNS feature (one Microsoft-proprietary and one vendor-neutral, respectively) that harden the DNS Server service.

DNSSEC basics

Domain Name System Security Extensions (DNSSEC) is an extension to the DNS protocol, de-fined by the Internet Engineering Task Force (IETF, of which Microsoft is a member), that uses public key cryptography to provide integrity and authentication to DNS zone records.

A digital signature is a mathematical method for validating the authenticity of a message. When you digitally sign a DNS zone in Windows Server 2016, a public-private key pair is used both to sign all resource records as well as to verify that each record has not been tampered with; hence DNSSEC's utility in defeating DNS cache poisoning attacks.

Deploying DNSSEC: a fast run-through

Following this procedure to quickly get a feel for how DNSSEC works in Windows Server 2016. Use a domain controller named dc1 and a member server named hyperv1.

1. On hyperv1, open an administrative PowerShell session and run a DNS query against dc1, its configured DNS server:

    ```
    Resolve-DnsName -Name dc1.contoso.local -Type A -DnssecOk

    Name                  Type    TTL    Section    IPAddress
    ----                  ----    ---    -------    ---------
    dc1.contoso.local     A       3600   Answer     10.0.0.1
    ```

    The DnssecOk switch parameter lets the DNS server know that the client is capable of working with DNSSEC. By the way, Windows Server 2012 R2, Windows 8.1, and Windows 10 are all DNSSEC-aware clients.

    The Type A parameter/value pair specifies that we're interested only in IPv4 for this exercise.

2. Open the DNS MMC console on dc1, right-click the domain's zone, and select DNSSEC | Sign The Zone from the shortcut menu.

3. In the Zone Signing Wizard, select Use Default Settings To Sign The Zone and then click Next to sign the zone using Microsoft's defaults. The only time you need to customize the DNSSEC settings is if you're required to do so for compliance regulation reasons.

4. As you can see in Figure 3-18, your zone has quite a few more resource records. Here are some highlights:

    ■ **DNSKEY**   This record stores the public key that is used to crytographically validate signed DNS records. In public key infrastructure (PKI), the DNS server signs the records with its private key, and validates the records' integrity by using its corresponding public key. Note that in DNSSEC it's the DNS server that performs the record validation on behalf of DNS clients.

    ■ **RRSIG**   This record is the digital signature for a particular DNS record. If a single bit is changed in a resource record (which would occur in a cache poisoning or spoofing attack), then the validation would break and resolution would fail for that request.

    ■ **NSEC3**   This record supports authenticated denial of existence. In other words, the DNS server can authoritatively claim that a given resource record does NOT exist.

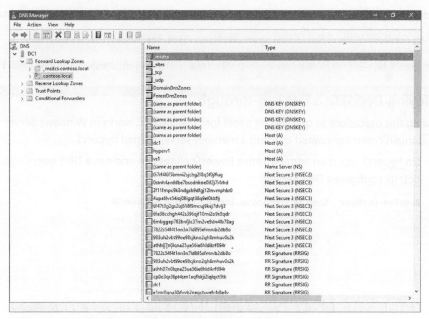

FIGURE 3-18 A signed DNS zone in Windows Server 2106

5. Now go back to the DNS client and re-run the Resolve-DnsName cmdlet:

```
Resolve-DnsName -Name dc1.contoso.local -Type A -DnssecOk
```

```
Name                             Type   TTL   Section    IPAddress
----                             ----   ---   -------    ---------
dc1.contoso.local                A      3600  Answer     10.0.0.1

Name         : dc1.contoso.local
QueryType    : RRSIG
TTL          : 3600
Section      : Answer
TypeCovered  : A
Algorithm    : 8
LabelCount   : 3
OriginalTtl  : 3600
Expiration   : 10/13/2016 2:34:12 PM
Signed       : 10/3/2016 1:34:12 PM
Signer       : contoso.local
Signature    : {58, 52, 246, 12...}
```

There is quite a bit more output, right?

Name Resolution Policy Table (NRPT)

We can use Group Policy to establish rules that affected nodes use when performing DNS queries. For example, we can force all domain nodes to request DNSSEC record validation whenever they reach one of your infrastructure DNS servers.

Configure NRPT rules in the following Group Policy path:

```
Computer Configuration\Policies\Windows Settings\Name Resolution Policy
```

The Name Resolution Policy has its own interface that you can check out in Figure 3-19.

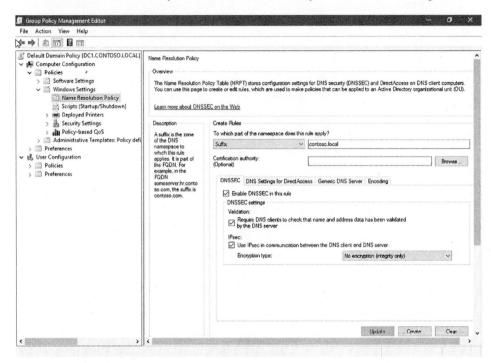

FIGURE 3-19 Configuring DNSSEC client policy in Group Policy

Under Create Rules, we can specify which DNS zone to scope for DNSSEC. Select Enable DNSSEC In This Rule to require that DNS clients check that name and address data has been validated by the server.

Optionally, select Use IPsec In Communication Between The DNS Client And The DNS Server. With the No Encryption (Integrity Only) option, we can layer IPSec into our DNS traffic without incurring the overhead penalty of data encryption.

DNS policies

The Microsoft development teams are innovating with their DNS server. Once again, it's too easy to take DNS for granted, it being such an old and globally used network protocol.

DNS policies in Windows Server 2016 enable administrators to control how their DNS servers handle different types of queries. To illustrate, review these typical use-case scenarios:

- **Split-brain DNS** Create zone scopes to make it easier to handle resolution of public and private zones with matching names (for example, constoso.com used internally with AD and externally to host the corporate website)

- **Traffic management**   DNS client traffic is automatically redirected to their geo-graphically closest DNS server
- **Filtering**   Malicious DNS queries are blocked and malicious DNS clients are blacklisted
- **Time of day redirection**   DNS queries forwarded to specific servers based on time of day

Intelligent DNS responses

In a theme that's rapidly becoming standard for Windows Server configuration, we use Windows PowerShell to define DNS policies. Let's run through a quick example in which we want to configure intelligent DNS responses based upon time of day.

We have two datacenters: one in the United States and another in Europe. Depending on the time, we redirect clients to hosts that reside closer to the client's location.

On one of our domain controllers, we create DNS client subnets for each region:

```
Add-DnsServerClientSubnet -Name 'USASubnet -IPv4Subnet '192.0.0.0/24, 182.0.0.0/24'
Add-DnsServerClientSubnet -Name 'EuropeSubnet' -IPv4Subnet '141.1.0.0/24, 151.1.0.0/24'
```

Next, define zone scopes. In DNS policy nomenclature, DNS zone scopes represent unique instances of a given DNS zone that can be configured in different ways.

```
Add-DnsServerZoneScope -ZoneName 'contoso.com' -Name 'USAZoneScope'
Add-DnsServerZoneScope -ZoneName 'contoso.com' -Name 'EuropeZoneScope'
```

Now define host records inside each zone scope. For instance, the following code defines records for Contoso's SharePoint Server:

```
Add-DnsServerResourceRecord -ZoneName 'contoso.com' -A -Name 'sharepoint' -IPv4Address
'192.0.0.1' -ZoneScope 'USAZoneScope'
Add-DnsServerResourceRecord -ZoneName 'contoso.com' -A -Name 'sharepoint' -IPv4Address
'141.1.0.3' -ZoneScope 'EuropeZoneScope'
```

Finally, create the actual DNS policy. The following PowerShell code specifies the following rules:

- European DNS clients receive the IP address of the SharePoint server in the Europe datacenter in their DNS query response.
- American DNS clients receive the IP address of the SharePoint server in the USA data-center in their DNS query response.
- Between 6 PM and 9 PM in Europe, 20 percent of the queries from European clients receive the IP address of the Web server in the USA datacenter in their DNS query response.
- Between 6 PM and 9 PM in the USA, 20 percent of the queries from the American clients receive the IP address of the Web server in the Europe datacenter in their DNS query response.
- Half of the queries from the rest of the world receive the IP address of the USA data-center and the other half receive the IP address of the Europe datacenter.

```
Add-DnsServerQueryResolutionPolicy -Name 'America6To9Policy' -Action ALLOW -ClientSubnet
'eq,USASubnet' -ZoneScope 'USAZoneScope,4;EuropeZoneScope,1' -TimeOfDay 'EQ,01:00-04:00'
-ZoneName 'contoso.com' -ProcessingOrder 1

Add-DnsServerQueryResolutionPolicy -Name 'Europe6To9Policy' -Action ALLOW -ClientSubnet
'eq,EuropeSubnet' -ZoneScope 'USAZoneScope,1;EuropeZoneScope,4' -TimeOfDay 'EQ,17:00-
20:00' -ZoneName 'contoso.com' -ProcessingOrder 2

Add-DnsServerQueryResolutionPolicy -Name 'AmericaPolicy' -Action ALLOW -ClientSubnet
'eq,USASubnet' -ZoneScope 'USAZoneScope,1' -ZoneName 'contoso.com' -ProcessingOrder 3

Add-DnsServerQueryResolutionPolicy -Name 'EuropePolicy' -Action ALLOW -ClientSubnet
'eq,EuropeSubnet' -ZoneScope 'EuropeZoneScope,1' -ZoneName 'contoso.com'
-ProcessingOrder 4

Add-DnsServerQueryResolutionPolicy -Name 'RestOfWorldPolicy' -Action ALLOW --ZoneScope
'EuropeZoneScope,1;USAZoneScope,1' -ZoneName 'contoso.com' -ProcessingOrder 5
```

Install and configure Microsoft Message Analzyer to analyze network traffic

Microsoft Message Analyzer (MMA) is Microsoft's free network protocol analyzer. MMA is the successor to the Network Monitor (Netmon) tool that's been a part of Windows since Windows NT 4.0. MMA represents a viable alternative to other popular protocol analyzers, such as Wireshark.

Not only does MMA give you frame-level visualization of network traffic flows, it also is a nifty log file reader. The tool's ever-expanding parser library can easily decode log files from Windows Server, Microsoft Azure, and third-party applications and protocols.

Go ahead and download MMA from the Microsoft Download Center. In our lab, we installed the tool on a Windows Server 2016 domain controller.

Let's run through an example in which we start an SMB-specific capture on dc1 and monitor SMB client/server communications.

1. Open Microsoft Message Analyzer and click New Session on the application Start page.

2. In the New Session dialog, give the session a meaningful name, like SMB transfer trace, and then click Live Trace. Notice in the interface that you can parse log data from Azure, the Event logs, SQL Server, or the Operations Management Suite (OMS).

3. On the Live Trace 1 tab, open the Select Scenario drop-down and type **smb** to view the built-in SMB-oriented scenarios. Scenarios make it easier to capture interesting traffic based on specific use cases. Figure 3-20 depicts the interface. Select the SMB2 Server Header Only scenario, ensure Localhost is set in the Target Computers: text box, and click Start to begin the capture.

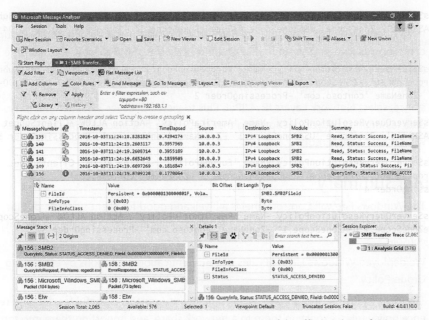

FIGURE 3-20 Scenarios make it easier to capture meaningful traffic in Microsoft Message Analyzer

4. Click the Stop button to halt the trace. Now the hard work comes in; namely, making sense of the output. Figure 3-21 contains an example.

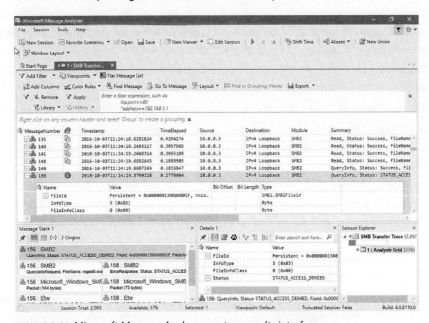

FIGURE 3-21 Microsoft Message Analyzer capture results interface.

5. Open the Layout menu and scroll to the File Sharing category. Once again, the MMA team offers presets to show you the fields that are most meaningful based on your use case. For example, you could try File Sharing Perf SMB2/SMB to view elapsed time and response time metrics.

6. Open the Viewpoints menu to observe the different protocol layer presets. For instance, select Network Layers IPv4/IPv6 Plus to view OSI Layer 3 header and payload data (assuming that you're capturing that data in the first place; MMA can't display what it hasn't captured).

Chapter summary

- The Windows Firewall Control Panel is all well and good for client systems, but for server security we need the power of the Windows Firewall with Advanced Security console.

- We deployed Windows Firewall rules and authentication exceptions by employing Group Policy.

- The local Windows Firewall with Advanced Security console is useful for defining reference policy rules, exporting them to a network share, and importing them into target GPOs.

- Connection security rules involve IPSec (specifically AH and ESP protocols) to provide confidentiality, integrity, and authentication on the network between specific hosts.

- We can work with Windows Firewall and connection security rules programmatically with Windows PowerShell or various MMC administrative console. There's also the ancient netsh command-line tool that still exists in Windows Server 2016.

- The trend with Microsoft is gradually exposing more and more Azure public cloud services to its on-premises customers.

- The new Network Controller role facilitates software-defined networking on-premises.

- Datacenter Firewall is a distributed, network-layer, stateful, multi-tenant firewall that protects access to virtual networks and individual VMs running on separate Hyper-V hosts.

- In Windows Server 2016, we're limited to managing the Network Controller and Distributed Firewall by using Windows PowerShell. However, System Center 2016 Virtual Machine Manager and Azure Stack give administrators a much more robust, graphical management surface.

- SMB 3.1.1 includes new security features that reduce the likelihood of man-in-the-middle (MITM) network attacks on SMB servers and clients.

- Windows Server 2016 DNS server continues to support DNSSEC; this technology leverages cryptographic signing to protect DNS resource records against spoofing and cache poisoning attacks.

- DNS policies, a new Windows Server 2016 feature, enable systems administrators to customize how DNS servers respond to client queries.

- Microsoft Message Analyzer is a free protocol analyzer that is the successor to Microsoft Network Monitor. The MMA development team actively develops add-ons and documentation to make the admittedly overwhelming capture output easier to comprehend.

Thought experiment

In this thought experiment, demonstrate your skills and knowledge of the topics covered in this chapter. You can find answer to this thought experiment in the next section.

You are a systems administrator for a scientific research institute at Woodgrove University. The institute is organized as a single Active Directory domain in which all infrastructure servers run Windows Server 2012 R2. You are halfway through an in-place upgrade process to Windows 10 Enterprise Edition for your users.

Two research groups within the institute have opened discussions with you concerning new business and operational requirements they are facing. The Jones research group secured a contract with the federal government which requires that their 3 servers and 21 desktop computers be isolated completely from the rest of the institute, the university, and even the Internet.

The Smith research group purchased a custom line of business (LOB) application server that communicates on TCP ports 47777 and 57777 and requires both authentication and data encryption. They need the software deployed on two servers, and communications needs to be supported between the two LOB app servers and the group's 14 desktop clients. Moreover, the LOB application is qualified for use only on Windows Server 2016.

1. Does your support of the Smith and Jones research groups require that you upgrade all the institute's infrastructure servers to Windows Server 2016?

2. What is your strategy to support the Smith group's business requirements?

3. What is your strategy to support the Jones group's business requirements?

Thought experiment answers

This section contains the solution to the thought experiment.

1. You are not required to upgrade all the institute's servers to Windows Server 2016 in this case. The Smith group's LOB application requires this version, so you need to perform upgrades for them. However, Windows Firewall with Advanced Security configuration hasn't changed between Windows Server 2012 R2 and Windows Server 2016, so you can employ the same Group Policy settings in either version.

2. To support the Smith group, you need to define an inbound Windows Firewall with Advanced Security Domain port rule for the two LOB servers that allows TCP 47777 and TCP 57777 connections from the Smith group's computers. Figure 3-22 depicts the rule's Properties page.

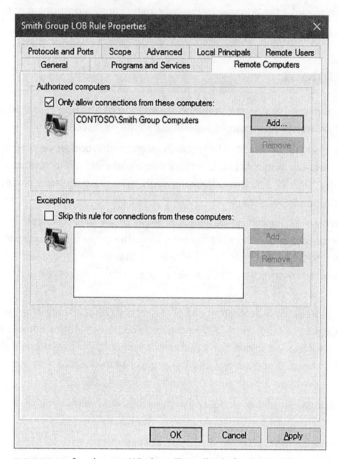

FIGURE 3-22 Scoping our Windows Firewall rule for the Smith research group

Because the Smith group calls for authentication and encryption, you need to enable the Allow The Connection If It Is Secure option for the rule to include IPSec in the configuration. Of course, the easiest way to deploy the rule is via a scoped GPO.

3. For the Jones group, you need to configure isolation for their entire network environment. While it is theoretically to isolate the group physically by reorganizing the institute's network hardware, we can accomplish this goal logically by (a) organizing the network segment as its own Active Directory domain; and (b) scoping a GPO to the group's 3 servers and 21 desktop clients that defines an IPSec connection security rule.

As is the case with Windows Server, there exists many different ways to arrive at the same result. One option is to define an Isolation connection security rule that includes the following properties:

- Endpoint 1 includes the IP addresses of the Jones group's 3 servers
- Endpoint 2 includes the IP addresses of the Jones group's 21 client workstations
- Authentication mode is Require Inbound And Outbound
- Authentication method is Computer And User (Kerberos V5)
- Protocols and ports are set to Any

## CHAPTER 4

Manage Privileged Identities

Cybersecurity attacks are commonly the result of administrative account penetration. Attackers can compromise privileged identities in a myriad of ways, some of which are simply not preventable using software and firmware tools, however sophisticated they become. Assuming that administrative accounts can conceivably be compromised, you should attempt to minimize the danger presented by such attacks by managing how privileged identities are used in the enterprise. Simply put, users requiring administrative access to perform certain tasks should employ administrative accounts only for those tasks, and those administrative accounts should have only the privileges needed to perform those tasks. Windows Server 2016 includes tools and architectures that enable you to control the privileges granted to administrative accounts, restrict the flow of administrative privileges, and limit the computers on which specific administrative accounts can be used.

Skills in this chapter:

- Implement an Enhanced Security Administrative Environment administrative forest design approach
- Implement Just-in-Time Administration
- Implement Just-Enough-Administration
- Implement Privileged Access Workstations and User Rights Assignments
- Implement Local Administrator Password Solution

Skill 4.1: Implement an Enhanced Security Administrative Environment administrative forest design approach

The *Enhanced Administrative Security Environment* (ESAE) is a reference architecture that is designed to protect administrative accounts and their credentials from exposure to malicious access by sequestering them in a separate Active Directory (AD) forest. ESAE is not a product, a role, or a feature. It is instead a collection of design principles that enables you to create a separate, single-domain forest that is dedicated to Active Directory management. Because the administrative forest sees limited use, you can harden it to a greater degree than your production forest(s).

Determine usage scenarios and requirements for implementing ESAE forest design architecture to create a dedicated administrative forest

The ESAE architecture calls for a separate AD forest that contains some or all of the administrative accounts with AD management privileges. By creating one-way forest trust relationships between the administrative forest and your production forest(s), as shown in Figure 4-1,
and by using other protective measures, such as selective authentication, you can exercise
more granular control over the authentication flow.

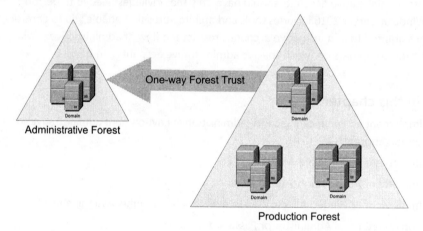

FIGURE 4-1 Trust relationships between administrative forest and a production forest

NOTE **LIMITING THE SCOPE OF THE ADMINISTRATIVE FOREST**

While it is possible to use the administrative forest for other management functions or applications, this is likely to increase the attack surface of the forest and reduce the effectiveness of the ESAE design. For maximum protection of the most privileged accounts in the
enterprise, do not use the administrative forest for any other purposes.

Active Directory administrative tiers

Although it is possible to place all of your administrative accounts into an administrative forest, many organizations use a tier model to separate AD administrative accounts based on their access. The typical model consists of three tiers, as follows:

- **Tier 0** Accounts that have direct administrative control over enterprise identities, including forests, domains, domain controllers, and their assets
- **Tier 1** Accounts that have direct administrative control over enterprise servers and applications
- **Tier 2** Accounts that have direct administrative control over user workstations and devices

Accounts in each tier have direct administrative access to servers in the same tier, but are permitted to access resources in lower tiers only when required by a specific administrative role, as shown in Figure 4-2. Accounts are blocked from accessing resources in higher tiers.

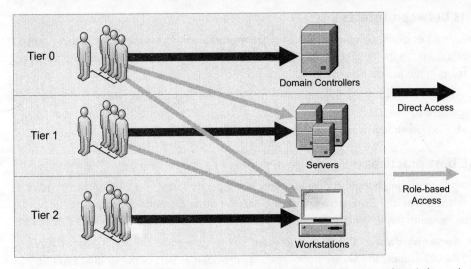

FIGURE 4-2 Administrative tiers limit account access to servers in the same tier or those in lower tiers

An ESAE architecture in a tiered environment typically places only the Tier 0 accounts in the administrative forest. Accounts that administer Tier 1 and Tier 2 assets remain as part of the production forest(s), as shown in Figure 4-3.

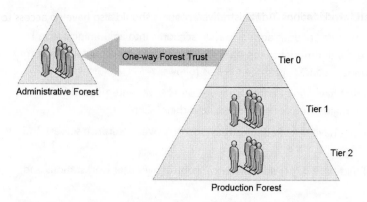

FIGURE 4-3 An ESAE architecture in a tiered enterprise can protect the Tier 0 administrative accounts by placing them in a separate forest

Trusts between forests

By creating a one-way domain or forest trust, the production forest trusts the administrative accounts stored in the administrative forest, enabling those accounts to manage Active Directory assets in the production forest.

There is no need for the administrative forest to trust the production forest for this AD management to take place. Therefore, a security breach in the production forest would not affect the administrative forest.

ESAE best practices

In addition to placing administrative accounts in a separate forest and limiting access using trust relationships, the ESAE architecture also calls for other methods of protecting the accounts, including the following:

- **Server hardware** Computers accessed by the accounts in the administrative forest should support the Secure Boot capability provided as part of the Unified Extensible Firmware Interface (UEFI) and have Trusted Platform Module (TPM) chips for the storage of BitLocker drive encryption keys.

- **Selective authentication** When you create a forest trust, you have the option of using forest wide or selective authentication. Selective authentication enables you to restrict the accounts in the administrative forest to specific servers in the production forest.

- **Multifactor authentication** All of the accounts in the administrative forest (except one) should require multifactor authentication, using smart cards or another secondary authentication mechanism. One account should be accessible using only a password, in the event of a problem with the multifactor authentication mechanism.

- **Limited privileges** Accounts in the administrative forest used to manage production forest resources should not have administrative privileges to the administrative forest, or its domains and workstations. Administrative accounts should also have no access to user resources that provide attack vectors, such as email and the Internet.

- **Server updates** All computers in the administrative forest should be automatically updated with all new security updates using Windows Server Update Services (WSUS) or another mechanism.

- **Clean source** All computers in the administrative forest should run the latest operating system version and should be installed using media that has been validated using the clean source principle.

- **Whitelisting** Computers accessed using administrative forest accounts should be restricted to safe applications using a whitelisting product such as AppLocker.

- **Intrusion detection and prevention** Systems in the administrative forest should be scanned regularly for potential security threats, using tools such as Attack Surface Analyzer or Advanced Threat Analytics.

Determine usage scenarios and requirements for implementing clean source principles in an Active Directory architecture

The *clean source principle* addresses the relationship between an object that you are trying to protect and a subject that is in control of the object. In this relationship, the security of the object is dependent on the security of the subject controlling it, as shown in Figure 4-4.

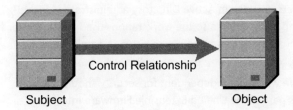

FIGURE 4-4 The security of an object is dependent on that of the subject controlling it

For example, you might take great pains to create a secure Active Directory architecture by hardening your domain controllers and creating dedicated administrative accounts. However, if you use one of those administrative accounts to log on at a workstation that is vulnerable to attack, then you are creating a security dependency between the workstation (the subject) and the domain controllers (the object). No matter how secure the domain controllers and the accounts are, the workstation becomes the weak link in the chain, and the administrative credentials could be compromised. The clean source principle dictates that for an object to be secure, all of its dependent subjects must be secure as well.

To implement the clean source principle in Active Directory, administrators must take control of system hardware, installation media, and the administrative architecture.

Transitive dependencies

Security dependencies are also transitive, meaning that an attack on a single subject can compromise objects all over the enterprise. For example, when system A has direct control of system B, and system B has direct control of system C, then an attacker compromising system A can gain direct control of system B and indirect control of system C in the process, as shown in Figure 4-5.

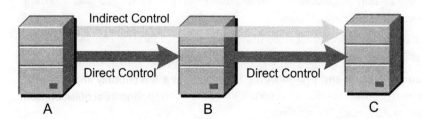

FIGURE 4-5 Security dependencies are transitive

Security dependencies are rarely as linear as in this diagram, however. An attack on a single system A can result in direct control over dozens of B systems and indirect control of hundreds of C systems.

Clean source for system hardware

The clean source principle extends ultimately to the hardware of the computers involved in secure transactions. All of the computers involved in Active Directory administration, including not only the domain controllers and servers, but also the workstations used to administer them, should be equipped with the hardware necessary to create a secure administration environment.

For example, all of the computers on which AD is dependent for security should support the Secure Boot capability provided as part of the Unified Extensible Firmware Interface (UEFI) and have Trusted Platform Module (TPM) chips for the storage of BitLocker drive encryption keys. A workstation that is not capable of providing a secure platform equal to that of the systems it administers is a violation of the clean source principle and a potential avenue of attack.

Clean source for installation media

Applying the clean source principle to an operating system or application installation casts the computer as the object to be protected and the installation medium as the subject, as shown in Figure 4-6. The computer is dependent on the uncompromised state of the installation medium for the security of the software in its initial install state.

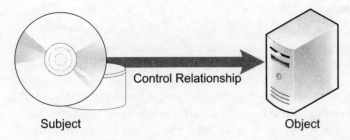

Subject   Control Relationship   Object

FIGURE 4-6 A computer is dependent for security on the media from which its software is installed

Theoretically, if an attacker tampers with your installation media, then all of the computers on which you install that software can be infected. Therefore, it is critically important to ensure that your installation media are protected from tampering during its acquisition from the source, during its storage prior to installation, and during the transfer from the storage medium to the system where you install it.

To ensure that the installation media you acquire are clean, you can use one of the following methods:

- Obtain the software on a physical medium (such as a DVD) directly from the manufacturer or from a reliable source.

- Download the software from the Internet that is validated with file hashed supplied by the vendor.

- Download the software from two independent locations on the Internet, using two separate computers with no security relationship, and compare the two copies using a tool like the Certutil.exe utility provided with the Certificate Services role.

Once you have acquired and validated the software, you must store it in such a way that it cannot be modified during the period before the actual installation. The physical or digital storage location should not be accessible by persons or computers with a lower security rating than the systems where it is ultimately installed.

When the installation media are stored for any appreciable length of time, they should also be revalidated immediately before installation.

Clean source for administrative architecture

To apply the clean source principle to the administrative architecture of an Active Directory installation, you must be certain that systems of a certain security level are never dependent on systems of a lower security level. A relatively insecure system that has direct control over a secure system compromises that security and provides an avenue for attack.

A control relationship between two systems can take many forms, including the following.

- Access Control Lists (ACLs)
- Group memberships
- Agents running as System
- Authentication

For example, logging on to an AD domain controller using a Tier 0 administrative account exposes the account credentials to the workstation you are using to log on. This creates a control relationship in which the workstation is the subject and the domain controller is the object, as shown in Figure 4-7. If that workstation is insecure and becomes compromised, then the Tier 0 account credentials are compromised as well. An attacker can then gain control over your domain controllers and the Active Directory database.

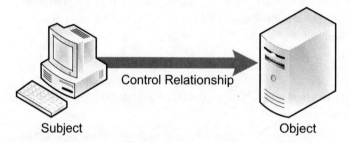

FIGURE 4-7 A domain controller dependent for security on every workstation used to log on to it

To apply the clean source principle to your administrative architecture, you should limit the number of workstations and other computers on which your Active Directory domain controllers have dependent relationships.

Skill 4.2: Implement Just-in-Time administration

No matter what security solutions administrators apply, account credentials will continue to be improperly shared or maliciously stolen. Whatever innovations the future brings, there are still users who share their passwords and administrators who use privileged accounts improperly. To address these issues, Microsoft has designed an environment in which access to administrative accounts is automatically restricted to specific tasks and limited periods of time. This is the basis for *just-in-time (JIT) administration*. *Privileged Access Management (PAM)* is an implementation of this JIT administration philosophy that is included as part of the Microsoft Identity Manager 2016 product.

Create a new administrative (bastion) forest in an existing Active Directory environment using Microsoft Identity Manager

A *bastion forest* is implementation of the separate administrative forest concept described earlier as part of the ESAE architecture. The Privileged Access Management tool in MIM 2016 enables you to establish a trust relationship between your production forest(s) and a new, separate forest that MIM then uses to store privileged administrative accounts and copies of privileged groups migrated from the production forest.

A bastion forest starts out as a standard Active Directory forest that you create using the Active Directory Domain Services role and the Active Directory Installation Wizard. The forest consists of a single domain, with at least one domain controller, and a member server on which you install MIM 2016.

At first, the new forest is not a bastion; it is completely separate from your production forest(s). It is not until after you create the forest and install MIM on the member server that you connect the bastion forest to your production forest(s) by establishing a trust relationship between the two.

The basic steps for creating a new administrative forest in an Active Directory environment are as follows:

1. On a new computer or virtual machine, install Windows Server and add the Active Directory Domain Services and DNS roles.

2. Create a new forest by promoting the server to a domain controller. The forest can have any name; it does not have to be part of the production forest naming structure.

3. On the domain controller, create the domain user accounts that are required to run MIM.

4. On another new computer or virtual machine, install another copy of Windows Server. This is the member server in the bastion forest domain that runs MIM 2016.

5. Join the server to the domain in the bastion forest.

6. On the member server, install and configure the prerequisites needed for MIM, including SQL Server, SharePoint, and Internet Information Services (IIS).

7. Install and configure Microsoft Identity Manager 2016.

Configure trusts between production and bastion forests

Once you have created the new AD forest to use as your bastion forest, and installed MIM on a member server, you must establish a trust relationship between the bastion forest and your production forest. This part of the bastion forest creation process consists of the three tasks, covered in the following sections.

Testing DNS connections

The bastion forest eventually contains administrative accounts moved from the production forest. Administrators whose accounts have been migrated must be able to seamlessly access production resources using the bastion forest accounts, and to do this, the systems in the production forest must be able to send DNS requests to the bastion forest DNS server.

To determine whether your production systems can contact the bastion DNS server, you can use the Nslookup tool at a Windows PowerShell or CMD prompt on any system in your production forest, with the DNS name of your bastion forest domain in place of server.domain.local:

```
nslookup -qt=ns server.domain.local
```

A successful result lists the name and IP address of the DNS server in the bastion forest, as shown in Figure 4-8.

```
PS C:\Users\Administrator> nslookup -qt=ns priv.contoso.com
DNS request timed out.
    timeout was 2 seconds.
Server:  UnKnown
Address:  ::1

Non-authoritative answer:
priv.contoso.com          nameserver = PRIVDC.priv.contoso.com

PRIVDC.priv.contoso.com internet address = 10.0.0.2
PS C:\Users\Administrator>
```

FIGURE 4-8 The nslookup command can test for a DNS connection between the production forest and the bastion forest

You can also use the Resolve-DnsName PowerShell cmdlet, as in the following example:

```
resolve-dnsname -name priv.contoso.com -type ns
```

If the nslookup command fails to identify the DNS server in the bastion forest, you have to create a name server (NS) resource record using DNS Manager on your production DNS server. Figure 4-9 shows such a record for a bastion forest domain called priv.contoso.com.

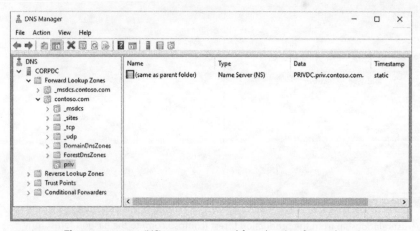

FIGURE 4-9 The name server (NS) resource record for a bastion forest domain

Create a PAM trust

In a PAM environment, privileged users are moved from the production forest to the bastion forest. For those users to be able to access resources in the production forest, you must create a trust relationship between the two forests. The trust relationship must be a one-way forest trust from the production domain to the bastion domain. In essence, the bastion domain must be trusted by the production domain, so that the administrative users in the bastion forest can access production resources.

MIM includes a collection of Windows PowerShell cmdlets, including one called NewPAM-Trust, which you run on the MIM server to create the required trust relationship between the forests. The syntax for the cmdlet is as follows:

```
New-PAMTrust -SourceForest "domain.local" -Credentials (Get-Credential)
```

Because you are executing this cmdlet from a computer in the bastion forest, the Source-Forest parameter identifies the production forest. You can use any standard Windows Power-Shell method to supply administrative credentials providing access to the production forest. If your environment contains more than one production forest, then you must run the cmdlet for each production forest in your enterprise.

The NewPAMTrust cmdlet does not provide any output, but if you look in the Active Directory Domains and Trusts tool on the production domain controller, you can see the bastion forest listed as an outgoing trust, as shown in Figure 4-10.

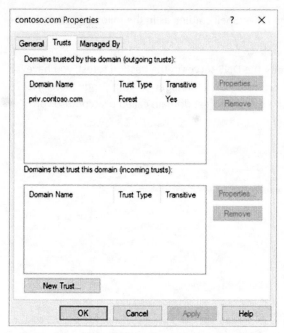

FIGURE 4-10 The trust relationship from the production forest (contoso.com) to the bastion forest (priv. contoso.com)

> **NOTE NEW-PAMTRUST AND NETDOM**
>
> The New-PAMTrust cmdlet performs three tasks: it creates the forest trust, it enables SID history for the trust and it disables SID filtering. Instead of using New-PAMTrust, you can perform these three tasks individually with the following commands using the netdom tool:
>
> ```
> netdom trust production.local /domain:bastion.local /userO:production\
> administrator /passwordO:password /add
> netdom trust production.local /domain:bastion.local /EnableSIDHistory:yes /
> userO:production\administrator /passwordO:password
> netdom trust production.local /domain:bastion.local  /Quarantine:no /
> userO:production\administrator /passwordO:password
> ```

After you create the trust between the forests, you must also run the New-PAMDomain-Configuration cmdlet for each domain in your production forest(s). The syntax for the cmdlet is as follows:

```
New-PAMDomainConfiguration -SourceDomain "domain" -Credentials (Get-Credential)
```

Create shadow principals in bastion forest

Shadow principals are the copies of production AD objects—users and groups—that PAM creates in a bastion forest. Unlike a simple copy, a shadow principal has the same security identifier (SID) as the original, which remains in the production forest and is no longer used. When a user has to perform an administrative task that requires the privileges of a specific group that has been shadowed in the bastion forest, the PAM server is able to grant the user membership in the shadowed group and issue a token with the same SID as the original group in the production forest. This enables the user to access resources in the production forest using a token that was actually issued by a separate bastion forest. The access control lists for the production resources do not have to change, because the bastion group has the same SID as the production group.

Because the bastion forest is less vulnerable to attack than the production forest, the shadow principals are well protected. In addition, the memberships in the shadow group can be limited to a specific duration, resulting in an implementation of the just-in-time administration principle.

To create shadow principals, you use Windows PowerShell cmdlets that are installed as part of the PAM implementation in MIM 2016, such as New-PAMUser and New-PAMGroup. These cmdlets perform the following tasks:

- **New-PAMGroup** Creates a new group in the bastion forest with the same SID as a group in the production forest. Then the cmdlet creates an object in the MIM Service database that corresponds to the new group in the bastion forest.

- **New-PAMUser** Creates a new user in the bastion forest with the same SID as a user in the production forest. Then the cmdlet creates two objects in the MIM Service database, corresponding to the original user account in the production forest and the new user account in the bastion forest.

To create a PAM group, use the New-PAMGroup cmdlet with the following syntax:

```
New-PAMGroup -SourceGroupName "group" -SourceDomain domainname -Credentials (Get-Credential)
```

This command creates a duplicate of the production group specified in the SourceGroup-Name parameter by accessing the domain specified in the SourceDomain parameter, using the supplied credentials.

To create a PAM user, you use the New-PAMUser cmdlet with the following syntax:

```
New-PAMUser -SourceDomain domain -SourceAccountName user -Credentials (Get-Credential)
```

This command creates a duplicate of the user account specified in the SourceAccount-Name parameter by accessing the domain specified in the SourceDomain parameter, using the supplied credentials.

Configure the MIM web portal

Once you have installed and configured the MIM prerequisites on the PAM server, including SQL Server and SharePoint, it is time to install and configure the Microsoft Identity Manager 2016 service and web portal. The web portal functions, shown in Figure 4-11, within the SharePoint environment and provides the administrative interface to all MIM functions, including PAM administration.

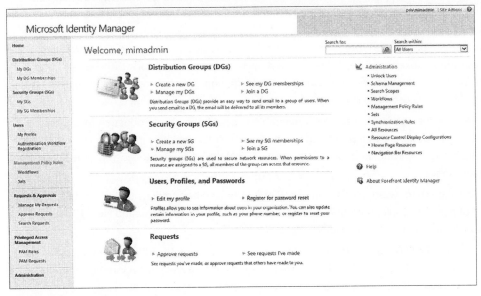

FIGURE 4-11 The MIM web portal main page

To install the web portal, you run the Setup.exe program from the Service and Portal folder in the MIM 2016 installation source files. This launches a standard Windows Installer setup wizard. To install a PAM server, you have to select the Privileged Access Management and MIM Portal components in the Custom Setup page.

The installation creates a new database in your SQL Server instance and intranet sites for the MIM administration portal and for the PAM REST application programming interface (API), which you can use to build applications that interact with the PAM server.

Request privileged access using the MIM web portal

Once the bastion forest is operational and MIM is installed and configured to provide PAM services, users can request privileged access in two ways: using the Windows PowerShell cmdlets included with the PAM client and using the MIM web portal.

To request access to a role using the MIM portal, you click the PAM Requests link on the main page to display the PAM Request page. Then, click the New icon to open the Create PAM Request page, as shown in Figure 4-12. On this page, you specify the role to which you want access.

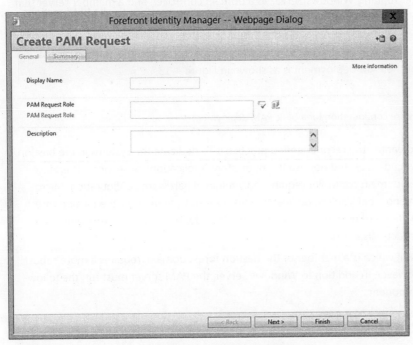

FIGURE 4-12 The Create PAM Request page in the MIM web portal

Determine requirements and usage scenarios for Privileged Access Management solutions

Privileges Access Management (PAM) is designed for enterprise installations that want to make it more difficult for potential attackers to compromise administrative credentials. For the sake of convenience, many users that perform administrative tasks only occasionally use their administrative credentials all the time. For the same reason, many of these users have access to administrative credentials that provide them with more privileges than they need to perform their assigned tasks. PAM is designed to provide these users with administrative access to specific resources for a limited amount of time. The users receive membership in administrative groups on request, and after a preset time limit, the group memberships expire.

In addition to limiting user access to administrative credentials, PAM also protects those credentials by storing them in an isolated bastion forest, where it is possible to implement security measures that would be impractical in a production forest.

Hardware and software requirements

Because it requires a separate bastion forest, PAM requires you to deploy at least one additional computer running Windows Server as a domain controller, and a member server that functions as the PAM server. These can be physical computers or virtual machines that are accessible to the rest of your network. The assumption is that you already have a production network that includes at least one domain controller plus user workstations. Thus, the basic configuration for the PAM deployment is as shown in Figure 4-13.

FIGURE 4-13 Hardware configuration for a basic PAM deployment

As mentioned earlier, the recommended practice is to dedicate the systems in the bastion forest to PAM functionality, and not use them for other applications or services. Therefore, the bastion forest domain controller requires only minimal hardware configuration. Microsoft also recommends that you use dedicated workstations to administer the bastion forest systems. Using a standard user workstation to administer highly secure systems puts the administrative credentials at risk.

The PAM server, which is a member of the bastion forest domain, requires a more robust configuration, however. In addition to Windows Server, the PAM server must run the following software components:

- Microsoft Identity Manager 2016
- Microsoft SQL Server 2014
- Microsoft SharePoint 2013 Foundation SP1

Using high availability

A server with 8 GB of memory and 120 GB of storage is to be considered the bare minimum for a PAM server deployment. However, if you intend to configure the PAM implementation for high availability, the network configuration becomes more complex. To run duplicate PAM servers, for example, you must have a shared storage solution, such as a storage area network (SAN), which is supported by SQL Server. As with all PAM hardware, it should be dedicated to the bastion forest and not used for other applications.

Create and implement MIM policies

In PAM, MIM contains tools that provide an implementation of a just-in-time administration philosophy, but it is up to the managers of the enterprise to create the policies with which those tools are used.

Looking at your existing Active Directory infrastructure, you should begin by identifying which of your groups have significant privileges that you might want to protect using PAM. Depending on your existing security policies, you might be able to migrate your current groups to the bastion forest, or you might have to consider designing new groups.

The primary goal of PAM is to limit the time during which groups with significant privileges are in use. However, you might also want to consider limiting the privileges assigned to each group. This way, you can create a just-enough philosophy at the same time as your just-in-time implementation.

You must also consider which of your users are going to require access to your privileged groups. All of the privileged groups you want to protect using PAM and the users that need them have to migrate to the bastion forest. Depending on the size of your enterprise, this can mean creating dozens or hundreds of PAM users and groups. If you already have a tiered security administration architecture, it might be relatively easy to decide which users and groups to migrate; if you do not, you might want to consider creating one.

Implement just-in-time administration principals using time-based policies

As an MIM administrator, once you have created the appropriate PAM users and groups in the bastion forest, you must create PAM roles corresponding to the administrative tasks that the users have to perform.

A PAM role is an object that associates one or more PAM users with specific PAM groups. The groups presumably have the privileges necessary to perform certain administrative tasks. Because the groups originated from the production forest and have the same SIDs as their production counterparts, the ACLs of the production resources respond to the PAM groups just as they would to the production groups.

Later, when users need to perform specific administrative tasks, they submit activation requests that name a specific role. When the MIM server grants a request, it adds the requesting user to the group(s) specified in the role for a specific length of time, which is also defined in the role.

Adding users to a role makes it possible for them to submit activation requests. Additional parameters for the cmdlet enable you to specify a description of the role's function, the Time-To-Live (TTL) for an activated PAM user's membership in the specified group(s), the times of day that the role is available, and the users who are permitted to approve requests for the role.

Creating a PAM role

To create a PAM role, you can use the New-PAMRole cmdlet with the following basic syntax:

```
New-PAMRole -DisplayName role -TTL time -Privileges group -Candidates users -Description
string
```

This command creates a role using the name specified in the DisplayName parameter. The group(s) to which the role provides membership are specified in the Privileges parameter, and the users who are permitted to request access to the role are specified in the Candidates parameter.

Depending on the size of your organization and the operational workflow, the use of the Description parameter might be an important part of the role creation process. If you have users who later have to locate the correct role for a specific administrative task, they can use the Get-PAMRoleForRequest cmdlet to search for a specific role.

It is also possible to create a role using the MIM portal installed as part of the PAM server implementation. From the Privileged Access Management Roles page, you can view and manage the existing roles on your PAM server, as well as create new roles using Create PAM Role page, as shown in Figure 4-14.

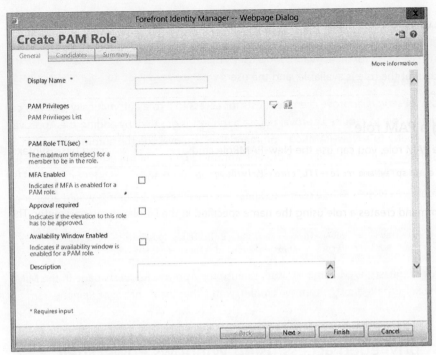

FIGURE 4-14 The Create PAM Role page on the MIM portal

Specifying time-based policies

To enable PAM to function as an implementation of just-in-time administration, the role also specifies how long the users remain members of the specified groups when MIM grants a request. You specify this time limit (in seconds) using the TTL parameter in the New-PAMRole cmdlet. The recommended minimum value for this parameter is 1800 seconds (30 minutes), but you can assign any value.

In addition to creating a time limit, you can also specify the time of day during which users are permitted to request the role. The AvailableFrom and AvailableTo parameters for the New-PAMRole cmdlet enable you to specify a range of time during which users are permitted to request access to the role. As with other Windows PowerShell cmdlets, these parameters accept date and time values in virtually any format, but the New-PAMRole cmdlet ignores any date values and uses only the times you specify. You must also include the AvailabilityWindowEnabled parameter for the cmdlet to recognize the times you specify.

Therefore, an example of a New-PAMRole command line that uses these parameters would appear as follows:

```
New-PAMRole -DisplayName "WebAdmins" -TTL 1800 -Privileges WebAdmins -Candidates JDaly
-Description "Web Administrators" -AvailabilityWindowEnabled -AvailableFrom "9:00 AM"
-AvailableTo "5:00 PM"
```

This command would create a role called WebAdmins that, when activated between 9:00 AM and 5:00 PM, would grant a user called JDaly membership in the WebAdmins group for 30 minutes.

Managing role access

By default, PAM servers approve client requests for access to a role automatically, but you can also configure a role to require approval before a request is granted. By adding the ApprovalEnabled parameter to a New-PAMRole command line, you override the automatic request processing. Requests for that role must then be approved by one of the users specified by the Approvers parameter, which you also must include in the command.

An example of a NewPAMRole command line that uses these parameters would appear as follows:

```
New-PAMRole -DisplayName "WebAdmins" -TTL 1800 -Privileges WebAdmins -Candidates JDaly
-Description "Web Administrators" -ApprovalEnabled -Approvers SDavis
```

To approve requests, PAM administrators can use the Approve Requests page in the MIM portal or the Set-PAMRequestToApprove cmdlet, with either the Approve or Reject parameter.

Request privileged access using Windows PowerShell

Once you have installed and configured MIM 2016 to provide PAM for your network, and you have created the required users, groups, and roles in the bastion forest, the server is ready to process access requests from users.

To provide users with the Windows PowerShell cmdlets they need to submit PAM requests, you must install the PAM client supplied with Microsoft Identity Manager 2016 on each user workstation. To do this, you run the Setup.exe program in the Add-ins and Extensions folder in the MIM 2016 installation source files. The package includes both x64 and x86 versions.

The Microsoft Identity Manager Add-ins and Extensions Setup Wizard includes a Custom Setup page on which you can select the components you want to install. Only the PAM Client module is required to install the Windows PowerShell cmdlets, as shown in Figure 4-15. To proceed with the installation, you must specify the name of the MIM server in your bastion forest.

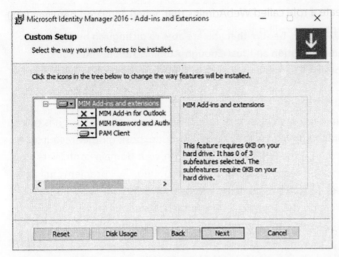

FIGURE 4-15 The Custom Setup page of the Microsoft Identity Manager Add-ins and Extensions Setup Wizard

Once the PAM Client is installed, workstation users that are logged on with an account that has been migrated to the bastion forest can open the Windows PowerShell interface, import the MIMPAM module to access the PAM client cmdlets, and create a new request. The syntax for the commands is as follows:

```
Runas /user:pamusername@pamdomain powershell
Import-Module MIMPAM
New-PAMRequest -role rolename
```

If your users do not know the name of the role they need, they can use the GetPAMRole-ForRequest cmdlet to list all of the roles available on the PAM server. By adding the Filter parameter, they can limit the list of roles to those that contain a specified text string.

Once the server approves the request, the user is added to the requested group(s) in the bastion forest and immediately receives the privileges to the production forest resources associated with those groups. At this point, the timing of the TTL value begins, and at the expiration of that value, the user's membership in the groups is revoked.

Skill 4.3: Implement Just-Enough-Administration

The just-in-time administration principle limits the time during which administrative users are granted access to elevated privileges. By contrast, Just-Enough-Administration (JEA, pronounced jee'-ah) is designed to limit administrative users to only the elevated privileges required to perform a given task. As with PAM, JEA provides users with privileges that time out after a specified period. Unlike PAM, JEA is a Windows PowerShell-based technique that you can implement easily on a server running Windows Server 2016. There is no need for a bastion forest or additional hardware or software.

Many organizations have implemented a form of role-based access control, but it is often difficult to grant administrators the privileges they need without exposing other resources to them as well. For example, if you run the DNS Server service on your domain controllers, you might be forced to grant the person responsible for troubleshooting DNS problems full access to the servers. This exposes your Active Directory domains to someone who has no need for those privileges. You are trusting the person to stick to the DNS components and to not make any changes in Active Directory. This arrangement is inherently insecure.

The fundamental problem with this arrangement is the prevalent use of graphical tools for system administration. It is difficult to grant a user access to the DNS Manager console without providing access to other administrative tools as well. Windows PowerShell, however, is much more granular in the tasks performed by specific cmdlets and other elements. With JEA, you can provide a user with access only to the Windows PowerShell cmdlets they need for DNS administration, and prevent them from accessing any others.

For some organizations, JEA represents a fundamental shift in administrative practices, from graphical tools to character-based ones. There can be a substantial learning curve involved in such a shift, but it can be a worthwhile one, both for the security of the organization and for the market value of the individual administrators.

This section covers how to:

- Enable a JEA solution on Windows Server 2016
- Create and configure session configuration files
- Create and configure role capability files
- Create a JEA endpoint
- Connect to a JEA endpoint on a server for administration
- View logs
- Download WMF 5.1 to a Windows Server 2008 R2
- Configure a JEA endpoint on a server using Desired State Configuration

Enable a JEA solution on Windows Server 2016

JEA is incorporated into Windows Server 2016 and Windows 10, and is also incorporated into Windows Management Framework 5.0, which you can download and install on computers running Windows Server 2012 R2, Windows Server 2012, and Windows 8/8.1.

JEA is based on the remote user capabilities built into Windows PowerShell. Users log on to Windows using unprivileged accounts and then use Windows PowerShell to establish a connection to a PowerShell *session configuration*, also known as a PowerShell *endpoint*. By connecting to an endpoint and entering into a session, the user is running as a remote user on the same computer. That remote user account has privileges (and possibly restrictions) that the user's own account does not have.

Stages in a JEA session

To connect to a PowerShell endpoint, you use the Enter-PSSession cmdlet, as shown in Figure 4-16. Notice that the command prompt changes as a result of the connection establishment, and the Get-UserInfo cmdlet displays both the user's unprivileged account (OperatorUser) and, under RunAsUser, the temporary virtual account to which the user is now connected (VA_2_CONTOSO_OperatorUser).

```
PS C:\Users\Administrator.CONTOSO> Enter-PSSession -ComputerName . -ConfigurationName
[localhost]: PS>get-userinfo

UserInfo                : System.Management.Automation.Remoting.PSPrincipal
ClientTimeZone          : System.CurrentSystemTimeZone
ConnectionString        : http://localhost:5985/wsman?PSVersion=5.1.14300.1000
ApplicationArguments    : {PSVersionTable}
ConnectedUser           : CONTOSO\OperatorUser
RunAsUser               : WinRM Virtual Users\WinRM VA_2_CONTOSO_OperatorUser


[localhost]: PS>
```

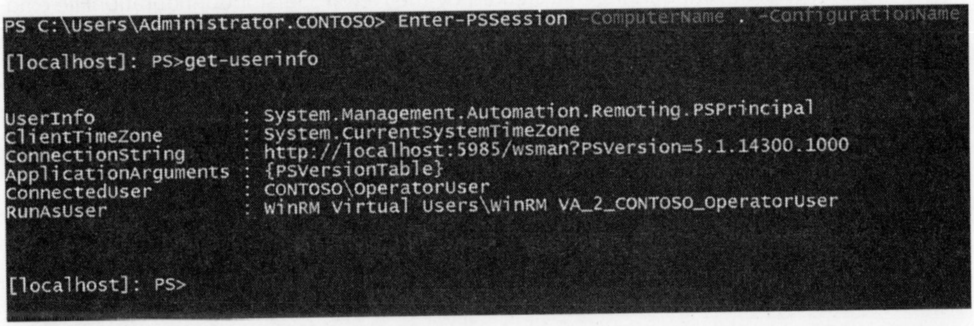

FIGURE 4-16 The result of an endpoint connection

While you are connected to the endpoint, you possess the privileges that have been granted to the virtual user account. In a typical session, the virtual user has access to a small subset of PowerShell cmdlets, only those required to perform the administrative tasks associated with a specific role. For example, a user responsible for web site administration might be granted the ability to restart IIS, but not the ability to restart the computer.

When you have completed your assigned tasks, you use the Exit-PSSession cmdlet to disconnect from the endpoint and return to your previous unprivileged state.

JEA components

To implement JEA on a computer running Windows Server 2016, you must create an endpoint. To do this, you must create and register two PowerShell script files, as follows:

- **Session configuration file** Script with a .pssc file extension that specifies the name of the endpoint to be created and identifies the role capabilities that should be assigned to specific groups.

- **Role capability file** Script with a .psrc file extension that specifies what cmdlets and other capabilities should be associated with a particular role.

Because these are script files that JEA administrators can change at any time, it is possible to adjust the capabilities being assigned to a particular role.

Create and configure session configuration files

The session configuration file is the key element of a JEA implementation, because it creates the endpoint to which users connect. To create your own session configuration file, you use the New-PSSessionConfigurationFile cmdlet.

The only required parameter for the New-PSSessionConfigurationFile cmdlet is Path, which you use to specify a location and file name for the new script file. Beyond that, there are two ways to configure the file. If you run the cmdlet with just a Path parameter, PowerShell creates a skeleton file, which you can then edit. There are also a great many optional parameters that you can include in the command, which configure the settings within the script file.

The default session configuration file created by the New-PSSessionConfigurationFile cmdlet appears as shown in Listing 4-1.

LISTING 4-1 A default session configuration file created by New-PSSessionConfigurationFile

```
@{
# Version number of the schema used for this document
SchemaVersion = '2.0.0.0'


# ID used to uniquely identify this document
GUID = 'eb70ac57-fb62-436f-a878-305bce71ae58'


# Author of this document
Author = 'Administrator'


# Description of the functionality provided by these settings
# Description = ''
# Session type defaults to apply for this session configuration. Can be
'RestrictedRemoteServer' (recommended), 'Empty', or 'Default'
SessionType = 'Default'


# Directory to place session transcripts for this session configuration
# TranscriptDirectory = 'C:\Transcripts\'


# Whether to run this session configuration as the machine's (virtual) administrator
account
# RunAsVirtualAccount = $true


# Scripts to run when applied to a session
# ScriptsToProcess = 'C:\ConfigData\InitScript1.ps1', 'C:\ConfigData\InitScript2.ps1'


# User roles (security groups), and the role capabilities that should be applied to
```

```
them when applied to a session
# RoleDefinitions = @{ 'CONTOSO\SqlAdmins' = @{ RoleCapabilities = 'SqlAdministration'
}; 'CONTOSO\ServerMonitors' = @{ VisibleCmdlets = 'Get-Process' } }


}
```

When you create a new session configuration file with no optional parameters, most of the commands in the script are commented out with a pound (#) symbol. When editing the script, you must remove the comment symbol on the lines you want to activate.

The most important commands in a session configuration file are as follows:

- **SessionType**   Specifies the preconfigured settings that the endpoint should use. JEA sessions typically use the RestrictedRemoteServer option, which supplies the user with a minimal set of eight cmdlets (Get-Command, Get-FormatData, Select-Object, Get-Help, Measure-Object, Exit-PSSession, Clear-Host, and Out-Default). This option also sets the PowerShell execution policy to RemoteSigned, which prevents the user from running downloaded scripts unless they are signed by a trusted publisher.

- **TranscriptDirectory**   Specifies a path to the location where PowerShell should maintain text-based transcripts (logs) of the activity during a session. Session information is also logged by the Windows Eventing engine.

- **RunAsVirtualAccount**   Specifies whether the user entering a session should employ the Windows Run As capability to obtain the privileges of a virtual account. By default, when you enable this setting, the virtual user is a member of the local Administrators group (or the Domain Admins group on a domain controller). JEA session configuration files typically use additional settings to override the default.

- **RoleDefinitions**   Specifies associations between role capabilities—as defined in separate role capability scripts—and specific security groups. This is the setting that is responsible for defining what the connected user is capable of doing when connected to the endpoint.

An example of an edited and functional session configuration script is shown in Listing 4-2. In this script, the members of the JEA_NonAdmin_Operator group receive the privileges defined in a role capability file called Maintenance.psrc.

LISTING 4-2 A completed session configuration script file

```
@{

# Version number of the schema used for this document
SchemaVersion = '2.0.0.0'

# ID used to uniquely identify this document
GUID = 'eaff40a4-73e1-450c-83b2-4ce537620f41'

# Author of this document
```

```
Author = 'Administrator'

# Description of the functionality provided by these settings
# Description = ''

# Session type defaults to apply for this session configuration. Can be
'RestrictedRemoteServer' (recommended), 'Empty', or 'Default'
SessionType = 'RestrictedRemoteServer'

# Directory to place session transcripts for this session configuration
TranscriptDirectory = 'C:\ProgramData\JEAConfiguration\Transcripts'

# Whether to run this session configuration as the machine's (virtual) administrator
account
RunAsVirtualAccount = $true

# Scripts to run when applied to a session
# ScriptsToProcess = 'C:\ConfigData\InitScript1.ps1', 'C:\ConfigData\InitScript2.ps1'

# User roles (security groups), and the role capabilities that should be applied to
them when applied to a session
RoleDefinitions = @{
    'contoso.com\JEA_NonAdmin_Operator' = @{
        'RoleCapabilities' = 'Maintenance' } }

}
```

Create and configure role capability files

As noted earlier, the session configuration script file contains references to role capability files. These are the script files that specify in detail what capabilities users have when they connect to the endpoint. The role capability file is essentially a whitelist; users receive access to the cmdlets and other capabilities specified in the file, and nothing else.

Creating role capability files is somewhat more involved than creating session configuration files, however. You might have noticed that the sample session configuration file shown earlier has a reference to a role capability file called Maintenance that has no path to the file's location or even a file name extension. This is because role capability files must be created in a folder called RoleCapabilities inside a valid PowerShell module.

Modules are PowerShell packages that can contain a variety of components, including cmdlets, functions, Desired State Configuration (DSC) resources, and role capabilities. When modules are located in one of the folders on the designated PowerShell path, the system searches those modules for the requested resources. These modules are how PowerShell finds the cmdlets you type on the command line, and how it finds the role capability files refer-enced in a session configuration script with no directory location.

The locations in the PowerShell path by default are as follows:

- C:\Users\Administrator.CONTOSO\Documents\WindowsPowerShell\Modules
- C:\Program Files\WindowsPowerShell\Modules
- C:\Windows\system32\WindowsPowerShell\v1.0\Modules

You can create a role capabilities file in an existing module in one of these locations or you can create a new module. In either case, you must create a RoleCapabilities subfolder in the module folder for your session configuration scripts to find it.

> **NOTE** **CREATING A ROLECAPABILITIES SUBFOLDER**
>
> You can create a RoleCapabilities subfolder using File Explorer in the usual manner, or you can create it using the New-Item cmdlet with the ItemType parameter, as in the following example:
>
> ```
> New-Item -Path "c:\Program Files\WindowsPowerShell\Modules\JEA\
> RoleCapabilities" -ItemType Directory
> ```

Once you have created the RoleCapabilities subfolder, you can create a blank role capabil-ity script file in it, using the New-PSRoleCapabilityFile cmdlet, as in the following example:

```
New-PSRoleCapabilityFile -Path "c:\Program Files\WindowsPowerShell\Modules\JEA\
Maintenance.psrc"
```

A blank role capability file is shown in Listing 4-3.

LISTING 4-3 A blank role capability file created by New-PSRoleCapabilityFile

```
@{
# ID used to uniquely identify this document
GUID = 'd9c9953d-9e6f-4349-ab40-b4c7701f6d59'

# Author of this document
Author = 'Administrator'

# Description of the functionality provided by these settings
# Description = ''

# Company associated with this document
CompanyName = 'Unknown'

# Copyright statement for this document
Copyright = '(c) 2016 Administrator. All rights reserved.'

# Modules to import when applied to a session
```

```
# ModulesToImport = 'MyCustomModule', @{ ModuleName = 'MyCustomModule'; ModuleVersion
= '1.0.0.0'; GUID = '4d30d5f0-cb16-4898-812d-f20a6c596bdf' }

# Aliases to make visible when applied to a session
# VisibleAliases = 'Item1', 'Item2'

# Cmdlets to make visible when applied to a session
# VisibleCmdlets = 'Invoke-Cmdlet1', @{ Name = 'Invoke-Cmdlet2'; Parameters = @
{ Name = 'Parameter1'; ValidateSet = 'Item1', 'Item2' }, @{ Name = 'Parameter2';
ValidatePattern = 'L*' } }

# Functions to make visible when applied to a session
# VisibleFunctions = 'Invoke-Function1', @{ Name = 'Invoke-Function2'; Parameters =
@{ Name = 'Parameter1'; ValidateSet = 'Item1', 'Item2' }, @{ Name = 'Parameter2';
ValidatePattern = 'L*' } }

# External commands (scripts and applications) to make visible when applied to a
session
# VisibleExternalCommands = 'Item1', 'Item2'

# Providers to make visible when applied to a session
# VisibleProviders = 'Item1', 'Item2'

# Scripts to run when applied to a session
# ScriptsToProcess = 'C:\ConfigData\InitScript1.ps1', 'C:\ConfigData\InitScript2.ps1'

# Aliases to be defined when applied to a session
# AliasDefinitions = @{ Name = 'Alias1'; Value = 'Invoke-Alias1'}, @{ Name = 'Alias2';
Value = 'Invoke-Alias2'}

# Functions to define when applied to a session
# FunctionDefinitions = @{ Name = 'MyFunction'; ScriptBlock = { param($MyInput)
$MyInput } }

# Variables to define when applied to a session
# VariableDefinitions = @{ Name = 'Variable1'; Value = { 'Dynamic' + 'InitialValue' }
}, @{ Name = 'Variable2'; Value = 'StaticInitialValue' }

# Environment variables to define when applied to a session
# EnvironmentVariables = @{ Variable1 = 'Value1'; Variable2 = 'Value2' }

# Type files (.ps1xml) to load when applied to a session
# TypesToProcess = 'C:\ConfigData\MyTypes.ps1xml', 'C:\ConfigData\OtherTypes.ps1xml'

# Format files (.ps1xml) to load when applied to a session
```

```
# FormatsToProcess = 'C:\ConfigData\MyFormats.ps1xml', 'C:\ConfigData\OtherFormats.
ps1xml'

# Assemblies to load when applied to a session
# AssembliesToLoad = 'System.Web', 'System.OtherAssembly, Version=4.0.0.0,
Culture=neutral, PublicKeyToken=b03f5f7f11d50a3a'
}
```

As with the New-PSSessionConfigurationFile cmdlet, there are a great many optional parameters you can include in the command to configure script elements. Alternatively, you can edit the script file and add settings that way.

Some of the most commonly used settings for JEA roles include the following:

- **VisibleCmdlets**   Specifies the cmdlets that you want to be made available to users inhabiting the role. These are in addition to the basic set of cmdlets supplied by the RestrictedRemoteServer session type in the session configuration file. You can list cmdlet names individually in this setting, use wildcard characters (as in Get-*, which grants access to all cmdlets beginning with the verb Get), or limit access to cmdlets used with specific parameters and values. For example, instead of just granting access to the Restart-Service cmdlet, which would enable users to restart any service, you can specify that access is only granted to the Restart-Service cmdlet when it is used with the Name parameter and the value Spooler, so that users can only restart that one service.

- **VisibleExternalCommands**   Specifies external commands that are to be made available to users inhabiting the role. You can identify commands by supplying the full path to an executable file or a PowerShell script.

- **FunctionDefinitions**   A PowerShell function is essentially a named block of code. You can provide endpoint users with access to functions by specifying them in the script and assigning them a name. For example, the Get-UserInfo command displayed earlier in Figure 4-16 is not a standard cmdlet; it is instead a function that has been defined with the name Get-UserInfo, so that users can run it as though it were a cmdlet.

An example of an edited role capability file is shown in Listing 4-4.

LISTING 4-4 A configured role capability file

```
@{

# ID used to uniquely identify this document
GUID = 'add6e229-647a-45a4-894b-cad514b9b7e0'

# Author of this document
Author = 'Contoso Admin'

# Company associated with this document
```

```
CompanyName = 'Contoso'

# Copyright statement for this document
Copyright = '(c) 2016 Contoso Admin. All rights reserved.'

# Cmdlets to make visible when applied to a session
VisibleCmdlets = 'Restart-Computer',
                 @{Name = 'Restart-Service'
                 Parameters = @{Name = 'Name'; ValidateSet = 'Spooler' }},
                 'Get-*'

# External commands (scripts and applications) to make visible when applied to a
session
VisibleExternalCommands = 'C:\Windows\system32\ipconfig.exe'

# Functions to define when applied to a session
FunctionDefinitions = @{
    'Name' = 'Get-UserInfo'
    'ScriptBlock' = { $PSSenderInfo } }
}
```

Create a JEA endpoint

Once you have created your session configuration and role capability script files, you must register the session with PowerShell using the Register-PSSessionConfiguration cmdlet. This creates the endpoint and prepares it for use.

The basic syntax of the cmdlet is as follows:

```
Register-PSSessionConfiguration -Name endpoint -Path location
```

In this command, you specify the location of the session configuration script file using the Path parameter, and you assign the endpoint a name using the Name parameter. This is the name that users specify in the ConfigurationName parameter when connecting to an end-point using the Enter-PSSession cmdlet.

At this point, the endpoint is ready to receive connections from users.

> **NOTE** **MODIFYING ROLE CAPABILITY FILES**
>
> Once you have registered an endpoint, you can make changes to the associated role ca-pability file, if necessary, without repeating the registration, because PowerShell loads the role capabilities each time a session starts. However, sessions that are already in progress when you modify the file retain their existing capabilities for the duration of the session.

Connect to a JEA endpoint on a server for administration

Once you have created and registered a PowerShell endpoint, users can connect to it using the Enter-PSSession cmdlet. The syntax for the cmdlet is as follows:

```
Enter-PSSession -ComputerName computer -ConfigurationName endpoint -Credentials
(Get-Credential)
```

In the Enter-PSSession command, the ComputerName parameter specifies the name of the system hosting the PowerShell endpoint. If that is the local system, you can use a period for this parameter, as in the following example. The ConfigurationName parameter specifies the name of the endpoint to which you are connecting, created when registering the session configuration file using the Register-PSSessionConfiguration cmdlet. The Credentials parameter can use any standard PowerShell method for supplying the account name and password of the user's unprivileged account. For example, calling the Get-Credential cmdlet generates a standard Windows PowerShell Credential Request dialog box.

An example of an Enter-PSSession command appears as follows:

```
Enter-PSSession -ComputerName . -ConfigurationName JEA -Credentials (Get-Credential)
```

Once you are successfully authenticated, the command prompt in your PowerShell window changes to specify the name of the computer hosting the endpoint to which you are connected (or LocalHost if it is the same computer on which you are working).

When you have completed your tasks, you can terminate the connection to the endpoint using the Exit-PSSession cmdlet with no parameters. When you do this, the session ends and the command prompt returns to its initial state.

View logs

In your session configuration file, there is a TranscriptDirectory setting that you use to specify a location where PowerShell should save transcripts of endpoint sessions. This is an automated implementation of a PowerShell feature called *over-the-shoulder transcription*, which generates text logs that are the functional equivalent of looking over the user's shoulder at the computer screen.

In PowerShell versions 4 and earlier, you created transcripts manually using the Start-Transcript cmdlet. In PowerShell 5, endpoints create transcripts automatically and save them to the location you specify in the session configuration file.

PowerShell creates a separate transcript file for each endpoint session, with the name of the computer hosting the endpoint and the date and time included in the file name. Each transcript begins with a header, as shown in Listing 4-5. The header specifies the start time of the session and the name of the computer hosting the endpoint. You can tell that this is a transcript of a JEA endpoint session by the difference between the Username and RunAs User values. In a transcript of a standard PowerShell session, these two values would be the same.

After the header, you can see a record of the commands issued by the user and their results. The transcript ends with the issuance of the Exit-PSSession command and a footer specifying the time the session ended.

LISTING 4-5 A JEA endpoint session transcript

```
***********************
Windows PowerShell transcript start
Start time: 20160831162904
Username: CONTOSO\OperatorUser
RunAs User: WinRM Virtual Users\WinRM VA_2_CONTOSO_OperatorUser
Machine: SERVERD (Microsoft Windows NT 10.0.14300.0)
Host Application: C:\Windows\system32\wsmprovhost.exe -Embedding
Process ID: 4012
PSVersion: 5.1.14300.1000
PSEdition: Desktop
PSCompatibleVersions: 1.0, 2.0, 3.0, 4.0, 5.0, 5.1.14300.1000
CLRVersion: 4.0.30319.42000
BuildVersion: 10.0.14300.1000
WSManStackVersion: 3.0
PSRemotingProtocolVersion: 2.3
SerializationVersion: 1.1.0.1
***********************
PS>CommandInvocation(Get-Command): "Get-Command"
>> ParameterBinding(Get-Command): name="Name"; value="Out-Default, Exit-PSSession"
>> ParameterBinding(Get-Command): name="CommandType"; value="Alias, Function, Filter,
Cmdlet, Configuration"
>> ParameterBinding(Get-Command): name="Module"; value=""
>> ParameterBinding(Get-Command): name="ArgumentList"; value=""
>> ParameterBinding(Get-Command): name="ListImported"; value="True"
>> ParameterBinding(Get-Command): name="ErrorAction"; value="SilentlyContinue"
>> ParameterBinding(Get-Command): name="ShowCommandInfo"; value="False"
>> CommandInvocation(Measure-Object): "Measure-Object"
>> ParameterBinding(Measure-Object): name="InputObject"; value=""
>> CommandInvocation(Select-Object): "Select-Object"
>> ParameterBinding(Select-Object): name="Property"; value="Count"
>> ParameterBinding(Select-Object): name="InputObject"; value=""
>> ParameterBinding(Measure-Object): name="InputObject"; value="Out-Default"
>> ParameterBinding(Measure-Object): name="InputObject"; value="Exit-PSSession"
PS>ParameterBinding(Select-Object): name="InputObject"; value="Microsoft.PowerShell.
Commands.GenericMeasureInfo"


Cmdlet          Restart-Service                              3.0.0.0
Microsoft.PowerShell.Management          CommandInvocation(Get-Help): "Get-Help"
>> ParameterBinding(Get-Help): name="Name"; value="restart-service"
>> ParameterBinding(Get-Help): name="Category"; value=""
```

```
>> CommandInvocation(Out-Default): "Out-Default"
>> ParameterBinding(Out-Default): name="InputObject"; value=""
>> TerminatingError(Get-Help): "Cannot find path '' because it does not exist."
>> CommandInvocation(Out-Default): "Out-Default"
>> ParameterBinding(Out-Default): name="InputObject"; value=""
>> ParameterBinding(Out-Default): name="InputObject"; value="Cannot find path ''
because it does not exist."
Cannot find path '' because it does not exist.
    + CategoryInfo          : ObjectNotFound: (:) [Get-Help], ItemNotFoundException
    + FullyQualifiedErrorId : PathNotFound,Microsoft.PowerShell.Commands.
GetHelpCommand

PS>CommandInvocation(Exit-PSSession): "Exit-PSSession"
>> CommandInvocation(Out-Default): "Out-Default"
>> ParameterBinding(Out-Default): name="InputObject"; value=""
************************
Windows PowerShell transcript end
End time: 20160831171037
************************
```

Download WMF 5.1 to a Windows Server 2008 R2

JEA is built into the Windows PowerPoint implementation in Windows Server 2016 and Windows 10. To use JEA on earlier Windows versions, including Windows Server 2012 R2, Windows Server 2012, Windows Server 2008 R2, Windows 8.1, Windows 8, and Windows 7 SP1, you must download and install Windows Management Framework (WMF) 5.0.

WMF 5.0 is available from the Microsoft Download Center at the following URL: *https://www.microsoft.com/en-us/download/details.aspx?id=50395*.

On Windows Server 2012 R2, Windows Server 2012, Windows 8.1, and Windows 8, you can simply download and install WMF 5.0. However, on Windows Server 2008 R2 and Windows 7 SP1, you must first install Windows Management Framework 4.0 and .NET Framework 4.5, and then install WMF 5.0.

> ***IMPORTANT*** **RUNNING JEA ON WINDOWS SERVER 2008 R2 AND WINDOWS 7 SP1**
>
> Windows Server 2008 R2 and Windows 7 do not provide full JEA functionality, even with WMF 5.0 installed. On these platforms, Windows PowerShell endpoints cannot create and assign virtual accounts to connected users.

Configure a JEA endpoint on a server using Desired State Configuration

The primary limitation of JEA is that it is a technology implemented using Windows PowerShell on individual systems. You have to create endpoints on each computer that you want users to manage in JEA sessions. Users can access endpoints from remote systems, but the session configurations themselves must be located on the computers to be managed.

How then can administrators in a large enterprise create JEA endpoints on many different computers without having to configure each one individually? One way is to use the Desired State Configuration (DSC) feature introduced as part of PowerShell in the Windows Server 2012 R2 release.

Desired State Configuration (DSC) is method for using declarative Windows PowerShell script files to apply, monitor, and maintain a specific system configuration. DSC resources take the form of PowerShell modules containing scripted configurations. Applying the module on a system implements the configuration, using PowerShell cmdlets and other resources called by the scripts.

The DSC Local Configuration Manager (LCM) is the component that applies and maintains a configuration using the DSC resources. The LCM monitors the system on a regular basis to ensure that a specific configuration is maintained. If it is not, the LCM uses the DSC resources to reapply the configuration. DSC configurations are idempotent, meaning that the scripts can be applied to a system repeatedly without generating errors or other undesirable results.

Deploying a DSC module

To deploy a DSC module, you run the Start-DSCConfiguration cmdlet. Depending on the parameters you include in this command, you can configure DSC to operate in one of two modes.

In Push mode, you run the cmdlet from a centralized DSC server where the module is stored and specify the names of the systems to receive the module using the ComputerName parameter. In Pull mode, you run the cmdlet from the computer to be managed, and it periodically retrieves the configuration from a centralized DSC server.

Using xJea

Microsoft has made available a PowerShell module called xJea that includes DSC resources you can use to implement JEA on your servers. The module is available from the PowerShell Gallery at *http://www.powershellgallery.com/packages/xJea*. To obtain the module, you perform the following cmdlet:

```
Install-Module -Name xJea
```

If you have not already done so, you have to approve a download of a NuGet provider, so that PowerShell can interact with the repository where the xJea module is stored.

The xJea module includes two resources that you can use to create JEA deployments, as follows. As with the session configuration and role capability files discussed earlier, you modify these files to create a JEA environment suifor your organization.

- **JEA Toolkit** Comparable to a role capability file, a JEA toolkit is a set of tasks that designated users can perform on a server when connected to a JEA endpoint.
- **JEA Endpoint** Comparable in part to a session configuration file, a JEA endpoint is created using one or more JEA toolkits and a list of users or groups that are provided access to the endpoint.

The advantage of using DSC to create endpoints is that you can create the resources once and deploy the module on computers all over the enterprise.

Skill 4.4: Implement Privileged Access Workstations and User Rights Assignments

Several of the security technologies described in this chapter include a recommendation that administrative users should only perform highly-privileged tasks using workstations that are dedicated to that purpose. *Privileged Access Workstation (PAW)* is a designation that Microsoft uses to define the hardware and software configurations required to create dedicated administrative workstations. Deploying PAWs properly is more than just a matter of purchasing new computers. The object of the PAW principle is to create a workstation environment that can only be used for administrative purposes, even if an administrator should try to do otherwise. This includes creating an Active Directory (AD) substructure devoted to PAW users and Group Policy settings that enforce the administrators' roles.

> **This section covers how to:**
> - Implement a PAWS solution
> - Configure User Rights Assignment group policies
> - Configure security options settings in Group Policy
> - Enable and configure Remote Credential Guard for remote desktop access

Implement a PAWS solution

As mentioned previously in this chapter, credential theft is one of the most serious security issues in today's computing environment. Using a standard user workstation to log on using highly-privileged credentials exposes those credentials to attack. By deploying PAWs on your network and dedicating them solely to administrative activity, the vulnerability of the administrative credentials is minimized.

The fundamental reasons for a PAW deployment are as follows:

- to prevent users from performing privileged tasks using unsecured workstations

- to prevent users from accessing vulnerable resources using administrative credentials

Thus, the problem is not only that administrators might use unprotected workstations to perform privileged tasks, they also might use their privileged credentials for dangerously insecure activities, such as web browsing and reading email.

The use of PAWs creates a separate, secure channel between dedicated administrative workstations and the sensitive resources that have to be managed. An administrative user then has two workstations and two user accounts, one for secure activities and one for everyday tasks, as shown in Figure 4-17.

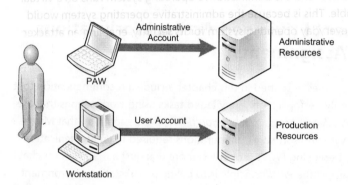

FIGURE 4-17 Administrative user with separate accounts and workstations for privileged and everyday use

Providing administrative users with PAWs does not necessarily mean that they use the workstations properly, however. Some might find the extra steps needed to maintain a secure administrative environment to be too inconvenient or too time-consuming, and end up reverting to the old habits of using their administrative accounts for everything. Therefore, a PAW deployment also includes an implementation of security groups and Group Policy settings that prevent PAWs from being used to access insecure resources.

PAW hardware profiles

A PAW calls for a separate instance of an operating system dedicated to administrative use. While the hardware implementation of this concept can call for two separate computers, this does not necessarily have to be the case. There are three possible hardware profiles that you can use to create PAWs for administrative use, as follows:

- **Dedicated hardware** Using separate computers for PAWs provides a complete separation of sensitive and everyday tasks. This option also enables the implementers to ensure that the PAW hardware is properly equipped and the supply chain secure.

However, a second computer for each administrative user consumes additional desk space and incurs additional expense. If the proximity of users allows it, it is possible for multiple administrative users (with separate accounts) to share one PAW without any additional security risk.

- Virtual machines   The Client Hyper-V capability in Windows 10 makes it possible for a single computer to run two instances of the operating system, one for secured administrative tasks and one for everyday, unsecured tasks. To do this, however, it is imperative that the secured administrative operating system be the host operating system on the computer, and the everyday user operating system be a virtual machine running on the host. The opposite configuration, in which the everyday user operating system runs on the host and the administrative operating system runs on a virtual machine, is unacceptable. This is because the administrative operating system would be dependent on the everyday operating system for its security, enabling an attacker to gain indirect control over the sensitive resources, due to the transitive nature of control relationships. This option reduces hardware expenditures by requiring only one computer, but the hardware itself must meet PAW requirements.

- Remote desktop   As an alternative to using client Hyper-V, it is also possible to separate administrative and everyday tasks by using a remote desktop or virtual application solution, either on-premises or in the cloud. For the same reason as in the Hyper-V solution, the computer must run the administrative operating system as its host environment and access the applications required for everyday production tasks using a Remote Desktop, RemoteApp, or other third-party solution. This way, the production applications are actually running on a remote server, and do not contaminate the control relationship between the host computer and the privileged resources. Apart from the reduced hardware expenditures, this option makes it possible to create a unified workstation environment for the user that does not require conscious switching between computers or virtual machines.

For any of these hardware profile, the computer hardware itself must be sufficient to support the PAW environment. Computers suifor use as PAWs should support Secure Boot and have Trusted Platform Module (TPM) chips for the storage of BitLocker drive encryption keys. For the Hyper-V option, the computers must have the hardware needed to support a hypervisor. If you plan to use multifactor authentication, the computers might also require card readers or biometric devices.

As dictated by the clean source principle described earlier in this chapter, the PAWs hardware must be acquired through a reputable supplier and stored in a secure location, so that unauthorized individuals cannot gain physical access to the computers, whether before, during, or after deployment.

PAW deployment phases

The deployment of a secured environment must be performed in a secure manner, It is therefore critical that the procurement, configuration, and distribution of PAWs be carefully planned and performed. The process of deploying PAWs should begin with the creation of usage scenarios that specify which users need secured workstations and the order in which they should get them.

If you already have a tiered administration model in place, as described earlier in this chapter, this task might be relatively easy. Tier 0 administrators are likely to be the first candidates for PAWs, with Tier 1 and possible Tier 2 administrators to follow. If you do not have an administrative model in place, you have to consider the individual administrative roles in your organization and prioritize them.

Microsoft has devised a three-phase plan for PAW deployment that provides for a gradual expansion of PAW distribution and security throughout the enterprise. The phases of the deployment are as follows:

- **Phase 1** Provides for rapid deployment of PAWs to the most critically important users, including Active Directory and other Tier 0 administrators. This first phase includes the creation of the Active Directory Organizational Units (OUs), security groups, and Group Policy objects needed to separate PAW users and computers from the rest of the enterprise. PAWs distributed during this phase should include only the management tools these administrators need.

- **Phase 2** Expands the scope of the project by deploying PAWs to users responsible for administration of application servers and cloud services, as well as other Tier 1 and Tier 2 administrative roles. This phase cannot begin until Phase 1 is completed, as it relies on the AD infrastructure created in Phase 1. PAWs distributed during Phase 2 is likely to require software and applications beyond those needed for Phase 1, due to the wider range of administrative roles being serviced. This phase might also include the creation of a request and distribution procedure for large-scale deployment of PAWs throughout the enterprise.

■ **Phase 3** Enhances the security of the PAWs deployed in Phases 1 and 2 by applying additional protections, such as multifactor authentication (the use of smart cards, virtual smart cards, biometrics, or other technologies), whitelisting (the limitation of trusted applications using Device Guard, AppLocker, or other products), and/or the use of secured containers (including the Protected Users security group and the Authentication Policies and Authentication Policy Silos objects in Active Directory). Other system hardening techniques you can consider include Credential Guard in Windows 10, full disk encryption, disabling Internet browsing (by configuring the browser to use a loopback address as a proxy server), and restricting the use of USB ports to non-media devices. This phase is not dependent on Phase 2, and can begin any time after the completion of Phase 1.

Configure User Rights Assignment group policies

As part of Microsoft's PAW deployment, you create a structure of Organization Units in your existing Active Directory domain to contain the computer objects representing your PAWs and the user objects representing your administrative accounts. You then use those OUs to deploy Group Policy objects containing user rights assignments and other settings.

> **NEED MORE REVIEW?** **DEPLOYING PAWS**
>
> Complete instructions for a PAW deployment, including details of the AD infrastructure modifications and Group Policy settings required, as well as scripts for creating them, are available at *https://technet.microsoft.com/windows-server-docs/security/securing-privileged-access/privileged-access-workstations*.

Configuring User Rights Assignments

To configure user rights assignments and other Group Policy settings for a PAW installation, you create a group policy object (GPO) and link it to an OU containing the AD objects (such as computer or users) that you want to configure. Any objects you then place in that OU receive the settings from the GPO.

To create and link a GPO, use the following procedure:

1. Open the Group Policy Management console on a domain controller or a workstation with Remote Server Administration Tools installed.

2. Browse to your domain and expand it.

3. Right-click the Group Policy Objects folder and, in the context menu that appears, select New. A New GPO dialog box appears.

4. Specify a name for the new GPO and click OK. The new GPO appears in the right pane.

5. In the left pane, browse to the OU you want to link to the GPO.

6. Right-click the OU and, in the context menu that appears, select Link an Existing GPO. A Select GPO dialog box appears.

7. Select the GPO you just created and configured and click OK. The GPO appears on the OU's Linked Group Policy Objects tab.

8. Right-click the new GPO you created and, in the context menu that appears, click Edit. A Group Policy Management Editor window appears.

At this point, you can browse through the structure of the GPO, which contains hundreds of settings that you can configure. For example, to configure user rights assignment settings for the computers to which the GPO is applied, you browse to the Computer Configuration\Policies\Windows Settings\Security Settings\Local Policies\User Rights Assignment container, as shown in Figure 4-18.

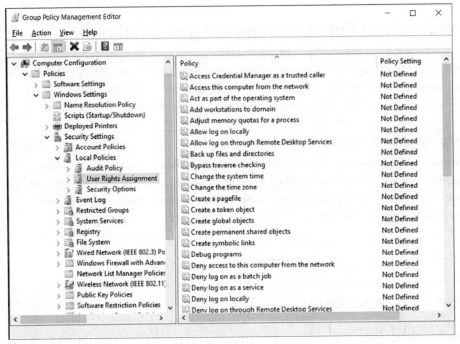

FIGURE 4-18 User rights assignment settings in a GPO

When you double-click one of the settings in the User Rights Assignments container, a Properties sheet appears, as shown in Figure 4-19. By default, all of the settings in a new GPO are blank, and the Properties sheet for each one contains controls that you can use to configure it. The controls vary for different types of settings, but User Rights Assignments settings typically have a checkbox to enable the setting and a list to which you can add the users or groups that you want to receive the setting.

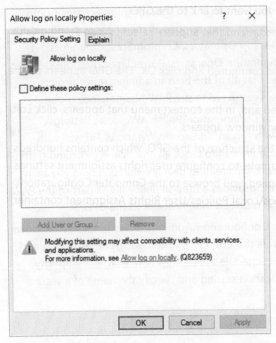

FIGURE 4-19 The Properties sheet for a user rights assignment setting in a GPO

Configuring a PAW computer GPO

As part of the Active Directory modifications for a PAW deployment, you create a new OU in which you place the computer objects representing all of the PAWs you intend to deploy, then you create a new GPO called PAW Configuration - Computer, in which you configure the settings that you want every PAW to receive.

- **Limit logon rights** In the Computer Configuration\Policies\Windows Settings\Security Settings\Local Policies\User Rights Assignment container, enable the Allow Log On Locally setting and add the PAW Users group. This group contains all of the administrative user accounts that are to be allowed to access PAWs. This setting prevents unprivileged accounts from logging on to PAWs.

- **Restrict maintenance access** In the Computer Configuration\Preferences\Control Panel Settings\Local Users and Groups container, select the Administrators (built-in) group, remove all of the existing member users and groups, and add the PAW Maintenance group and the local Administrator. The PAW Maintenance group contains all of the user accounts that are to be allowed to administer the security environment of the PAWs. This prevents unauthorized users (including PAW users themselves, unless they are members of the PAW Maintenance group) from modifying the PAWs' security settings.

- Restrict local group membership In the Computer Configuration\Preferences\Control Panel Settings\Local Users and Groups container, remove all member users and groups from the following built-in groups: Backup Operators, Cryptographic Operators, Hyper-V Administrators, Network Configuration Operators, Power Users, Remote Desktop Users, Replicator. This setting ensures that all of the built-in administrative groups remain empty. Administrative access is restricted to the PAW Maintenance group.

- Block inbound traffic In the Computer Configuration\Policies\Windows Settings\Security Settings\Windows Firewall with Advanced Security\Windows Firewall with Advanced Security node, configure the firewall to block all unsolicited incoming traffic, prevent local Administrators members from creating new firewall rules, and log all incoming and outgoing traffic. Microsoft provides a firewall policy file as part of the PAW deployment instructions that adds the required modifications to the GPO.

- Configure updates   In the Computer Configuration\Administrative Templates\Windows Components\Windows Updates, enable the Configure Automatic Updates setting and select option 4 - Auto Download and Schedule the Install. Then, enable the Specify Intranet Microsoft Update Service Location setting and specify the name of a secure WSUS server on your network.

Restricting administrator logons

In the previous section, you configured settings on the PAWs that prevent unprivileged users from logging on. The converse situation also applies, however: you must also prevent privileged users from logging on to unprivileged workstations. To do this, you create a GPO containing the following user rights assignments and link the GPO to the OUs containing computer objects other than PAWs:

- Deny Log On Locally
- Deny Log On As a Batch Job
- Deny Log On As a Service

Enable each of these user rights assignment settings and add all of the domain administrative groups that might contain PAW users, including the following:

- PAW Users
- Enterprise Admins
- Domain Admins
- Schema Admins
- Administrators
- Account Operators
- Backup Operators
- Print Operators
- Server Operators

- Domain Controllers
- Read-Only Domain Controllers
- Group Policy Creators Owners
- Cryptographic Operators

By applying these settings to the unsecured computers on the network, you prevent users from logging on to them with administrative accounts. Administrators can still access these systems, but they must use their standard user account.

Configure security options settings in group policy

In addition to the user rights assignments and other settings shown in the previous section, group policy objects also include a container called Security Options, which has dozens of settings that you can use to harden the security of your workstations and servers.

To configure these settings using the Group Policy Management Editor, browse to the container located at Computer Configuration\Policies\Windows Settings\Security Settings\Local Policies\Security Options, as shown in Figure 4-20.

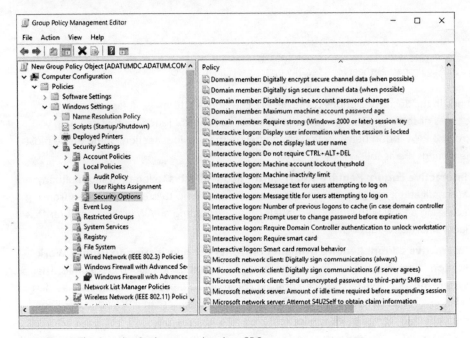

FIGURE 4-20 The Security Options container in a GPO

As with user rights assignment settings, double-clicking on a security option setting opens a Properties sheet, as shown in Figure 4-21. However, because security options apply to the entire computer, not to specific users and groups, there is no account list. Instead, security options can have various types controls that configure the functionality of the setting, such as the spin box in this example.

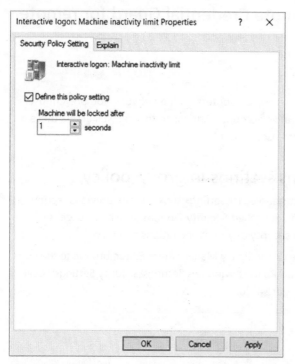

FIGURE 4-21 The Properties sheet for a security options setting in a GPO

Settings in the Security Options container are categorized, to make it easier to locate specific types of settings. The Interactive Logon settings control functions that can help you to control the PAW logon behavior you configured in the previous section. Some of the most valuable settings are as follows:

- **Interactive Logon: Require Smart Card** Requires users to log on using multifactor authentication, in the form of a smart card. This can help to prevent attackers from accessing a PAW with stolen credentials or impersonating a PAW with a computer that lacks smart card support.

- **Interactive Logon: Require Domain Controller Authentication to Unlock Workstation** Prevents the computer from being unlocked using cached credentials. The system must be able to contact a domain controller to perform an interactive authentication, or it remains locked. This can help to prevent access to a PAW that has been disconnected from the network or removed from the premises.

- **Interactive Logon: Machine Inactivity Limit** Enables the computer to invoke the screen saver after a specified period of inactivity, forcing the user to supply credentials to reactivate the system. This can prevent an attacker from gaining access to a PAW that has been left unattended.

Enable and configure Remote Credential Guard for remote desktop access

Credential Guard is a security feature first introduced in Windows 10 Enterprise and Windows Server 2016 that protects user credentials by storing them in a virtualized container that is separate from the operating system. Windows traditionally stores credentials in the Local Security Authority (LSA), which uses process memory. Credential Guard creates a container called the isolated LSA process that is virtualized using the same hypervisor that Hyper-V uses. An attacking program running on the system with administrative privileges cannot access credentials stored in the isolated LSA process.

A variation on this concept, called *Remote Credential Guard*, was added in Windows 10, version 1607, and Windows Server 2016. Remote Credential Guard is designed to protect your credentials when you connect to another Windows system using Remote Desktop.

Normally, in a Remote Desktop connection, the target system authenticates the incoming user, and therefore gains access to the user's credentials. In the case of a help desk operator, providing support often requires a Remote Desktop connection to an unsecured client workstation that might already be compromised, which results in the operator's credentials being compromised as well. Remote Credential Guard works by redirecting the connector's Kerberos authentication requests back to the source system. Because the credentials never reach the target computer, they are not endangered.

To use Remote Credential Guard, both systems involved in the Remote Desktop connection must meet the following requirements:

- Both systems must be running Windows 10, version 1607 or later, or Windows Server 2016.
- Both systems must be members of the same Active Directory domain, or two separate domains joined by a trust relationship.
- Both systems must be configured to use Kerberos authentication.
- The connecting system must use the Remote Desktop classic Windows app.

Enabling Remote Credential Guard

The first step required to use Remote Commercial Guard is to enable it in the registry on both computers. To do this, use the following procedure:

1. Open Registry Editor.
2. Browse to the HKEY_LOCAL_MACHINE\System\CurrentControlSet\Control\Lsa container.
3. Add a new DWORD value with the name DisableRestrictedAdmin and the value 0.

You can also do this by executing the following command at an administrative command prompt:

```
reg add HKLM\SYSTEM\CurrentControlSet\Control\Lsa /v DisableRestrictedAdmin /d 0 /t
REG_DWORD
```

Configuring Remote Credential Guard

Once you have enabled Remote Credential Guard, you must turn it on before you can establish a secured connection. You can do this using a Group Policy setting, or you can use a command line parameter when running the Remote Desktop Connection client.

To configure Remote Credential Guard using Group Policy, use the following procedure:

1. Open a Group Policy object in Group Policy Management Editor that are applied to the connecting computer.

2. Browse to the Computer Configuration\Administrative Templates\System\Credentials Delegation folder.

3. Double-click the Restrict Delegation of Credentials to Remote Servers setting. The Restrict Delegation of Credentials to Remote Servers Properties sheet appears.

4. Click Enabled and, in the Use the Following Restricted Mode drop-down list, select Require Remote Credential Guard, as shown in Figure 4-22.

5. Click OK.

6. Close Group Policy Management Editor.

7. From a command prompt, run gpupdate.exe /force to apply the policy settings.

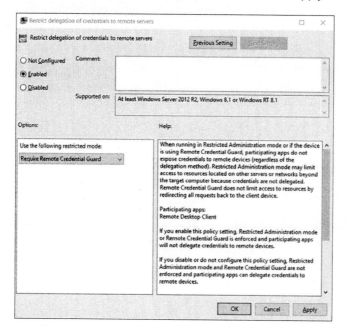

FIGURE 4-22 CONFIGURING REMOTE CREDENTIAL GUARD USING GROUP POLICY

Instead of using Group Policy, you can also activate Remote Credential Guard when you launch the Remote Desktop Connection client from the command prompt, using the following command:

```
mstsc.exe /remoteGuard
```

Skill 4.5: Implement Local Administrator Password Solution

Active Directory provides a protected, centralized store for domain user accounts and their passwords, but there are some situations when domain users must log on to their workstations using local accounts. This creates a problem for IT management.

Leaving control of the local account passwords to the users is not practical. Some organizations use a single local account and password for all of the workstations, which is a security hazard. There are third-party password management solutions, but these cost money, often require additional hardware and software, and add another product for IT to manage.

Local Administrator Password Solution (LAPS) is a free Microsoft product that enables workstations to automatically change the passwords on local accounts and store those passwords as attributes of the computer objects in Active Directory. Using permissions, you can control which users are allowed to read the passwords and change them.

This section covers how to:

- Install and configure the LAPS tool
- Secure local administrator passwords using LAPS
- Manage password parameters and properties using LAPS

Install and configure the LAPS tool

LAPS is a client/server tool that runs as a Group Policy client-side extension on your computers. The program is packaged as a single Microsoft Installer file, with an .msi extension, which you must download from the Microsoft Download Center. Both x64 and x86 versions are provided in the download, along with documentation.

Deploying LAPS on your network consists of three basic steps: installing the LAPS management tools, modifying your Active Directory schema, and deploying the LAPS client to your workstations. Fortunately, all of the components required for all three steps are provided in the single installer file.

Installing LAPS management tools

To install LAPS on a computer you are using for management, you download the appropriate LAPS installer file for your computer platform (LAPS.x64 or LAPS.x86) and run it to launch the Local Administrator Password Solution Setup Wizard. By default, the wizard is configured to install only the AdmPwd GPO Extension, as shown in Figure 4-23. This is the client side of the program that go on every computer you intend to manage. For the systems you use to manage LAPS, you must also select the Management Tools component and all of its subcomponents. This includes a graphical client interface, the PowerShell module, and the Group Policy templates.

FIGURE 4-23 Installing LAPS

You can install the management tools on other workstations later, but you need one to gain access to the tools for modifying the Active Directory schema.

Modifying Active Directory

As noted earlier, LAPS stores local account passwords in Active Directory. To do this you must modify the AD schema to add two attributes to the computer object type, as follows:

- **msMcsAdmPwd**   Stores the local account password
- **msMcsAdmPwdExpirationTime**   Stores the expiration date time for the current password

You do this using a Windows PowerShell cmdlet supplied with the LAPS management tools.

> ***NOTE* MODIFYING THE ACTIVE DIRECTORY SCHEMA**
>
> Active Directory consists of objects representing network resources, and objects consist of attributes, which store information about the object. It is the schema that defines the types of objects you can create in AD and the attributes each object type supports. By default, the computer object does not have an attribute for local account password storage, so by extending the schema, LAPS creates one.

To extend the schema you must open a Windows PowerShell window using an account that is a member of the Schema Admins group in your domain. This is only necessary once. All of the LAPS PowerShell cmdlets, for managers and clients, are supplied in a single module, which you must import before you can access them.

To import the module, use the following command:

```
Import-Module AdmPwd.PS
```

Adding the verbose parameter to the command displays a list of all the cmdlets included in the module, as shown in Figure 4-24.

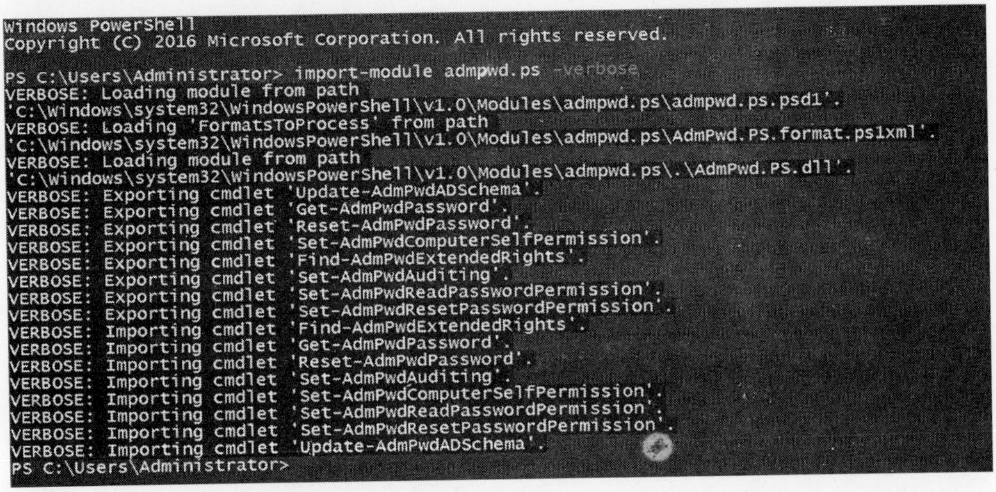

```
Windows PowerShell
Copyright (C) 2016 Microsoft Corporation. All rights reserved.

PS C:\Users\Administrator> import-module admpwd.ps -verbose
VERBOSE: Loading module from path
'C:\Windows\system32\WindowsPowerShell\v1.0\Modules\admpwd.ps\admpwd.ps.psd1'.
VERBOSE: Loading 'FormatsToProcess' from path
'C:\Windows\system32\WindowsPowerShell\v1.0\Modules\admpwd.ps\AdmPwd.PS.format.ps1xml'.
VERBOSE: Loading module from path
'C:\Windows\system32\WindowsPowerShell\v1.0\Modules\admpwd.ps\.\AdmPwd.PS.dll'.
VERBOSE: Exporting cmdlet 'Update-AdmPwdADSchema'.
VERBOSE: Exporting cmdlet 'Get-AdmPwdPassword'.
VERBOSE: Exporting cmdlet 'Reset-AdmPwdPassword'.
VERBOSE: Exporting cmdlet 'Set-AdmPwdComputerSelfPermission'.
VERBOSE: Exporting cmdlet 'Find-AdmPwdExtendedRights'.
VERBOSE: Exporting cmdlet 'Set-AdmPwdAuditing'.
VERBOSE: Exporting cmdlet 'Set-AdmPwdReadPasswordPermission'.
VERBOSE: Exporting cmdlet 'Set-AdmPwdResetPasswordPermission'.
VERBOSE: Importing cmdlet 'Find-AdmPwdExtendedRights'.
VERBOSE: Importing cmdlet 'Get-AdmPwdPassword'.
VERBOSE: Importing cmdlet 'Reset-AdmPwdPassword'.
VERBOSE: Importing cmdlet 'Set-AdmPwdAuditing'.
VERBOSE: Importing cmdlet 'Set-AdmPwdComputerSelfPermission'.
VERBOSE: Importing cmdlet 'Set-AdmPwdReadPasswordPermission'.
VERBOSE: Importing cmdlet 'Set-AdmPwdResetPasswordPermission'.
VERBOSE: Importing cmdlet 'Update-AdmPwdADSchema'.
PS C:\Users\Administrator>
```

FIGURE 4-24 Importing the LAPS PowerShell module

To extend the schema, you use the following cmdlet, with no parameters.

UpdateAdmPwdADSchema

Modifying the schema adds the new attributes to all of your existing computer objects and to the object type that AD uses to create new computer objects as well, as shown in Figure 4-25.

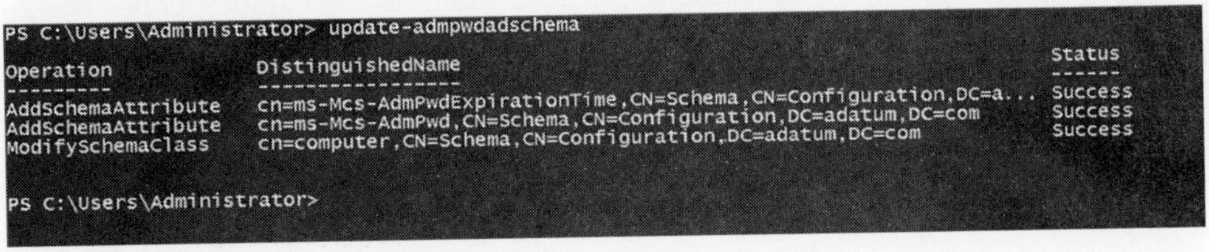

```
PS C:\Users\Administrator> update-admpwdadschema

Operation            DistinguishedName                                                        Status
---------            -----------------                                                        ------
AddSchemaAttribute   cn=ms-Mcs-AdmPwdExpirationTime,CN=Schema,CN=Configuration,DC=a...        Success
AddSchemaAttribute   cn=ms-Mcs-AdmPwd,CN=Schema,CN=Configuration,DC=adatum,DC=com             Success
ModifySchemaClass    cn=computer,CN=Schema,CN=Configuration,DC=adatum,DC=com                   Success

PS C:\Users\Administrator>
```

FIGURE 4-25 Modifying the AD schema for LAPS

As with files and directories, Active Directory objects and attributes have permissions, in the form of access control lists (ACLs). Using these permissions, you specify who can access the new attributes you created and what the users can do with them.

For LAPS client computers to be able to update their passwords, they must have the Write permission to the attributes LAPS created. To deploy these permissions, you use the Set-Ad-mPwdComputerSelfPermission cmdlet to apply them to the Active Directory organizational unit (OU) objects which contain your LAPS client workstations. Applying the permissions to the OUs causes them be inherited by all of the subordinate objects in those OUs, including other OUs.

To assign the Write permission for the two LAPS attributes to the SELF built-in account on your clients, you use the following PowerShell command syntax:

```
Set-AdmPwdComputerSelfPermission -Identity:OUname
```

You must repeat this command with the name of every OU containing the computer objects of LAPS clients, unless the OU is subordinate to another OU that you have already configured.

To grant users or groups the permissions needed to read the passwords stored in the AD attributes, you use the Set-AdmPwdReadPasswordPermission cmdlet, with the following syntax:

```
Set-AdmPwdReadPasswordPermission -OrgUnit OUname -AllowedPrincipals username
```

In this command, the OrgUnit parameter specifies the name of the OU that delegate the permissions (that is, the OU containing the client computers), and the AllowedPrincipals parameter specifies the names of the users or groups that should receive the permission. You can specify multiple users or groups in one command, separated by commas.

Granting users or groups the Write permission for the ms-Mcs-AdmPwdExpirationTime attribute enables them to force a reset of a local account password stored in AD using LAPS. The cmdlet that does this is Set-AdmPwdResetPasswordPermission, and the syntax is as follows:

```
Set-AdmPwdResetPasswordPermission -OrgUnit OUname -AllowedPrincipals username
```

LAPS client deployment

To deploy LAPS on your client workstations, you use the same installer as for your management systems. You can simply run the installer on each client computer manually, but because LAPS is packaged as an .msi file, there are also many ways to automate the installation process for a large enterprise.

To script the installation, you can use one of the following command lines, replacing the path variable with the location of the file:

```
msiexec /i path\LAPS.x64.msi /quiet
msiexec /i path\LAPS.x86.msi /quiet
```

By default, the package installs only the client, so there are no other parameters required. You can insert this command into a logon script or a batch file, but one of the easiest ways to perform a mass deployment of a Windows Installer package is to use Group Policy Software Installation.

To install the LAPS package using Group Policy, open a group policy object and, in the Computer Configuration\Policies\Software Settings\Software Installation container, right-click and choose New\Package. After you supply the location of the package file (using a network path, so the client computers can access it), a new package appears in the right pane, as shown in Figure 4-26.

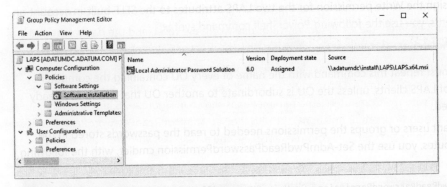

FIGURE 4-26 A LAPS software installation package

Once you have added the package, you link the GPO to the container where the computer objects for your intended clients are located. Once the GPO is in place, the next time the computers in that container restart, the LAPS package is automatically installed.

Secure local administrator passwords using LAPS

When you install the GPO Editor Templates with the LAPS management tools, the installer adds Group Policy settings that you can use to enable password management and configure LAPS. To enable LAPS on your clients, use the following procedure:

1. In Group Policy Management, create a new Group Policy object and link it to the OUs containing your LAPS client computers.

2. Open the new GPO in Group Policy Management Editor and browse to the Computer Configuration\Policies\Administrative Templates\LAPS folder, as shown in Figure 4-27.

3. Double-click the Enable Local Admin Password Management setting.

4. In the Enable Local Admin Password Management Properties sheet, select Enabled and click OK.

5. Close Group Policy Management Editor.

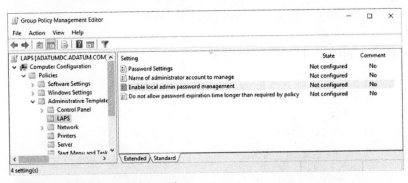

FIGURE 4-27 LAPS Group Policy settings

The next time your client computers restart (or you run `gpupdate.exe /force` on them) the LAPS client is enabled, the local Administrator passwords are reset, and the passwords and expiration dates are stored in their computer objects in Active Directory.

To demonstrate that LAPS is enabled on a client computer, you can open a PowerShell window, import the AdmPwd.PS module, as you did earlier, and run the Get-AdmPwdPassword cmdlet with the ComputerName parameter, as shown in Figure 4-28. If your user account has the appropriate permissions (set with the Set-AdmPwdReadPasswordPermission), the output from the PowerShell command displays the actual password stored in the AD computer object.

FIGURE 4-28 Output of the Get-AdmPwdPassword cmdlet

LAPS also includes a graphical client tool, which you can choose to install by selecting the Fat Client UI component in the Local Administrator Password Solution Setup Wizard. By running the tool, which appears as LAPS UI in the list of installed applications, and searching for the computer name, you see the display shown in Figure 4-29.

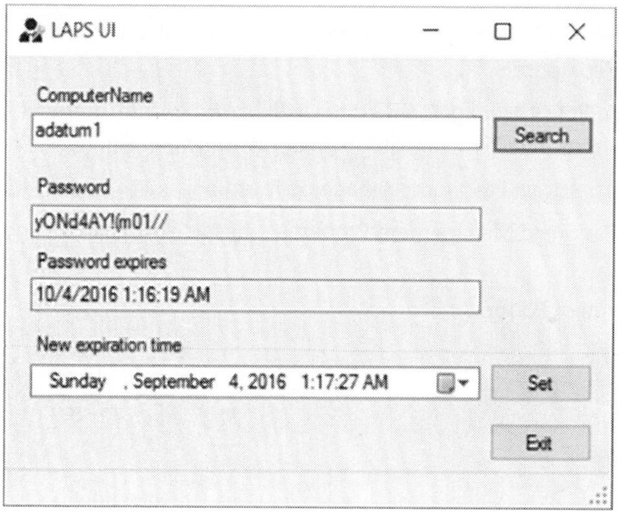

FIGURE 4-29 The LAPS UI tool

Manage password parameters and properties using LAPS

In addition to enabling LAPS, you can also use Group Policy settings to configure its behavior. You can control the nature of the passwords that LAPS assigns to local administrator accounts, and you can specify the name of the account that LAPS should protect.

Configuring password settings

When LAPS assigns passwords to the local Administrator account, it defaults to creating passwords that are 14 characters long and consist of a combination of capital and lowercase letters, numbers, and symbols. The default expiration date for each password is 30 days after its creation.

You can modify these defaults by enabling the Password Settings policy. To do this, double-click the Password Settings policy in a GPO, to display the Properties sheet shown in Figure 4-30.

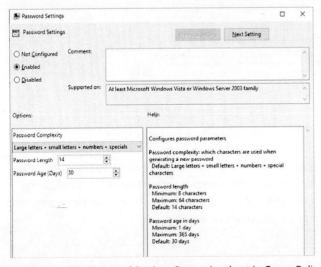

FIGURE 4-30 The Password Settings Properties sheet in Group Policy

When you click the Enabled button, controls appear that you can use to select the length of the passwords LAPS creates, choose a level of complexity, and specify a password age after which it expires.

Changing the account name

LAPS assigns passwords to the local Administrator account, which it can identify by its well-known SID. In some organizations, it is common practice to rename the local Administrator account, to prevent attackers from trying to compromise it. However, the account's security identifier (SID) remains the same, so LAPS still assigns passwords to that account.

By default, the Windows workstation operating systems have the local Administrator account disabled, as a security measure. When you create a local account while installing the operating system, that account receives administrator privileges. If you want to configure LAPS to assign passwords to an account other than Administrator, you can do so using the Name of Administrator Account to Manage setting in Group Policy.

To use this setting, you double-click the Name of Administrator Account to Manage policy in a GPO, to open the Properties sheet shown in Figure 4-31. Click the Enabled button and specify the name of the local account you want LAPS to manage in the Administrator Account Name field.

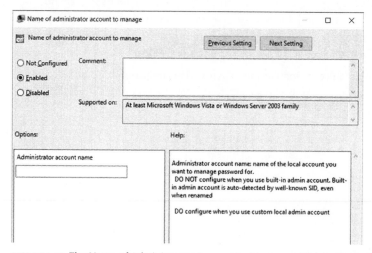

FIGURE 4-31 The Name of Administrator Account to Manage setting in Group Policy

Do not enable this setting and specify the name of the Administrator account, even if you have renamed it. LAPS can always identify the Administrator account by its SID. Configuring this policy setting causes LAPS to manage another local account instead of Administrator, not in addition to it. LAPS can only protect one account on a system.

Chapter summary

- Enhanced Administrative Security Environment (ESAE) is a reference model for a network security architecture that protects highly privileged accounts by storing them in a separate Active Directory forest, dedicated solely to that purpose.

- The clean source principle defines the nature of the relationships between objects that require protection and subjects that control the object. In practical terms, this principle calls for highly privileged resources to be administered using workstations that are equally privileged, and software installations to be performed using source media that is securely obtained and stored.

- Just-in-time administration is an administrative philosophy that calls for users to receive elevated privileges only when they are needed to perform certain tasks. The privileges are then revoked after a set time interval, protecting the credentials that provide those privileges.

- Privileged Access Management (PAM) is an implementation of the just-in-time concept included in the Microsoft Identity Manager (MIM) 2016 product. PAM calls for the creation of a bastion forest, a separate, hardened Active Directory forest that is joined to the production forest by a one-way trust relationship.

- The most highly-privileged administrative accounts are migrated to the bastion forest in the form of shadow principals, which are copies of the user and group objects that have the same security identifiers (SIDs) as the originals in the production forest.

- In addition to MIM, a PAM server installation requires Microsoft SQL Server in order to store information about the bastion forest, and Microsoft SharePoint in order to provide a web portal that functions as the PAM administrative interface.

- Once the PAM server and the bastion forest are in place, users can request privileges using Windows PowerShell cmdlets or the MIM web portal.

- Just-enough administration (JEA) is a Windows PowerShell feature implemented in Windows Server 2016, Windows 10, and Windows Management Framework 5.0. It does not require any other additional software or hardware.

- JEA is a server-based technology that provides users with elevated privileges on a temporary basis. Users employ a PowerShell cmdlet connect to a JEA endpoint with an unprivileged account and are assigned a temporary Run As account that provides them with elevated privileges for the duration of the session. When they disconnect from the endpoint, the users return to their unprivileged state.

- To create a JEA endpoint, you must have a session configuration script file and a role capability script file. These files specify who is permitted to connect to the endpoint and what privileges they are eligible to receive. Registering the session configuration using a PowerShell cmdlet makes the endpoint available for use.

- Each server to be administered must have its own endpoints, though users can connect to them from remote systems. Using Desired State Configuration (DSC), you can perform a mass deployment of JEA endpoints throughout the enterprise.

- A Privileged Access Workstation (PAW) is a highly-secure computer that is intended for use only to manage secure resources. Based on the clean source principle, administrative credentials should not be exposed to systems that are insecure. A PAW provides a hardened software and hardware configuration that is not to be used for any activities that can potentially jeopardize the credentials, such as web browsing and email.

- In addition to the configuration of the computer itself, a PAW deployment calls for user rights assignments and other policies that prevent the PAW from accessing unprotected resources and protect sensitive resources from administrative access by any workstation other than a PAW.

- Remote Credential Guard is a feature of Windows Server 2016 and Windows 10 that prevents sensitive credentials from being transmitted to host computers during Remote Desktop connections. The Kerberos authentication requests are redirected back to the connecting system instead.

- LAPS is a tool that automatically assigns local Administrator passwords to client computers and stores the passwords in the Active Directory computer objects.

- To deploy LAPS, you must install the client package, extend the AD schema using the PowerShell cmdlets provided, and set permissions granting access to the clients' computer objects.

- Extending the schema for LAPS creates two new attributes in the computer object, which LAPS users to store the local Administrator password and its expiration date.

- To enable the installed LAPS clients, use the settings added to Group Policy by the installer. You can also use the settings to control the length and complexity of the passwords and configure LAPS to protect a different local account.

- Confirm that LAPS is operating on the client using the Get-AdmPwdPassword cmdlet or the graphical LAPS UI client tool.

Thought experiment

In this thought experiment, demonstrate your skills and knowledge of the topics covered in this chapter. You can find answer to this thought experiment in the next section.

Most of the technologies described in this chapter are designed to prevent the credentials that administrators use to access and manage sensitive resources from being compromised by attackers. For each of the following technologies, explain how it prevents highly privileged credentials from being compromised.

1. Privileged Access Management

2. Just-enough administration

3. Privileged access workstations

4. Remote Credential Guard

5. Local Administrator Password Solution

Thought experiment answers

This section contains the solution to the thought experiment.

1. Privileged Access Management protects privileged credentials by storing them in a bastion forest, a dedicated Active Directory forest that is connected to the production forest using a one-way trust relationship. The bastion forest is hardened and used only for PAM. Privileged users and groups are migrated to the bastion forest using shadow principals, copies of the objects that have the same security identifiers as the originals. Because of the trust relationship and the duplicate SIDs, the bastion forest can generate Kerberos tickets that are accepted by resources in the production forest.

2. Just-enough administration is a Windows PowerShell technology that protects privileged credentials by assigning them only to temporary user accounts that are assigned to users that connect to a PowerShell endpoint. The user establishes a remote connection to the endpoint and, while connected, runs as privileged user. When the connection is terminated, so is the user's access to the privileged account.

3. Privileged access workstations protect privileged credentials by providing a secure workstation platform that can only be used for administrative tasks. A PAW cannot be used to access insecure resources, such as the open Internet, and unprivileged users cannot log on to a PAW.

4. Remote Credential Guard protects the privileged credentials often used to establish Remote Desktop connections. Instead of transmitting the credentials to the target system for Kerberos authentication, Remote Credential Guard redirects the credentials back to the connecting system, for authentication there.

5. Local Administrator Password Solution (LAPS) eliminates the need for IT personnel to assign the same local Administrator password on multiple workstations, a solution that is prone to credential theft. LAPS automatically assigns unique passwords to each computer, stores them in Active Directory computer objects, and resets them with new passwords at periodic intervals.

## CHAPTER 5

Implement threat detection solutions

Network administrators in today's world must face a constant escalation of security threats, and one of the most difficult things about those threats is that they can easily occur without obvious signs of an attack. There are a variety of security tools available that monitor and record the condition of the network and alert administrators to unusual conditions that might indicate an attack in progress, which we'll cover in this chapter.

Skills in this chapter:

- Configure advanced audit policies
- Install and configure Microsoft Advanced Threat Analytics
- Determine threat detection solutions using Operations Management Suite

Skill 5.1: Configure advanced audit policies

In today's business environment, enterprise administrators often devote a great deal of time, money, and effort into acquiring, deploying, and maintaining security technologies. In addition to these tasks, however, it is also important to ascertain the effectiveness of these technologies. One way of doing this is through auditing.

The auditing capabilities built into the Windows operating systems enable you to log successful and failed security events, such as logons, account accesses, and object accesses. You can use auditing to track both user activities and system activities. Planning to audit requires that you determine the computers to be audited and the types of events you want to track.

When you consider an event to audit, such as account logon events, you must decide whether to audit successful logon attempts, failed logon attempts, or both. Tracking successful events enables you to determine how often users access network resources. This information can be valuable when planning your resource usage and budgeting for new resources. Tracking failed events can help you determine when security breaches occur or are attempted. For example, if you notice frequent failed logon attempts for a specific user account, you might want to investigate the possibility of an attack.

When an audited event occurs, Windows writes an event to the Security log on the domain controller or the computer where the event took place. If it is a domain logon attempt or another Active Directory-related event, the event is written to the event log on the domain controller. If it is a computer event, such as a drive access, the event is written to the local computer's event log. Planning an auditing policy for your organization is a matter of deciding which resources on your network you want to monitor and how you analyze the data collected by the auditing process.

This section covers how to:

- Determine the Differences and Usage Scenarios for Using Local Audit Policies and Advanced Auditing Policies
- Implement Auditing Using Group Policy and Auditpol.exe
- Implement Auditing Using Windows PowerShell
- Create Expression-Based Audit Policies
- Configure the Audit PNP Activity Policy
- Configure the Audit Group Membership Policy
- Enable and Configure Module, Script Block, and Transcription Logging in Windows PowerShell

Determine the differences and usage scenarios for using local audit policies and advanced auditing policies

To create an effective auditing policy, you must decide which computers, resources, and events to audit. You should balance the need for auditing against the potential information overload that would be created if you audited every possible type of event. The basic steps involved in creating an auditing policy for your organization are as follows:

1. Identify the sensitive resources in your enterprise that are most in need of monitoring.

2. Identify the computer, user groups, and other objects that provide access to the sensitive resources you identified in step 1.

3. Select the audit policy settings that you can use to monitor the computers, groups, and other objects you identified in step 2.

4. Decide whether it is more beneficial to audit successes, failures, or both, for the auditing policy settings you have selected.

5. Create an audit policy deployment strategy, in which you decide how many Group Policy objects (GPOs) to use, which AD objects to link them to, and what audit policy settings to configure in each one.

6. Configure the size of your security logs based on the number of events that you anticipate logging. Consider also archiving your security logs to provide a documented history of your audits. Keeping a history of event occurrences can provide you with supporting documentation of resource usage and potential security breach attempts.

> **NOTE   CONFIGURING EVENT LOG SETTINGS**
>
> You can configure Event Log policy settings in the Computer Configuration\Windows Settings\Security Settings\Event Log container of any Group Policy object.

To implement an auditing policy on an Active Directory network, you define your desired policy settings in Group Policy objects (GPOs) and link them to domain, organizational unit (OU), or site objects. Part of the process of developing an archiving policy includes deciding whether to use local audit policies or advanced audit policies.

Each GPO contains two sets of audit policies: a basic one that has nine settings and an advanced one that has 60. The resources monitored by the two sets of policies overlap, but as you might imagine, the advanced audit policies provide more granular control over the events that are recorded in the Security log.

For example, the basic settings, located in the Computer Configuration\Policies\Windows Settings\Security Settings\Local Policies\Audit Policy container of a GPO, include an Audit Account Logon Events setting, as shown in Figure 5-1. Enabling this setting audits the success and/or failure of all logon attempts.

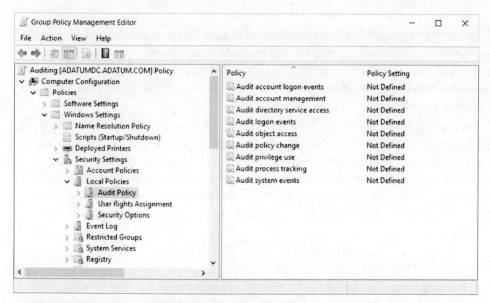

FIGURE 5-1 Basic audit policy settings in a Group Policy object

The advanced settings, located in the Computer Configuration\Policies\Windows Settings\ Advanced Audit Policy Configuration container of a GPO, includes four Account Logon settings, as shown in Figure 5-2. These settings distinguish between credential validations, Kerberos authentication activities, and other account logon events. These four advanced settings, combined, are the equivalent of the one basic Account Logon Events setting.

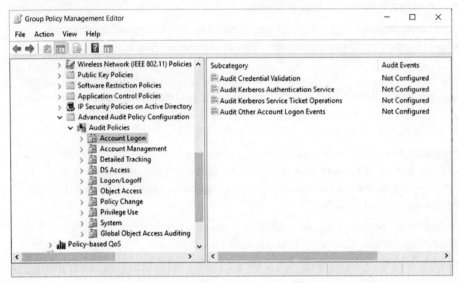

FIGURE 5-2 Advanced audit policy settings in a Group Policy object

One of the mistakes that many administrators make at first is auditing too much, assuming that more data is always better. Some of the audit policy settings can generate enormous amounts of data, which can quickly fill up your Security logs, place an undue burden on the computers doing the auditing, and provide far more information that the administrators can practically process.

For example, if you want to audit the read accesses to a file or folder, make sure you audit the Read events, not Full Control. Auditing Full Control triggers writes to the log for every action on the file or folder. Auditing uses system resources to process and store events. Therefore, auditing unnecessary events creates overhead on your server and makes it difficult to monitor the logs. The advanced audit policy settings enable you to be more selective in the events and resources you choose to audit, keeping your logs more manageable in the process.

Basic audit policies

Deciding whether to use basic or advanced audit policies requires an understanding of the types of information each policy setting audits. The basic audit policy settings are as follows:

- **Audit Account Logon Events**   Logs events related to successful user logons to a domain. The events are logged to the domain controller that processes the request.

- **Audit Account Management**   Logs events related to user or group account creation, deletion, renaming, enabling, or disabling.

- **Audit Directory Service Access**   Logs user attempts to access Active Directory objects, such as users or OUs, which have system access control lists (SACLs) specified. To generate a log entry for a specific object, a user specified in the SACL must attempt to access the object using one of the permissions granted to that user in the SACL.

- **Audit Logon Events**   Logs events related to user logons on a member server or workstation computer. The events are logged on the computer that processes the request.

- **Audit Object Access**   Logs user attempts to access non-Active Directory objects, such as files, folders, registry keys, and printers, which have system access control lists (SACLs) specified. To generate a log entry for a specific object, a user specified in the SACL must attempt to access the object using one of the permissions granted to that user in the SACL.

- **Audit Policy Change**   Logs events such as user rights assignment changes, establishment or removal of trust relationships, IPsec policy agent changes, and granting or removal of system access privileges.

- **Audit Privilege Use**   Logs each instance of a user attempting to exercise user rights. Several user rights are excluded from the settings because they would generate a great many logged events if audited.

- **Audit Process Tracking**   Logs process-related events, such as process creation, process termination, handle duplication, and indirect object access.

- **Audit System Events**   Logs events such as system startups and shutdowns; system time changes; system event resources exhaustion, such as when an event log is filled and can no longer append entries; security log cleaning; or any event that affects system security or the Security log.

The basic audit policy settings can generate a large number of event log entries, because they are less granular, making it more difficult to analyze the Security log.

Advanced audit policies

The Advanced Audit Policy Configuration folder in a GPO contains ten categories that contain several settings each. Many of the categories correspond to the basic audit settings, but split the auditing capabilities among multiple settings. This enables you to configure an audit policy similar to that of the basic settings, but with greater specificity. You can some of the settings in a category to log successes or failures, while leaving other settings unconfigured.

You can also mix configurations within a category by auditing successes for some settings and failures for others.

The advanced audit policy categories are as follows:

- **Account Logon**   Contains settings that audit authentication activities based on the account databases the activities use. For example, you can configure settings that audit only Kerberos authentications or only Security Account Manager (SAM) authentications.

- **Account Management**   Contains individual settings that enable you to audit changes to user accounts, computer accounts, and each type of group separately.

- **Detailed Tracking**   Contains settings that audit specific application and user activities, including Data Protection Application Programming Interface (DPAPI) encryption and decryption, Plug-and-Play hardware detection, process creation and termination, and incoming Remote Procedure Call (RPC) connections.

- **DS Access**   Contains settings that audit attempts to access, replicate, and modify Active Directory Domain Services objects. All events generated by these settings are logged on domain controllers.

- **Logon/Logoff**   Contains settings that audit individual aspects of interactive and network logon and logoff activities, including account lockouts, IPsec connections, and Network Policy Server connections.

- **Object Access**   Contains separate settings that audit attempts to access specific objects or object types, including files, shares, certificates, handles, kernel objects, registry settings, removable storage, and SAM accounts, which have system access control lists (SACLs) specified. To generate a log entry for a specific object, a user specified in the SACL must attempt to access the object using one of the permissions granted to that user in the SACL.

- **Policy Change**   Contains settings that audit changes to individual types of security policies, including audit, authentication, authorization, Windows Filtering Platform (WFP), and Microsoft Protection Service (MPSSVC) policies.

- **Privilege Use**   Contains settings that audit the use of sensitive and non-sensitive permissions by the users and computers to which they have been assigned.

- **System**   Contains settings that audit security-related system changes not included in other categories, including IPsec driver, security state, and system integrity modifications.

- **Global Object Access Auditing**   Contains settings that enable you to configure and apply global SACLs to all file system or registry objects. Unlike other audit policy settings, these two include an Advanced Security Settings dialog box in which you create auditing entries, as shown in Figure 5-3. If a file, folder, or registry setting has an SACL applied to it individually, the permissions in the individual SACL are combined with those in the global SACL.

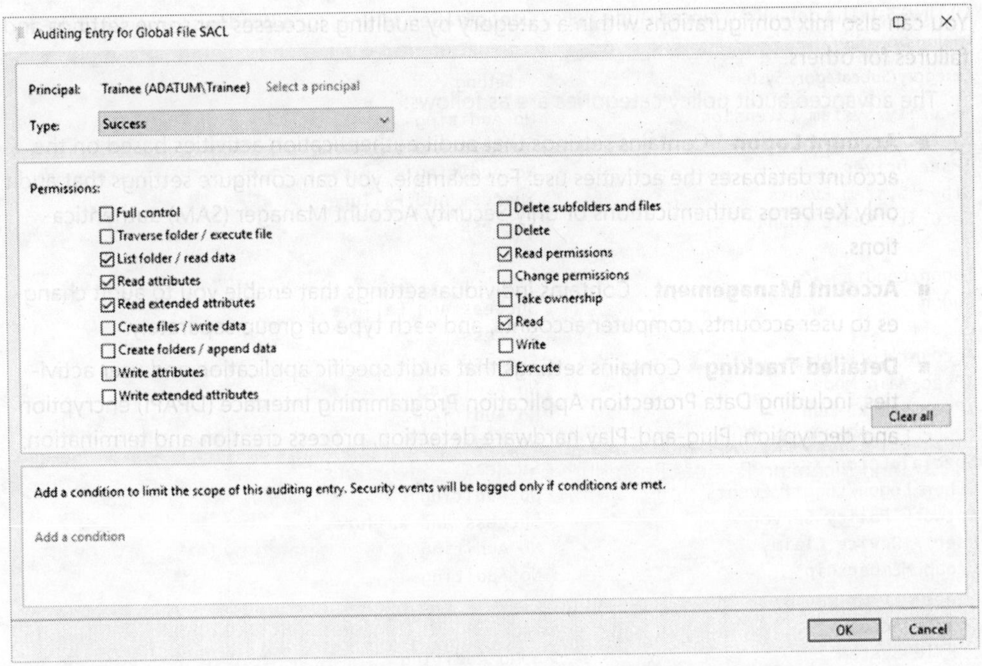

FIGURE 5-3 Auditing Entry dialog box in a global object access auditing policy setting

> **NOTE CONFIRMING OBJECT AUDITING**
>
> One of the prominent maintenance issues in Windows auditing has always been the inability to determine which objects have correct SACLs applied to them, except by viewing each object individually. Global object access auditing makes it possible for administrators to confirm that all elements are appropriately configured with SACLs by viewing the Advanced Security Settings dialog box associated with the policy setting.

Windows Server 2016 has some of the advanced auditing policies applied to it by default. You cannot view the existing audit policy settings in the Group Policy objects, but you can display them by running the Auditpol.exe program from the command prompt. Listing 5-1 displays an Auditpol.exe output containing the default audit policy settings for a Windows Server 2016 domain controller.

LISTING 5-1 The default Advanced Audit Policy Configuration settings for a Windows Server 2016 domain controller

Category/Subcategory System	Setting
Security System Extension	No Auditing
System Integrity	Success and Failure
IPsec Driver	No Auditing
Other System Events	Success and Failure
Security State Change	Success
Logon/Logoff	
Logon	Success and Failure
Logoff	Success
Account Lockout	Success
IPsec Main Mode	No Auditing
IPsec Quick Mode	No Auditing
IPsec Extended Mode	No Auditing
Special Logon	Success
Other Logon/Logoff Events	No Auditing
Network Policy Server	Success and Failure
User / Device Claims	No Auditing
Group Membership	No Auditing
Object Access	
File System	No Auditing
Registry	No Auditing
Kernel Object	No Auditing
SAM	No Auditing
Certification Services	No Auditing
Application Generated	No Auditing
Handle Manipulation	No Auditing
File Share	No Auditing
Filtering Platform Packet Drop	No Auditing
Filtering Platform Connection	No Auditing
Other Object Access Events	No Auditing
Detailed File Share	No Auditing
Removable Storage	No Auditing
Central Policy Staging	No Auditing
Privilege Use	
Non Sensitive Privilege Use	No Auditing
Other Privilege Use Events	No Auditing
Sensitive Privilege Use	No Auditing
Detailed Tracking	
Process Creation	No Auditing
Process Termination	No Auditing
DPAPI Activity	No Auditing
RPC Events	No Auditing
Plug and Play Events	No Auditing

```
Policy Change
    Authentication Policy Change          Success
Authorization Policy Change               No Auditing
MPSSVC Rule-Level Policy Change           No Auditing
Filtering Platform Policy Change          No Auditing
Other Policy Change Events                No Auditing
Audit Policy Change                       Success

Account Management
User Account Management                   Success
Computer Account Management               Success
Security Group Management                 Success
Distribution Group Management             No Auditing
Application Group Management              No Auditing
Other Account Management Events           No Auditing

DS Access
Directory Service Changes                 No Auditing
Directory Service Replication             No Auditing
Detailed Directory Service Replication    No Auditing
Directory Service Access                  Success

Account Logon
Kerberos Service Ticket Operations        Success
Other Account Logon Events                No Auditing
Kerberos Authentication Service           Success
Credential Validation                     Success
```

Audit policy priorities

The basic set of local audit policy settings are included in all Group Policy objects, and in the Local Security Policy tool on every computer. This means that you can configure the basic settings on an individual computer or deploy them to a large number of computers using Group Policy in Active Directory.

The advanced audit policies are only provided in Group Policy objects, so you can only deploy them that way. The basic and advanced audit policies are not compatible with each other. If you configure advanced audit settings in a GPO, any existing basic audit settings are cleared on a computer before the advanced settings are applied. Choosing between the basic and advanced audit policy settings is essentially a matter of how granular you want your auditing to be.

Operating system versions

The basic auditing policies were introduced in Windows 2000, and are therefore applicable to any server or workstation computers running Windows 2000 or later. The advanced auditing policy settings were only introduced in Windows Server 2008 and Windows 7. You can therefore apply those settings only to computers running those operating systems or later.

If you have Windows computers running old and new operating systems on your network, you can place them in separate OUs and create individual GPOs with basic settings for the older operating systems and advanced settings for the newer ones. You can also create a single GPO that contains both basic and advanced audit policy settings, keeping in mind that the older operating systems ignore the advanced settings and the newer ones do not apply the basic settings.

Implement auditing using Group Policy and Auditpol.exe

The best way to implement auditing on computers throughout a network is to deploy the desired settings using Group Policy. By configuring the audit policy settings you want to use in a Group Policy object, you can link the GPO to any domain, site, or organizational unit (OU) object in your Active Directory installation. All of the computers contained in the object to which you have linked the GPO receives and applies the audit policy settings the next time they restart.

The assumption here is that you have already decided what audit policies you intend to deploy and what computers on your network should receive them. Based on these decisions, your audit policy deployment might consist of a single GPO applied to an entire domain, or many GPOs with different auditing configurations, linked to various OUs.

> **NOTE** **AUDIT MANAGEMENT PREREQUISITES**
>
> To set up and administer an audit policy, you must possess the Manage Auditing and Security Log user right for the computer on which you want to configure a policy or review a log. This right is granted by default to the Administrators group. However, to delegate this task to another user, such as a container administrator, that person must possess the specific right. In addition, any files or folders to be audited must be located on NTFS volumes.

Creating a new auditing GPO

To create a new GPO and configure it to deploy advanced audit policy settings, use the following procedure:

1. Log on to a domain controller using an account with domain Administrator privileges.
2. Open the Group Policy Management console, expand the forest container, and browse to your domain.
3. Expand the domain container, right-click the Group Policy Objects folder and, in the context menu, select New. The New GPO dialog box appears.
4. Create a new GPO with an appropriate name.
5. Right-click the new GPO and click Edit. A Group Policy Management Editor window for this policy appears.

6. Browse the Computer Configuration\Policies\Windows Settings\Security Settings\ Advanced Audit Policy Configuration\Audit Policies container. The audit policy categories appear.

7. Select a category and double-click one of the subcategory settings in the right pane. The Properties sheet for the policy you chose appears, as shown in Figure 5-4.

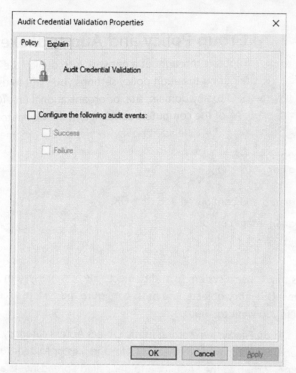

FIGURE 5-4 The Audit Credential Validation Properties sheet

8. Select the Configure the Following Audit Events check box.

9. Select the appropriate check box(es) to audit Success events, Failure events, or both.

10. Click OK to close the setting's Properties sheet.

11. Repeat steps 7 to 10 to configure additional policy settings.

12. Close the Group Policy Management Editor console.

13. In the Group Policy Management console, browse to the domain, site, or OU object containing the computers you want to configure.

14. Right-click the object and, from the context menu, select Link To An Existing GPO. The Select GPO dialog box appears, as shown in Figure 5-5.

FIGURE 5-5 Select GPO dialog box

15. Select the GPO you just created and configured and click OK.

16. Close the Group Policy Management console.

Auditing objects

When you enable policy settings that cause a system to audit objects, such as file system elements, registry settings, and Active Directory objects, you must configure the system access control lists (SACLs) for the objects you want to audit.

For example, if you enable the Audit File System setting in the Object Access category, not Security log, events are generated until you configure the SACLs for the files or folders you want to audit. If you add the Trainee group to the SACL for a folder called Spreadsheets and grant it the Read permission, then a Security log event is generated every time a member of the Trainee group reads a file in the Spreadsheets folder. Users who are not members of the Trainee group are be audited when they access the Spreadsheets folder. Members of the Trainee group are not audited when they access files not in the Spreadsheets folder.

To configure the SACLs on file system objects, use the following procedure:

1. Log on to a domain controller, using an account with domain Administrator privileges.

2. Open File Explorer, browse to the file or folder you want to audit, and open its Properties sheet.

3. Click the Security tab, and then click Advanced. The Advanced Security Settings dialog box appears.

4. Click the Auditing tab, and then click Continue to confirm your administrative access.

5. Click Add. The Auditing Entry page appears.

6. Click Select a Principal. The Select User, Computer, Service Account, or Group dialog box appears. Specify the users or groups to be audited and click OK. The users or groups appear in the Auditing Entry dialog box for the object.

7. From the Type drop-down list, specify whether you want to audit failures, successes, or both.

8. Select the basic permissions you want to audit for this object and click OK. The new Auditing entry appears in the Advanced Security Settings dialog box, as shown in Figure 5-6.

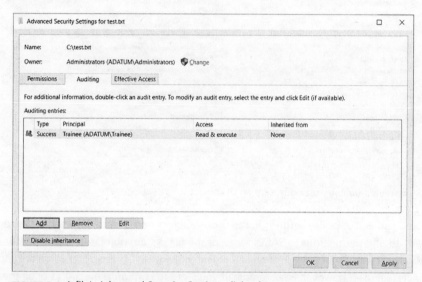

FIGURE 5-6 A file's Advanced Security Settings dialog box

9. Create additional auditing entries, if desired, and click OK.

10. Click OK to close the object's Advanced Security Settings dialog box.

11. Click OK to close the object's Properties sheet.

12. Close the File Explorer window.

The process of configuring SACLs for registry settings and Active Directory objects is roughly the same as for file system elements. All of the objects have Properties sheets with a Security tab, which provides access to an Advanced Security Settings dialog box. The difference between the object types is the permissions that you can select for an SACL. For example, the Auditing Entry dialog box for an organizational unit object in Active Directory has many more permissions to choose from than a file, as shown in Figure 5-7.

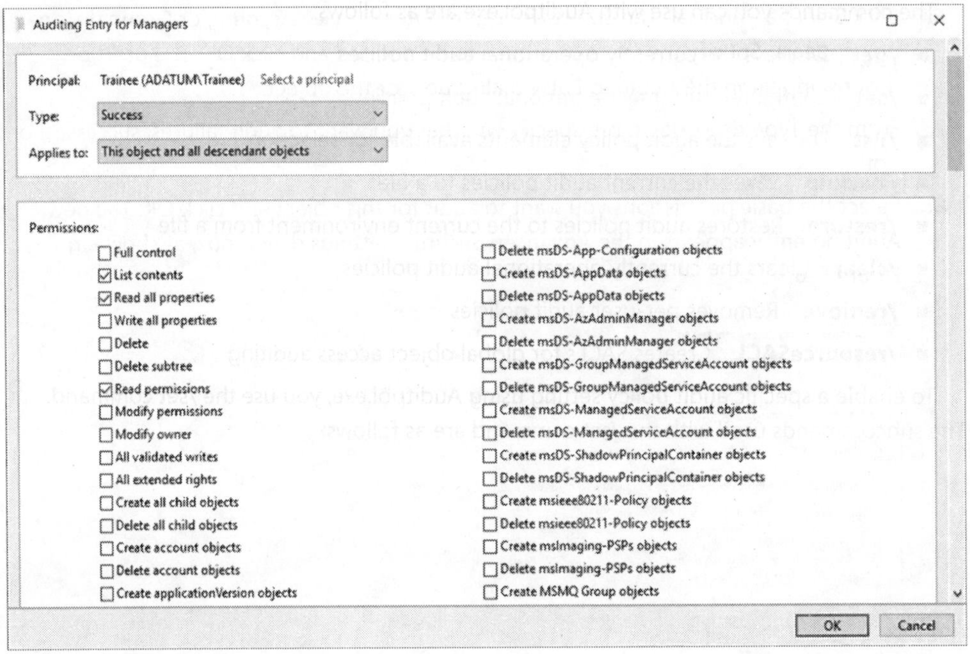

FIGURE 5-7 The Auditing Entry dialog box for an OU object

As noted earlier, the policy settings in the Global Object Access Auditing category provide a means of adding permissions to SACLs for all of the file system objects or registry settings on a computer, rather than configuring each object individually. These policies are only applicable for certain uses, however. For example, if you were to configure the SACLs of all the files on a computer with the Read permission for the Domain Users group, the system would add an enormous number of events to the Security log. However, if you wanted to monitor all of the files deleted by your organization's new hires, you could use Global Object Access Auditing to grant the Delete permission to the Trainee group for all of your file system objects.

Using auditpol.exe

Auditpol.exe is a command prompt utility that you can use to configure audit policy settings directly on a computer or from a script. Auditpol does not modify the settings in a Group Policy object; it applies changes to the actual operating environment of the computer on which you run it.

The basic syntax of Auditpol.exe is as follows:

```
Auditpol.exe command subcommand options
```

The commands you can use with Auditpol.exe are as follows:

- **/get**   Displays the currently operational audit policies
- **/set**   Configures currently operational audit policies
- **/list**   Displays the audit policy elements available for selection
- **/backup**   Saves the current audit policies to a file
- **/restore**   Restores audit policies to the current environment from a file
- **/clear**   Clears the currently operational audit policies
- **/remove**   Removes per-user audit policies
- **/resourceSACL**   Creates SACLs for global object access auditing

To enable a specific audit policy setting using Auditpol.exe, you use the /set command. The subcommands used with the /set command are as follows:

- **/category:categoryname**   Specifies one of the nine audit policy categories, either by name or by globally unique identifier (GUID). When you specify a category on the command line with no subcategory, Auditpol configures all of the policy settings in that category.
- **/subcategory:subcategoryname**   Specifies one of the available audit policy settings, either by name or by GUID.
- **/success:enable**   Configures the specified policies for success auditing. This is the default if the command line lacks both the /success and the /failure options. The /success:disable parameter prevents the policies from performing success auditing.
- **/failure:enable**   Configures the specified policies for failure auditing. The /failure:disable parameter prevents the policies from performing failure auditing.

Therefore, an example of an Auditpol command that would configure a system to audit all failed logon attempts would be as follows:

```
auditpol /set /subcategory:"logon" /failure:enable
```

When specifying categories or subcategories on the command line, you must use the correct name or substitute a GUID. To display the correct names and GUIDs for the audit policy settings, you can use the following command:

```
auditpol /list /subcategory:* /v
```

Auditpol.exe supports the use of wildcard characters in the /category and /subcategory parameters. The /v parameters (for verbose) causes the program to list the GUIDs as well as the names of the categories and subcategories. Listing 5-2 shows the output of this command.

LISTING 5-2 The category and subcategory names for Advanced Audit Policy Configuration settings, with GUID values

```
Category/Subcategory,GUID
System,{69979848-797A-11D9-BED3-505054503030}
    Security State Change,{0CCE9210-69AE-11D9-BED3-505054503030}
    Security System Extension,{0CCE9211-69AE-11D9-BED3-505054503030}
    System Integrity,{0CCE9212-69AE-11D9-BED3-505054503030}
    IPsec Driver,{0CCE9213-69AE-11D9-BED3-505054503030}
    Other System Events,{0CCE9214-69AE-11D9-BED3-505054503030}
Logon/Logoff,{69979849-797A-11D9-BED3-505054503030}
    Logon,{0CCE9215-69AE-11D9-BED3-505054503030}
    Logoff,{0CCE9216-69AE-11D9-BED3-505054503030}
    Account Lockout,{0CCE9217-69AE-11D9-BED3-505054503030}
    IPsec Main Mode,{0CCE9218-69AE-11D9-BED3-505054503030}
    IPsec Quick Mode,{0CCE9219-69AE-11D9-BED3-505054503030}
    IPsec Extended Mode,{0CCE921A-69AE-11D9-BED3-505054503030}
    Special Logon,{0CCE921B-69AE-11D9-BED3-505054503030}
    Other Logon/Logoff Events,{0CCE921C-69AE-11D9-BED3-505054503030}
    Network Policy Server,{0CCE9243-69AE-11D9-BED3-505054503030}
    User / Device Claims,{0CCE9247-69AE-11D9-BED3-505054503030}
    Group Membership,{0CCE9249-69AE-11D9-BED3-505054503030}
Object Access,{6997984A-797A-11D9-BED3-505054503030}
    File System,{0CCE921D-69AE-11D9-BED3-505054503030}
    Registry,{0CCE921E-69AE-11D9-BED3-505054503030}
    Kernel Object,{0CCE921F-69AE-11D9-BED3-505054503030}
    SAM,{0CCE9220-69AE-11D9-BED3-505054503030}
    Certification Services,{0CCE9221-69AE-11D9-BED3-505054503030}
    Application Generated,{0CCE9222-69AE-11D9-BED3-505054503030}
    Handle Manipulation,{0CCE9223-69AE-11D9-BED3-505054503030}
    File Share,{0CCE9224-69AE-11D9-BED3-505054503030}
    Filtering Platform Packet Drop,{0CCE9225-69AE-11D9-BED3-505054503030}
    Filtering Platform Connection,{0CCE9226-69AE-11D9-BED3-505054503030}
    Other Object Access Events,{0CCE9227-69AE-11D9-BED3-505054503030}
    Detailed File Share,{0CCE9244-69AE-11D9-BED3-505054503030}
    Removable Storage,{0CCE9245-69AE-11D9-BED3-505054503030}
    Central Policy Staging,{0CCE9246-69AE-11D9-BED3-505054503030}
Privilege Use,{6997984B-797A-11D9-BED3-505054503030}
    Sensitive Privilege Use,{0CCE9228-69AE-11D9-BED3-505054503030}
    Non Sensitive Privilege Use,{0CCE9229-69AE-11D9-BED3-505054503030}
    Other Privilege Use Events,{0CCE922A-69AE-11D9-BED3-505054503030}
Detailed Tracking,{6997984C-797A-11D9-BED3-505054503030}
    Process Creation,{0CCE922B-69AE-11D9-BED3-505054503030}
    Process Termination,{0CCE922C-69AE-11D9-BED3-505054503030}
```

```
  DPAPI Activity,{0CCE922D-69AE-11D9-BED3-505054503030}
  RPC Events,{0CCE922E-69AE-11D9-BED3-505054503030}
  Plug and Play Events,{0CCE9248-69AE-11D9-BED3-505054503030}
Policy Change,{6997984D-797A-11D9-BED3-505054503030}
  Audit Policy Change,{0CCE922F-69AE-11D9-BED3-505054503030}
  Authentication Policy Change,{0CCE9230-69AE-11D9-BED3-505054503030}
  Authorization Policy Change,{0CCE9231-69AE-11D9-BED3-505054503030}
  MPSSVC Rule-Level Policy Change,{0CCE9232-69AE-11D9-BED3-505054503030}
  Filtering Platform Policy Change,{0CCE9233-69AE-11D9-BED3-505054503030}
  Other Policy Change Events,{0CCE9234-69AE-11D9-BED3-505054503030}
Account Management,{6997984E-797A-11D9-BED3-505054503030}
  User Account Management,{0CCE9235-69AE-11D9-BED3-505054503030}
  Computer Account Management,{0CCE9236-69AE-11D9-BED3-505054503030}
  Security Group Management,{0CCE9237-69AE-11D9-BED3-505054503030}
  Distribution Group Management,{0CCE9238-69AE-11D9-BED3-505054503030}
  Application Group Management,{0CCE9239-69AE-11D9-BED3-505054503030}
  Other Account Management Events,{0CCE923A-69AE-11D9-BED3-505054503030}
DS Access,{6997984F-797A-11D9-BED3-505054503030}
  Directory Service Access,{0CCE923B-69AE-11D9-BED3-505054503030}
  Directory Service Changes,{0CCE923C-69AE-11D9-BED3-505054503030}
  Directory Service Replication,{0CCE923D-69AE-11D9-BED3-505054503030}
  Detailed Directory Service Replication,{0CCE923E-69AE-11D9-BED3-505054503030}
Account Logon,{69979850-797A-11D9-BED3-505054503030}
  Credential Validation,{0CCE923F-69AE-11D9-BED3-505054503030}
  Kerberos Service Ticket Operations,{0CCE9240-69AE-11D9-BED3-505054503030}
  Other Account Logon Events,{0CCE9241-69AE-11D9-BED3-505054503030}
  Kerberos Authentication Service,{0CCE9242-69AE-11D9-BED3-505054503030}
```

 **Quick check**

> If you create a Group Policy object that contains both basic and advanced audit
> policy settings, and you deploy it to an entire domain, what are the effective poli-
> cies on a computer running Windows 10? On a computer running Windows XP?

Quick check answer

> On the computer running Windows 10, any basic auditing policies on the
> computer would be cleared, and the basic policy settings in the GPO would be
> ignored. On the computer running Windows XP, the advanced auditing policy
> settings in the GPO would be ignored, and the basic policy settings applied.

Implement auditing using Windows PowerShell

The native capabilities of Windows PowerShell are limited when it comes to security auditing. You can run Auditpol.exe from a PowerShell prompt, but there are no cmdlets you can use to configure audit policy settings, either directly or in GPOs. However, when you are using Object Access policy settings, you can use PowerShell to configure SACLs for specific objects.

The Get-Acl cmdlet displays the security descriptor for an object, such as a file, folder, or registry key. The security descriptor contains all of the object's access control lists (ACLs), including the SACL. The syntax for a simple Get-Acl command is as follows:

```
Get-acl -path filename -audit | format-list
```

- **path**   Specifies the object whose security descriptor you want to display. The -path parameter can specify a folder name, a full path to a specific file, or a location in the registry. Wildcard characters are allowed.

- **audit**   Causes the cmdlet to display the SACL information in the security descriptor.

- **FormatList**   This is not a parameter, but rather another cmdlet that presents the output of the GetAcl cmdlet in a more readable manner, as shown in Figure 5-8. When you run GetAcl without piping the output to Format-List, the output is displayed as a table in which long values are truncated.

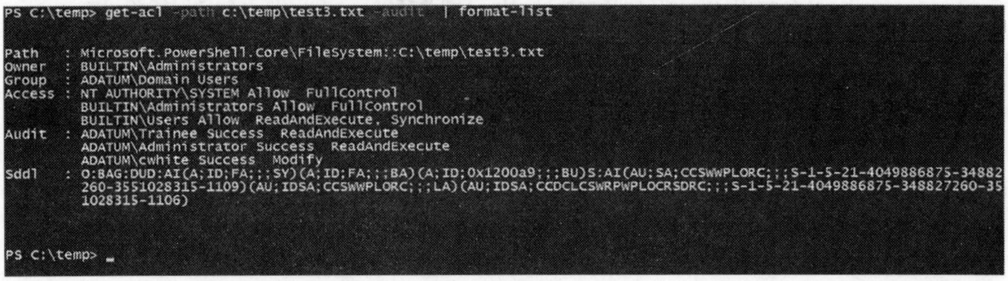

FIGURE 5-8 Output of the Get-Acl cmdlet

By itself, Get-Acl is interesting and even useful, but its greatest value appears when you use it with the Set-Acl cmdlet, which adds a security descriptor to an object. Using these two cmdlets in combination, you can copy the security descriptor, including the SACL, from one object to another.

By piping the output of Get-Acl for one file to Set-Acl, specifying another file, you can copy the entire security descriptor from one to the other. The command would appear as in the following example:

```
Get-acl -path "c:\docs\oldfile.txt" -audit | set-acl -path "c:\docs\newfile.txt"
```

You can also achieve the same result by saving the Get-Acl output to a variable and feeding it to Set-Acl, as in the following example:

```
$oldsacl = get-acl -path "c:\docs\oldfile.txt" -audit
Set-acl -path "c:\docs\newfile.txt" -aclobject $oldsacl
```

Create expression-based audit policies

When you create audit policies to monitor file system elements of registry settings, you use SACLs to specify which elements you want to monitor. You can, for example, monitor access to specific files by specific users or groups. Expression-based audit policies expand this capability by enabling you to specify additional criteria for auditing. Instead of selecting specific files or folders for auditing, you can select documents for auditing based on attributes you have previously defined, such as the country or department with which the documents are associated.

The interface for defining the conditions under which files are audited is part of the Auditing Entry dialog box found in the Global Object Access Auditing policy settings, as well as individual file system elements. For example, using Global Object Access Auditing, you can create a policy that generates audit events for all files from the Finance department that have been modified, or all files from a particular country. You create your own criteria for the expressions using Dynamic Access Control (DAC).

To create an expression-based audit policy, use the following procedure:

1. Open a GPO in the Group Policy Management Editor console.
2. Configure the File System policy in the Global Object Access Auditing category.
3. Open the Advanced Security Settings dialog box.
4. Add an auditing entry.
5. Select a principal.
6. Choose whether to audit Success or Failure.
7. Select the permissions you want to monitor.
8. Click Add a Condition.

At this point, a series of drop-down lists appears at the bottom of the dialog box, with which you can create an expression that limits the scope of the audit policy. The values that appear in the drop-down lists are based on the claim types and resource properties that you configure in Dynamic Access Control. You can create multiple expressions, and the interface provides Boolean operators you can use to control the evaluation of the expressions, as shown in Figure 5-9.

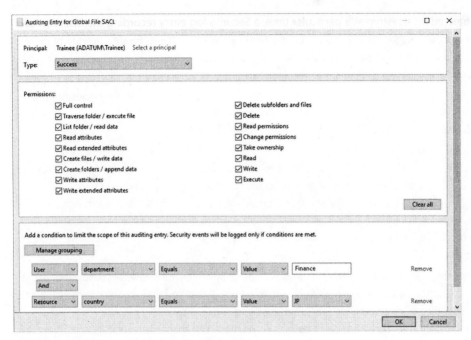

FIGURE 5-9 Creating expression-based audit policies

Configure the audit PNP activity policy

Social engineering is a major threat to network security. One of the most common attack vectors associated with social engineering practices is the use of external data storage devices, such as USB flash drives. An attacker provides a user with a document conveniently stored on a flash drive, and when the user inserts it into his or her computer, the system can be compromised by any sort of malware.

In versions prior to Windows Server 2016 and Windows 10, an event log entry was created the first time a user inserted a particular USB device. The log entry identified the device and recorded its first use. However, the system did not create additional log entries when the device was removed and re-inserted.

Windows Server 2016 and Windows 10 have a new audit policy setting that addresses this shortcoming. The Audit PNP Activity policy, found in the Detail Tracking category, generates an event in the Security log each time Plug and Play (PNP) detects the connection of an external device of any type. The policy even generates a new event each time a user connects the same device to the system.

The value of this policy is that administrators can correlate the insertion of a PNP device with other activities on the system. For example, when the introduction of a malware infection is detected on a system at a particular time, a Security log entry recording the insertion of a USB flash drive at approximately the same time can indicate the malware's avenue of ingress.

The Audit PNP Activity policy setting in a GPO, shown in Figure 5-10, has the same appearance as most other policy settings, but there is a difference in how the system employs it. Despite having checkboxes for both Success and Failure auditing, the policy does not record Failure events, so selecting the failure checkbox has no effect.

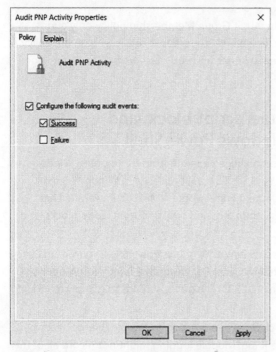

FIGURE 5-10 The Audit PNP Activities Properties sheet

Configure the Audit Group Membership policy

One of the most commonly used audit policies is Audit Logon, which tracks the users who log on to a system by generating events in the Security log. This policy enables administrators to monitor and record who accesses a particular system. There is also another policy in the Logon/Logoff category that can provide additional information for this analysis.

The Audit Group Membership policy generates event log entries that list the group memberships of the users that log on to the computer. For an interactive logon, the events are created on the local system. For a network logon, such as a connection to a shared folder, the events are created on the system hosting the resource.

The events generated by the Audit Group Membership policy contain a list of both the local and domain groups to which the logged on user belongs. If the list of groups is too long for one event, the system creates multiple events.

The value of this policy derives from the ability to see which groups have members logging on to a particular computer. In the case of a privileged access workstation, for example, you can use this auditing policy to confirm that all of the users logging on to the workstation belong to the proper group.

As with the Audit PNP Activity policy, the Audit Group Membership policy only audits successes, despite its having a Failure checkbox on its Properties sheet. To enable the policy, you must configure it in a GPO in the normal manner, and you must enable the Audit Logon policy as well.

Enable and configure module, script block, and transcription logging in Windows PowerShell

Windows PowerShell has its own logging capabilities, separate from those of the Windows auditing policies. Starting with Windows PowerShell 5.0, first released in Windows Server 2008 R2, Windows 7, and Windows Management Framework (WMF) 5.0, PowerShell has enhanced logging capabilities that records commands and scripts, output, code blocks, and transcripts of sessions.

To enable and configure the logging capabilities of Windows PowerShell, you Group Policy settings found in the Computer Configuration\Policies\Administrative Templates\Windows Components\Windows PowerShell folder in any GPO. The policy settings that apply to logging are as follows:

- **Turn On Module Logging** Records pipeline execution events for the specified modules in the Windows PowerShell event log. Module logging might not record all of the commands issued in a session, but it can capture details that the other logging options do not. When you enable the policy, as shown in Figure 5-11, you can click the Show button to specify the modules you want to log, or insert an asterisk (*) to log all modules. Module logging can generate a large number of events, so you should configure your maximum log size accordingly. This policy is the functional equivalent of setting the LogPipelineExecutionDetails property for a module to True. This policy is also present in the User Configuration folder of a GPO, but the Computer Configuration setting takes precedence.

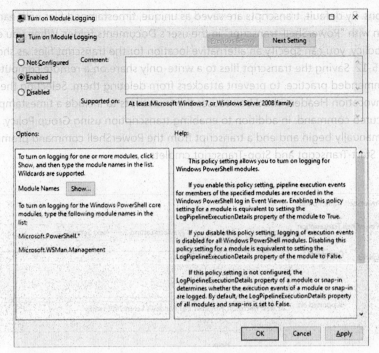

FIGURE 5-11 The Turn On Module Logging Properties sheet

- **Turn On PowerShell Script Block Logging** Records blocks of code as the PowerShell engine executes them, including commands and scripts. This policy can record code obfuscated with Base64, XOR, ROT13, or encryption, and includes the unobfuscated code as well. However, script block logging does not record the output generated by the executed code. Logs are recorded as events in the Windows PowerShell event log. For long script blocks, two or more event log entries might be required.

NOTE **LOGGING SUSPICIOUS CODE**

Windows PowerShell automatically logs blocks of code that contain suspicious commands or scripts, even if you do not enable the Turn On PowerShell Script Block Logging policy. These event log entries are flagged with a Warning status, while the entries generated by the enabled policy are flagged as Information or Verbose. If you explicitly disable the policy, no code blocks are recorded to the log, including suspicious ones.

- **Turn On PowerShell Transcription** Creates text transcriptions of every PowerShell session, including all of the input and output visible on the PowerShell terminal. A transcript does not include output resulting from executed scripts or written to other destinations. By default, transcripts are saved as unique, timestamped files with names that begin with "PowerShell_transcript" in the user's Documents folder. When you enable the policy, you can specify an alternative location for the transcript files, as shown in Figure 5-12. Saving the transcript files to a write-only share on a remote computer is a recommended practice, to prevent attackers from deleting them. Selecting the Include Invocation Headers checkbox causes the transcripts to include a timestamp for each executed command. In addition to enabling transcription using Group Policy, you can also manually begin and end a transcript from the PowerShell command prompt, using the Start-Transcript and Stop-Transcript cmdlets.

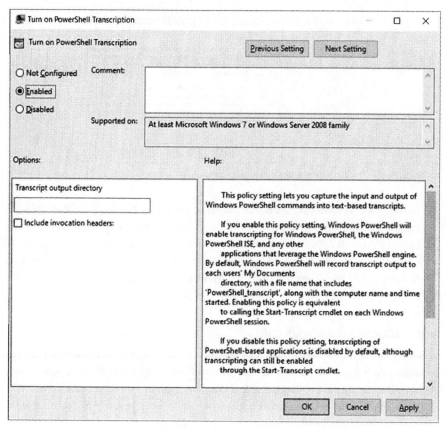

FIGURE 5-12 The Turn On PowerShell Transcription Properties sheet

Skill 5.2: Install and configure Microsoft Advanced Threat Analytics

Microsoft Advanced Threat Analytics (ATA) is a security product that helps to protect an enterprise network from advanced forms of cyberattack. ATA gathers information from Windows logs and uses deep packet inspection techniques to evaluate trends in network traffic to and from domain controllers and the behavior of users, devices, and resources. This way, ATA can detect suspicious activity generated by the various phases of an attack and generate alerts that specify the type of attack that might be in progress and the systems that are involved.

When you first install ATA, it detects evidence of known attack types immediately. Then, in a matter of weeks, ATA begins to recognize the normal behavior of your network and is able to detect suspicious deviations from the norm.

> **This section covers how to:**
> - Determine Usage Scenarios for ATA
> - Determine Deployment Requirements for ATA
> - Install and Configure ATA Gateway on a Dedicated Server
> - Install and Configure ATA Lightweight Gateway Directly on a Domain Controller
> - Configure Alerts in ATA Center When Suspicious Activity Is Detected
> - Review and Edit Suspicious Activities on the Attack Time Line

Determine usage scenarios for ATA

ATA is designed to detect activity in the various phases of what some cybersecurity experts refer to as the kill chain. Originally a military term, the *kill chain* represents the stages of an attack, from the initial reconnaissance to the attacker's final actions on the compromised plan. ATA analysis of the data it collects from domain controller traffic and event logs can alert you to activities occurring at any phase of the kill chain.

Some of the most critical phases of an attack that are detectable by ATA are described in the following sections.

Reconnaissance

In a military kill chain, reconnaissance is the selection of a vulnerable target. The same is true in a cybersecurity kill chain. Attackers attempt to identify user accounts that might be susceptible to attack by using various techniques.

These techniques can include sending false requests to a domain controller, to determine if a specific user exists, to obtain a list the users involved in active Server Message Blocks (SMB) sessions, or to obtain Domain Name System (DNS) information. All of these techniques can provide an attacker with the names and IP addresses of active user accounts.

ATA can detect the request messages that attackers use to gather these types of information, and recognize them for what they are.

Compromised credentials

There are various network traffic patterns that can indicate attempts to compromise account credentials or utilize credentials that have already been compromised. ATA uses traffic and behavioral analysis to detect unusual activity that emulates well-known attack techniques.

For example, ATA can recognize when an account displays anomalous resource access patterns, logins during non-working hours, and abnormal numbers of logins. These phenomena can indicate that an account has already been compromised, and the attacker is attempting to make use of it.

ATA can also detect potentially compromising communications, such as passwords transmitted in plain text, and attempts to compromise credentials with brute force methods and authentication requests that don't conform to the normal protocol.

ATA can also make use of a specialized dummy account called a honey token. This is an unused user account that serves as a lure and a trap for attackers. Any activity occurring that uses the honey token account is certain to be illicit, and ATA can gleam a great deal from the attempts to use that account.

Lateral movement

Lateral movement is an attempt by an attacker in possession of stolen credentials to gain access to other resources using those credentials. ATA detects these attempts by examining account traffic patterns, looking for signs of connections to unusual resources, logons from different workstations, or the use of abnormal devices.

ATA also examines Kerberos and NTLM authentication traffic, looking for signs of common intrusion techniques in which attackers use illicitly obtained Kerberos ticket-granting tickets (TGTs) or NTLM hashes to access additional resources. Attacks like Pass-the-Ticket and Pass-the-Hash are some of the most commonly used means of compromising user account credentials today, and ATA detects them by analyzing not just the packets themselves, but the way in which they are used.

Privilege escalation

Attackers in possession of stolen credentials might try to increase the privileges of those credentials by altering Kerberos TGTs to grant themselves additional permissions. A TGT contains an authorization header that specifies the permissions granted to the user account. By altering this header, the attacker can conceivably use an account that is relatively unprivileged to access highly sensitive resources. ATA can detect these attempts by examining the network packets containing the TGTs for alterations and by analyzing the differences in the ways that the account is being used.

Domain dominance

ATA can detect attackers that attempt to compromise a domain controller directly by posing as another domain controller. By spoofing an authentication ticket encrypted and signed by the KRBTGT service account on a domain controller (also known as the Kerberos Golden Ticket), the attacker can be confirmed as another domain controller, and can then issue TGTs for any resource, request replication of the Active Directory database, and remotely execute code on the domain controller computer.

Determine deployment requirements for ATA

ATA is a wholly on-premise product that does not require cloud resources. It is a standalone product that gathers information from the domain controllers in your enterprise, stores it, and analyzes it for potential threats.

ATA Center

The focal point of the Ata product is a dedicated server known as the ATA Center. This computer is the receiver of the information gathered from your domain controllers, and the place where the threat analysis occurs. The ATA Center performs the following functions:

- **ATA Gateway configuration** Manages the configuration settings for ATA gateways and ATA Lightweight Gateways.
- **Data storage** Uses MongoDB to store all ATA configuration data, information received from gateways, network activity behavior, and threat analysis results.
- **Threat analysis** Parses and analyzes network traffic, analyzes the network's default behavior patterns, detects well-known attack behaviors.
- **ATA Console hosting** Uses Internet Information Services (IIS) to host the ATA Console intranet site, which provides an ATA configuration interface and displays the results of ATA's threat analyses.
- **Alert generation** Creates emails and system events to notify administrators when ATA detects suspicious activity.

In most cases, one ATA Center computer can service an entire Active Directory forest. If your enterprise consists of multiple forests, you need one ATA center for each one. In the case of especially large forests, more than one ATA center might be required. Microsoft provides a sizing tool that you can use to determine the correct ATA installation for your enterprise, based on the packet transmission rates of your domain controllers.

The computer that functions as the ATA Center should have two IP addresses on the same subnet, and Internet Information Services (IIS) must be installed. One of the addresses is used to communicate with the network (receive the traffic from the gateways) and one is for IIS, to host the ATA Console.

ATA Gateways

The ATA Center receives the information it uses to perform its analyses from ATA gateways on your network. ATA supports two types of gateways, as follows:

- **ATA Gateway**   Runs on a standalone server and gathers information from domain controllers using port mirroring and event forwarding
- **ATA Lightweight Gateway**   Runs on a domain controller itself and gathers information locally

Both gateway types perform many of the same functions, including the following:

- Capture network traffic transmitted to and from domain controllers
- Receive Windows Event information through Windows Event Forwarding
- Access Active Directory user and computer object information
- Transfer all gathered information to the ATA Center

The standalone ATA Gateway can service multiple domain controllers, up to a maximum of 50,000 packets per second of domain controller traffic. You can install multiple ATA gateways on a network, if more capacity is required. Apart from its capacity, the standalone gateway provides a security advantage; because it is separate from the domain controllers, potential attackers have a harder time learning that ATA is installed on the network. The main disadvantage is that the standalone ATA Gateway requires a server, and a server license, of its own.

ATA Lightweight Gateways service only the domain controllers on which they are installed, and support up to 10,000 packets per second. ATA Lightweight Gateways continually monitor the CPU and memory utilization on the domain controllers where they are running, and throttle their resource usage to ensure that the native functions of the domain controller are not affected.

Less expensive, because a separate server is not required, ATA Lightweight Gateways are an ideal solution for branch offices and cloud-based virtual domain controllers.

Administrators are free to mix ATA Gateways and ATA Lightweight Gateways, all feeding their information to an ATA center, as shown in Figure 5-13.

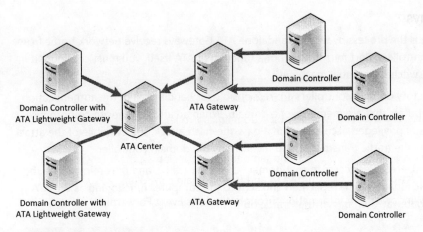

FIGURE 5-13 ATA architecture

Computers functioning as ATA Gateways must have at least two network adapters, one for standard management traffic and one for the incoming domain controller traffic supplied by the port mirroring process. Both of the adapters should have static IP addresses. The management adapter should have the usual DNS server and Default Gateway addresses configured, and the DNS Suffix For This Connection text box on the DNS tab of the Advanced TCP/IP Settings dialog box should specify the name of the domain you are monitoring, as shown in Figure 5-14. The port mirroring adapter should have no Default Gateway or DNS server addresses. These settings are to ensure that all traffic but the incoming port mirroring traffic uses the management adapter.

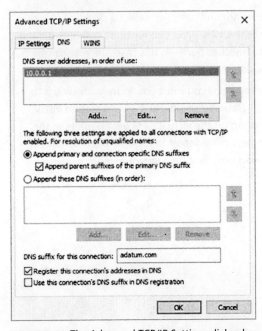

FIGURE 5-14 The Advanced TCP/IP Settings dialog box

Port Mirroring

Port mirroring is the process by which standalone ATA Gateways receive network traffic from the domain controllers. Port mirroring is not a function of ATA itself; you must configure it in your network switches or virtual machines.

Active Directory domain controllers are responsible for handling all of the authentication traffic for computers that are members of a domain. When an attacker tries to compromise the credentials of privileged accounts, as in a pass-the-hash attack, the evidence of the attack can be found in the traffic transmitted and received by the domain controller.

Therefore, ATA requires access to that domain controller traffic, and port mirroring is the process by which that traffic is replicated and sent to the computer functioning as the ATA Gateway. The gateway then passes that traffic on to the ATA Center.

> **NOTE** **PORT MIRRORING AND ATA GATEWAYS**
>
> Only standalone ATA Gateways use port mirroring to receive network traffic from domain controllers. ATA Lightweight Gateways run on the domain controllers, so they already have access to the required traffic.

Under normal conditions, on a physical network, switches are the hardware components that connect the computers together. Each computer is connected to a port on a switch. Network packets transmitted by a computer enter the switch through one of its ports and are forwarded out through another port, the one to which the destination computer is connected. The result is that the only computers that have access to a network packet are the one transmitting it and the one receiving it.

Port mirroring is a switch feature that enables administrators to select a port—in this case, the one to which the domain controller is connected. And you also have a copy of the traffic passing through that port in either direction to another port—in this case, the one to which the computer functioning as the ATA Center is connected.

If you are implementing ATA on physical computers, you must configure your switch to mirror the domain controller traffic to your ATA Gateway computer. If you are using virtual machines, you can usually configure port mirroring on the virtual network adapters in the virtual machines. For example, in Hyper-V, the network adapter in each virtual machine has an Advanced Features page in the Settings dialog box, as shown in Figure 5-15.

FIGURE 5-15 Advanced network adapter settings in a Hyper-V virtual machine

When you enable port mirroring, you use the Mirroring Mode drop-down list to specify whether you want that adapter to be the Source or the Destination of the mirrored traffic. If your domain controller and your ATA Gateway are both virtual machines on the same host, you would configure the domain controller as Source and your ATA Gateway as Destination.

When the computers involved in the port mirroring relationship are connected to different switches, or are virtual machines on different hosts, or when one is a physical computer and one a virtual machine, the process of configuring port mirroring is more complicated, and usually involves consulting the documentation for your switching hardware.

Event Forwarding

When the event ID 4776 appears in a computer's Security log, this indicates that someone tried to log on using NTLM authentication. The message that appears in the log looks like the following:

```
The domain controller attempted to validate the credentials for an account.
Authentication Package: MICROSOFT_AUTHENTICATION_PACKAGE_V1_0
Logon Account: administrator
Source Workstation: WIN-R9H529RIO4Y
Error Code: 0xc0000064
```

Despite the wording of the message, it is not only domain controllers that log this event. Member servers and workstations generate this when users log on with local SAM accounts. Domain controllers log this event only when they authenticate users with NTLM, not Kerberos.

ATA requires access to these events to detect credential attacks such as Pass-the-Hash. Therefore, you must configure your computers to forward these event messages to your ATA Gateways. There are two ways to do this, as follows:

- **Security identification and event management (SIEM)/syslog** If you have a SIEM or syslog server on your network, you can configure it to forward 4776 events to your ATA Gateway, and configure the ATA Gateway to listen for events forwarded from the server.

- **Windows Event Forwarding** Windows has an Event Forwarding capability that enables you to create a subscription for the ATA Gateway and configure it to select the 4776 events and transmit them.

Install and Configure ATA Gateway on a Dedicated Server

ATA is packaged as a single installation disk or disk image with one Microsoft ATA Center Setup application on it. To deploy ATA in your enterprise, you must first install the ATA Center software on a member server using the disk. Then, you download the ATA Gateway software from within the ATA console interface.

Installing ATA Center

To install ATA Center on your server, use the following procedure:

1. Log on to the server with administrative privileges and run the Microsoft ATA Center Setup file on the ATA installation disk.

2. Select the language to use for the installation and accept the terms of the license agreement.

3. On the Center Configuration page, shown in Figure 5-16, the system's two IP addresses should appear in the two fields. You can change the proposed location of the database, if desired, and select an SSL certificate generated by your certification authority, if your network has one.

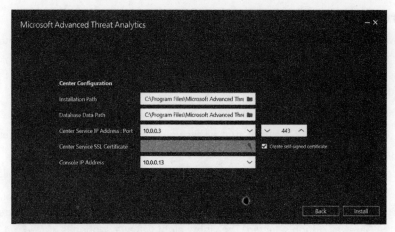

FIGURE 5-16 The ATA Center Configuration page

4. When the installation is completed, click Launch to open a browser window and display the Microsoft Advanced Threat Analytics home page, as shown in Figure 5-17.

FIGURE 5-17 The Microsoft Advanced Threat Analytics home page

5. Log on to the site using the same account you used to log on to the server.

6. On the Directory Services page, supply credentials for an account with domain administrator privileges.

7. Click the Gateways link on the left side of the page.

8. Click Download Gateway Setup and save the downloaded file to a location on your local drive.

Install ATA Gateway

Once you have installed the ATA Center and downloaded the ATA Gateway software, you can proceed to install an ATA Gateway on another member server. This server should already be configured as the recipient of the port mirroring traffic from the domain controller you plan to service with the gateway.

To install an ATA Gateway, use the following procedure:

1. Copy the Microsoft ATA Gateway Setup.zip file you downloaded on the ATA Center computer and copy it to the server on which you install ATA Gateway.

2. Extract the contents of the zip file and run the Microsoft ATA Gateway Setup application.

3. Specify the language you want to use and, on the Gateway Deployment Type page, leave the Gateway option selected. The Lightweight Gateway option is grayed out unless you are installing the software on a domain controller.

4. In the Gateway Configuration settings, select an alternate location for the installation and the SSL certificate you used for the ATA Center installation, if desired.

5. In the Gateway Registration section, as shown in Figure 5-18, enter credentials for a member of the local Administrators or Advanced Threat Analytics Administrators group on the ATA Center computer.

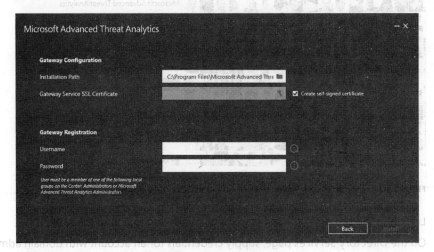

FIGURE 5-18 The Microsoft ATA Gateway Setup application

6. When the installation is completed, return to the ATA Center computer, sign on the ATA Console again, and click the Gateways link on the left side of the page. The new gateway should appear in the display with a Not Configured status, as shown in Figure 5-19.

FIGURE 5-19 The ATA Console with an unconfigured gateway

7. Click the gateway in the listing to open the configuration screen for your ATA gateway computer, as shown in Figure 5-20.

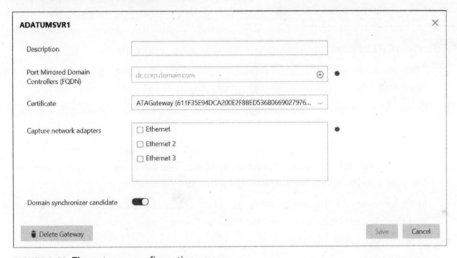

FIGURE 5-20 The gateway configuration screen

8. In the Port Mirrored Domain Controllers (FQDN) field, specify the fully qualified domain name of your domain controller (that is, adatumdc.adatum.com, not just adatumdc).

9. In the Capture Network Adapters box, select the adapter that you have configured to receive the port mirroring traffic from the domain controller.

10. Click Save, and the main console screen appears again, this time with the gateway's Status showing as Starting. In a few minutes, the Status changes to Running.

Once the ATA Center and the ATA Gateway are operational, you must leave them to run, so that they can establish a baseline for the behavior of your network and begin to track anomalous behavior.

Install and Configure ATA Lightweight Gateway Directly on a Domain Controller

The Microsoft ATA Gateway Setup file you downloaded in the previous section can install either an ATA Gateway or a ATA Lightweight Gateway. As you saw when installing the gateway software on a member server, the ATA Lightweight Gateway option was grayed out. When you run Microsoft ATA Gateway Setup on a domain controller, the program recognizes the computer as such and allows the ATA Lightweight Gateway installation.

To install the ATA Lightweight Gateway on a domain controller, the computer must have a processor with at least two cores and also a minimum of six gigabytes of memory. Unlike an ATA Gateway installation, you do not have to configure port mirroring on the switch or the network adapter because the domain controller already has access to the required traffic.

If you are using a virtual machine for your domain controller, be sure to allocate the full amount of memory required and do not use the Dynamic Memory feature in Hyper-V or any similar memory management feature. ATA does not support the use of these technologies.

To install ATA Lightweight Gateway, use the following procedure:

1. Copy the Microsoft ATA Gateway Setup.zip file you downloaded on the ATA Center computer and copy it to the server on which you install ATA Gateway.

2. Extract the contents of the zip file and run the Microsoft ATA Gateway Setup application.

3. Specify the language you want to use and, on the Gateway Deployment Type page, leave the Lightweight Gateway option selected. The Gateway option is grayed out because you installing the software on a domain controller.

4. In the Gateway Configuration settings, select an alternate location for the installation and the SSL certificate you used for the ATA Center installation, if desired.

5. In the Gateway Registration section, enter credentials for a member of the local Administrators or Advanced Threat Analytics Administrators group on the ATA Center computer.

When the installation is completed, the ATA Lightweight Gateway is added to the Gateways page in the ATA Console, and immediately progresses from the Starting to the Running status. There is no need for a configuration procedure, as with the standalone ATA Gateway installation.

Configure alerts in ATA Center when suspicious activity is detected

Once you have installed and configured the ATA components, you can configure the ATA Center to notify you by generating emails or syslog events when it detects suspicious activity. These procedures assume that you already have the mail and/or syslog servers installed, configured, and available for use.

Configuring mail server settings

The first step in configuring ATA to generate mail alerts is to configure the mail server settings the ATA Center uses to send the messages. To configure these settings, use the following procedure:

1. Sign on to the ATA Console and, in the Settings menu (three vertical dots), click Configuration.

2. Click the Mail Server link on the left side of the screen, to display the Mail Server panel, as shown in Figure 5-21.

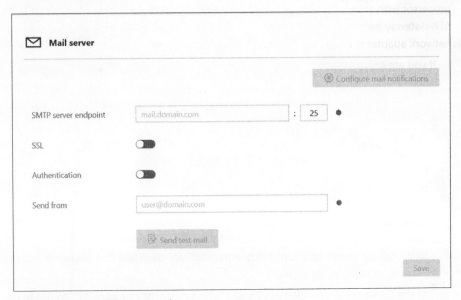

FIGURE 5-21 The Mail Server panel

3. In the SMTP Server Endpoint fields, enter the fully qualified domain name and port number of your outgoing mail server.

4. If your mail server requires a Secured Sockets Layer (SSL) connection, click the SSL switch and, if necessary, the Accept Any Server Certificate switch.

5. If your mail server requires authentication, click the Authentication switch and enter valid credentials in the Username and Password fields.

6. In the Send From field, enter the email address you want to appear in the From field of the messages.

7. Click Save.

Configuring syslog server settings

As with mail alerts, the first step in configuring ATA to generate syslog alerts is to configure the syslog server settings the ATA Center uses. To configure these settings, use the following procedure:

1. Click the Syslog Server link on the left side of the screen, to display the Syslog Server panel, as shown in Figure 5-22.

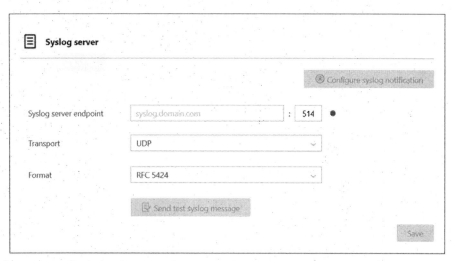

FIGURE 5-22 The Syslog Server panel

2. In the Syslog Server Endpoint fields, enter the fully-qualified domain name and port number of your syslog server.

3. In the Transport drop-down list, choose which protocol you want ATA to use to communicate with the server: UDP, TCP, or TLS (Secured Syslog).

4. In the Format drop-down list, choose whether you want ATA to use the RFC5424 or RFC3164 format.

5. Click Save.

Configuring Notification settings

Once you have saved your Mail Server configuration settings, the Configure Mail Notifications button at the top right is enabled. In the same way, saving the Syslog Server settings activates a Configure Syslog Notifications button. Both of these buttons take you to the same place, the Notification Settings panel, which you can also access by clicking the Settings link in the Notifications section on the main ATA Console Configuration page.

To configure the notification settings, use the following procedure:

1. Click the Configure Mail Notifications or Configure Syslog Notifications button, or click the Settings link. The Notification Settings panel appears, as shown in Figure 5-23.

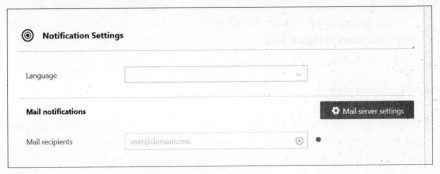

FIGURE 5-23 The Notification Settings panel

2. In the Language drop-down list, select the language you want ATA to use for the notifications.

3. In the Mail Recipients field, enter the email addresses of the people you want to receive the alert notifications.

4. Click the three switches to specify whether ATA should send notifications in the event of suspicious activity, health issues, and/or available updates.

5. In the Syslog Notifications section, click the three switches to specify whether messages should be sent for new suspicious activity, existing suspicious activity, and/or new health issues.

6. Click Save.

Review and edit suspicious activities on the Attack Time Line

Once ATA is installed and operational, the primary source of information about its results is the Timeline page in the ATA Console. The timeline tracks the suspicious activities that occur on your network day by day, as shown in Figure 5-24. It takes up to a month after the initial installation for ATA to construct a baseline for your network activity, but once this is done, behavior that is out of the norm is reported.

FIGURE 5-24 The Timeline page in the ATA Console.

For example, if an administrative user account is only used for interactive logons to a domain every day between 9:00 AM and 5:00PM, and ATA suddenly starts detecting remote logons using that account during the overnight hours, it would flag that as suspicious behavior. It's not just the remote logon itself that is suspicious, but the atypicality of the timing. ATA then generates an entry on the timeline providing the details of the activity, as shown in Figure 5-25.

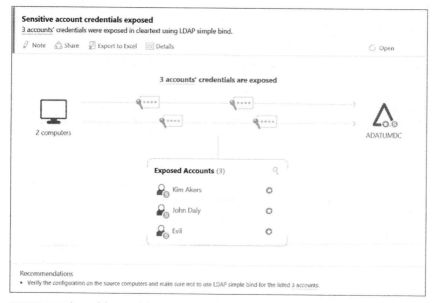

FIGURE 5-25 A suspicious activity report on the Timeline page in the ATA Console

Each timeline entry includes information about what resource was accessed, what computers accessed it, what accounts were used to gain the access, and what actions you might consider taking to address the issue. When you click the avatar of a user or computer, the console displays available information about it, as shown in Figure 5-26.

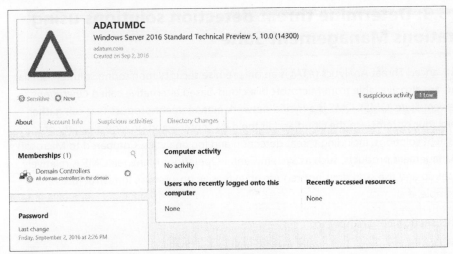

FIGURE 5-26 A server information page in the ATA Console

In the timeline, suspicious activities are graded by severity: high, medium, and low, and there is a status indicator you can use to grade your own investigation of the event: open, resolved, or dismissed.

Each timeline entry also has controls that enable you to do the following:

- Add your own notes to the activity event.
- Share the information in the event by emailing it.
- Export the information in the event to a Microsoft Excel spreadsheet.
- Display a detailed summary of the event, as shown in Figure 5-27.

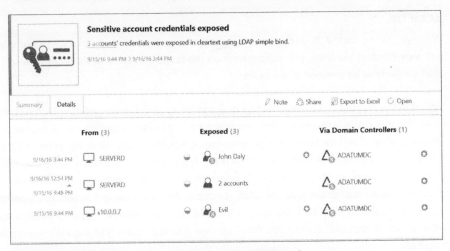

FIGURE 5-27 A detailed event summary page in the ATA Console

Skill 5.3: Determine threat detection solutions using Operations Management Suite

While Advanced Threat Analytics (ATA) is an on-premise security monitoring solution, similar functions are also available from Microsoft in a cloud-based alternative called *Operations Management Suite* (OMS). OMS is a hybrid network management product that can gather data from your systems—in the cloud and in the data center—and provide a variety of management solutions, including threat detection and log analytics. Compared to Microsoft's other management products, such as System Center Operations Manager, OMS is relatively easy to set up and use, and does not require an extensive on-premise infrastructure.

> **This section covers how to:**
> - Determine usage and deployment scenarios for OMS
> - Determine security and auditing functions available for use
> - Determine log analytics usage scenarios

Determine Usage and Deployment Scenarios for OMS

OMS is the latest incarnation of a product that was originally called System Center Advisor (SCA) and then Azure Operational Insight. SCA was a tool that provided server configuration best practices advice, and Azure Operational Insight added log analytics capabilities. OMS now adds security and compliance monitoring, as well as backup and disaster recovery services, to make the product into a full-fledged suite.

EXAM TIP

When preparing for the 70-744 exam, be sure that when you are studying a large, complex software product like OMS, you concentrate on the features related to threat detection that are likely to be covered in the exam.

Based in the cloud, OMS is essentially a management-as-a-service product that has all of the benefits of a cloud implementation, such as frequent updates and universal availability, while being able to service both your on-premise computers and your cloud servers. OMS is agent-based. You install the Microsoft Monitoring Agent (MMA) software on the computers you want to manage, and the agent sends information, including system logs, network traces, and performance counter data, to the OMS service in the cloud using the Secure Hypertext Transfer Protocol (HTTPS). Then, working in the OMS portal, shown in Figure 5-28, you select the management modules (called solutions) you want to use to analyze the information by the agents.

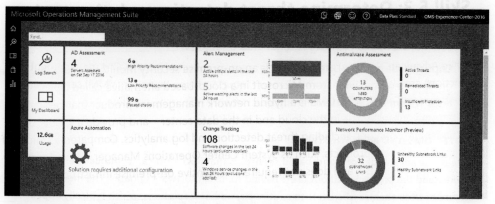

FIGURE 5-28 The Operations Management Suite (OMS) portal

> **NOTE** **USING OMS WITH SYSTEM CENTER OPERATIONS MANAGER**
>
> OMS can function in tandem with the System Center Operations Manager (SCOM) product, funneling all of the agent data through an on-premise SCOM server to the OMS service, or it can function independently, with the data going directly from the agents to OMS. Hybrid implementations are also possible.

Some of the OMS solutions that are currently available include the following:

- **Alert management** Collects alert information from one or more SCOM management groups and provides search, tuning, remediation, and root cause analysis capabilities.

- **Antimalware assessment** Using System Center Endpoint Protection on the client systems, collects information on malware protection status and detected threats

- **Change tracking** Using software inventory information gathered by the agents, displays recent software modifications, broken down by software type, by application, and by computer.

- **Security and audit** Using security, application, and firewall event log information gathered by the agents, provides an overview of potential security issues, including the presence of malware, identity threats, missing updates, and malicious traffic.

- **Wire data** Using only network traffic metadata gathered by the agents, provides network traffic analysis functions without performing packet captures.

- **Backup** Using backup status information gathered from Azure Backup and Windows Server agents, provides a combined interface for backup and recovery processes on both Azure and on-premise servers.

- **System update assessment** Using system state data gathered by the agents, provides a summary of missing updates on the network computers, broken down by computer, update type, and specific update.

- **AD assessment** Using Windows Management Instrumentation (WMI), registry, and performance data gathered by the agents, identifies problems with Active Directory configurations and provides recommended solutions.

- **Capacity planning** Using performance data collected from SCOM management groups integrated with System Center Virtual Machine Manager (VMM) servers, analyzes system usage patterns and predicts future resource utilization.

> **NOTE** **OMS AND NEW SOLUTIONS**
>
> One of the advantages of cloud-based services is that Microsoft can continually enhance and extend the product, without users having to install software updates. The modular nature of OMS enables Microsoft to continually add new solutions, which typically appear on the portal's Solutions Gallery page during the latter stages of their development.

Deploying OMS

Compared with the System Center products, deploying OMS on your network is an extremely simple process. The steps for a full hybrid installation are as follows:

1. Log on using a Microsoft account.
2. Create a new workspace.
3. Confirm your email address.
4. Link an Azure subscription.
5. Associate an organization with the workspace.
6. Onboard SCOM.
7. Onboard Windows systems.
8. Onboard Linux systems.
9. Add solutions.

A full hybrid OMS installation monitors both on-premise and Microsoft Azure servers, but an Azure subscription is not required to use OMS. You can create a simple OMS workspace and connect it to your on-premise servers using the following procedure.

1. Open the *http://microsoft.com/oms* page in your browser and click the Try For Free button and then the Get Started button.
2. Log on using a Microsoft account.
3. Create a new OMS workspace by filling out the form shown in Figure 5-29.

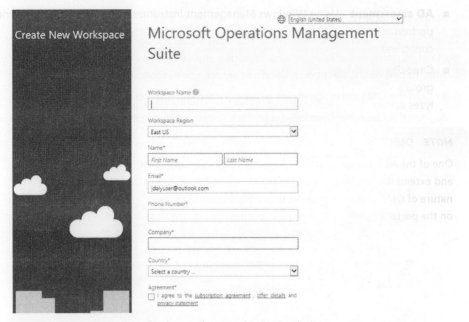

FIGURE 5-29 The Create New Workspace form on the OMS web site

4. Confirm your email address by responding to the message sent to your Microsoft account.

5. Open the initial Microsoft Operations Management Suite portal page (see Figure 5-30).

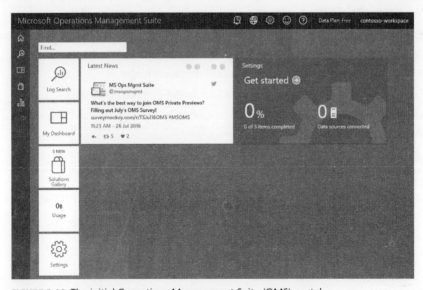

FIGURE 5-30 The initial Operations Management Suite (OMS) portal

Deploying agents

To add on-premise computers to OMS, you must install the agents provided in the OMS portal. The portal includes agents for Windows and Linux servers, as well as Azure and System Center. To deploy the agent on a Windows server, use the following procedure:

1. On the OMS portal Overview page, click the Get Started pane.

2. On the Overview | Settings page, click Connected Sources and Windows Servers (see Figure 5-31).

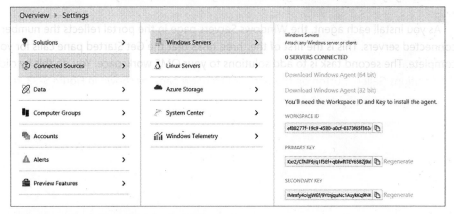

FIGURE 5-31 The Settings page in the OMS portal

3. Click the Download Windows Agent link for the appropriate platform and note the Workspace ID and Workspace Key values. You need them to install the agent.

4. Copy the downloaded agent file to the first computer you want to add to OMS and execute it. The Microsoft Monitoring Agent Setup Wizard launches.

5. Accept the license terms and the default Destination folder.

6. Select the Connect the Agent to Azure Log Analytics (OMS) checkbox.

7. On the Azure Log Analytics page (see Figure 5-32), paste in the Workspace ID and Workspace Key values you noted earlier.

FIGURE 5-32 The Azure Log Analytics page of the Microsoft Monitoring Agent Setup Wizard.

8. Accept the default Windows Update setting.

9. Click Install, and then click Finish.

10. Repeat the process on all the computers you want to onboard.

> **NOTE MASS AGENT DEPLOYMENT**
>
> OMS provides the agents as Windows Installer packages, which makes it a simple matter to deploy them to multiple computers using virtually any software distribution product, including System Center Configuration Manager and Group Policy.

As you install each agent, the Windows Servers page in the portal reflects the number of connected servers. This is the first of the three tasks that the Get Started pane calls for you to complete. The second task is to add solutions to your OMS workspace. You do this by clicking the Solutions Gallery button on the portal's Overview page, as shown in Figure 5-33, selecting the solution you want to use, and click Add on the Details page that appears.

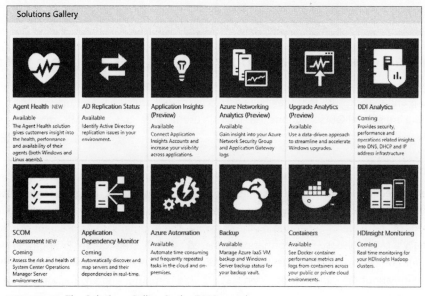

FIGURE 5-33 The Solutions Gallery in the OMS portal

The last of the three tasks that OMS requests you to complete is to specify the Azure subscription you want to connect to OMS. As mentioned earlier, this is not a requirement to use OMS.

When you open the Settings page and click Accounts and Azure Subscription & Data Plan, you can click the Link This Workspace to Azure Subscription hyperlink, a Link Azure Subscription page appears, as shown in Figure 5-34. Here you can link to an existing subscription, create a new subscription, or bypass the page.

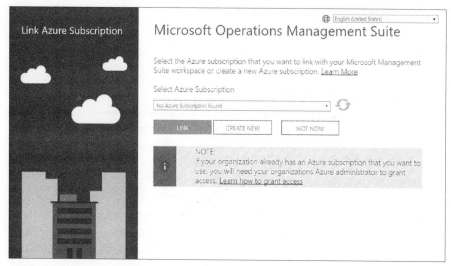

FIGURE 5-34 The Link Azure Subscription page

Determine security and auditing functions available for use

Once you have OMS operational, using it for threat detection is a matter of selecting the right solutions and making sure that they have access to the right information from your computers. There are several OMS solutions that provide useful threat detection information, some directly and others indirectly.

Antimalware assessment

Malware detection software is the first line of defense against attack, but on a large network, administrators do not want to have to check each server individually, or even plow through hundreds of status alerts generated by the software. The Antimalware Assessment solution is essentially a clearinghouse for information gathered by the System Center Endpoint Protection agent, which you must have installed on your servers. This agent provides OMS with information about the current protection status of the computer and any malware threats it has detected.

On receiving information from the agents, OMS populates the solution with information for the entire network, including a list of the computers with threats detected, a list of threats detected, and lists of computers with and without antimalware protection, as shown in Figure 5-35.

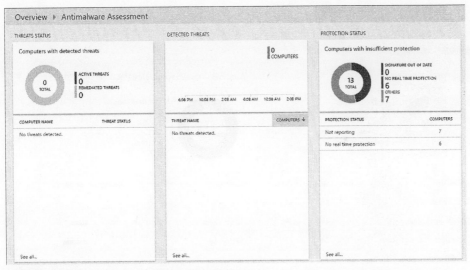

FIGURE 5-35 The Antimalware Assessment solution

System Update Assessment

Ensuring that your computers have the latest operating system and application security updates installed is one of the most important ways to prevent attacks. Even if your enterprise has an internal protocol in place for testing and deploying updates, using a solution such as Windows Server Update Services (WSUS), the System Update Assessment solution in OMS can provide a valuable overview of what updates are available and which have been installed.

The System Update Assessment solution gathers system state information provided by the agents, and also accesses the Microsoft Update servers to determine what updates have been released. This assessment occurs every 24 hours. OMS then compares the information from the two sources and populates the solution with composite graphs based on the perspectives of the computers and the updates, as shown in Figure 5-36.

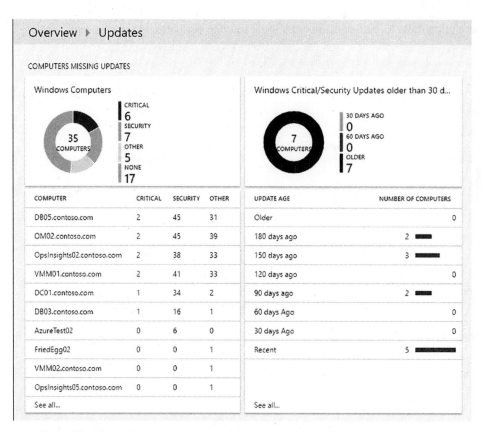

Overview ▶ Updates

COMPUTERS MISSING UPDATES

Windows Computers

35
COMPUTERS

CRITICAL	6
SECURITY	7
OTHER	5
NONE	17

Windows Critical/Security Updates older than 30 d...

7
COMPUTERS

30 DAYS AGO	0
60 DAYS AGO	0
OLDER	7

COMPUTER	CRITICAL	SECURITY	OTHER
DB05.contoso.com	2	45	31
OM02.contoso.com	2	45	39
OpsInsights02.contoso.com	2	38	33
VMM01.contoso.com	2	41	33
DC01.contoso.com	1	34	2
DB03.contoso.com	1	16	1
AzureTest02	0	6	0
FriedEgg02	0	0	1
VMM02.contoso.com	0	0	1
OpsInsights05.contoso.com	0	0	1
See all...			

UPDATE AGE	NUMBER OF COMPUTERS
Older	0
180 days ago	2
150 days ago	3
120 days ago	0
90 days ago	2
60 days Ago	0
30 days Ago	0
Recent	5
See all...	

FIGURE 5-36 The System Update Assessment solution

Security and Audit

The Security and Audit solution uses information gathered from the Security Event log, the Application Event log, and the Windows Firewall log to assess several different security conditions, some of which overlap with those provided by other solutions. The agents on the computers always send this log information directly to the OMS service, even when the computers are part of a System Center Operations Manager (SCOM) group.

> **NOTE** **USING OMS SECURITY AND AUDIT WITH SCOM COMPUTERS**
>
> When computers are members of an SCOM management group, most of the information collected by the agent goes to the SCOM server first, which then relays it to the OMS service. However, depending on the auditing options you select, the logs required by the Security and Audit solution can accumulate extremely large amounts of data, and sending that data directly to OMS can prevent an unnecessary burden on the SCOM server.

By analyzing these logs, the Security and Audit solution evaluates information such as the accounts used to perform logons, the IP addresses of the connecting computers, and their baseline traffic patterns, and performs a threat intelligence assessment, as shown in Figure 5-37.

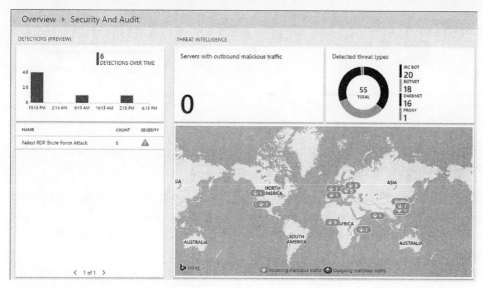

FIGURE 5-37 The Security and Audit solution

The solution also has additional capabilities. For example, it can compare the IP addresses of the connecting computers with a list of known malicious IP addresses provided by the Microsoft Threat Intelligence Center.

Determine log analytics usage scenarios

OMS is essentially a log analysis tool that displays its results in a graphical format. The real power of OMS is found in its searching capability, which enables you to perform precise searches to locate specific information. In many cases, clicking a graph on one of the solution pages takes you to a Log Search page, populated with the search string that provided the data for the graph, as shown in Figure 5-38. On this page, you can modify the parameters of the search to display different information, and save the search to a list of favorites.

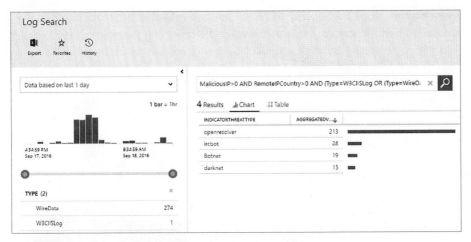

FIGURE 5-38 An OMS Log Search page

The results obtained from a log analysis obviously depend on the types of log data provided to OMS. For the Security and Audit solution to function, for example, you must configure your servers to capture pertinent information to the Application, Security, and Windows Firewall logs.

As shown earlier in this chapter, the Windows Security Event log depends on the system's auditing policy settings for its content, and so therefore does OSM. To supply OSM with the Security log data it needs, you must configure the advanced auditing policies on your servers using Group Policy.

> **NEED MORE REVIEW?** **RECOMMENDED AUDITING POLICY SETTINGS**
>
> For a detailed listing of Microsoft's recommendations for advanced auditing policy settings, see *https://technet.microsoft.com/windows-server-docs/identity/ad-ds/plan/security-best-practices/audit-policy-recommendations*.

For Application log data, you should configure your servers to log information on which executable files, installer scripts, and packages are used in your network. To do this, configure the following settings in a Group Policy object and deploy it to your OSM computers:

- Browse to the Computer Configuration\Policies\Windows Settings\Security Settings\ Application Control Settings folder, open the Properties sheet for the AppLocker and, on the Enforcement tab, select the Configured checkbox and the Audit Only setting for all of the policies there, as shown in Figure 5-39.

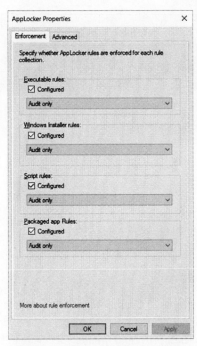

FIGURE 5-39 The AppLocker Properties sheet

- Browse to the Computer Configuration\Policies\Windows Settings\Security Settings\ Application Control Settings\AppLocker folder and create a new rule for each of the four types (Executable Rules, Windows Installer Rules, Script Rules, and Packaged App Rules) using the default settings, the Path option, and an asterisk (*) for the Path value.

- Browse to the Computer Configuration\Policies\Windows Settings\Security Settings\ System Services folder and configure the Application Identity service to start automatically.

By default, Windows Firewall does not log any of its activities at all, so you must enable its logging by configuring the policy settings as follows:

1. Browse to the Computer Configuration\Policies\Windows Settings\Security Settings\ Windows Firewall with Advanced Security folder.

2. Right-click the Windows Firewall with Advanced Security policy and open its Properties sheet.

3. One each of the three profile tabs, click Customize in the Logging box and, in the Customize Logging Settings dialog box, shown in Figure 5-40, configure the following settings:

   - Size limit (KB): 100

   - Logged dropped packets: Yes

   - Log successful connections: Yes

FIGURE 5-40 The Customize Logging Settings dialog box for Windows Firewall

Chapter summary

- Audit policies enable you to record specific events in a computer's Security event log. Earlier Windows versions included only nine basic audit policy settings, but Windows Server 2016 now had 60 advanced audit policies, providing greater specificity in the events and objects to be audited.

- To enable and configure auditing on Windows computers, you can use Group Policy or the Auditpol.exe command prompt utility.

- To audit file system elements, registry settings, and Active Directory objects, you must enable an audit policy and configure a system access control list (SACL) for each object you want to audit. Global Object Access Auditing is a feature that enables you to use Group Policy to create SACLs for an entire file system or registry. You can also create expression-based policies based on criteria you configure in Dynamic Access Control (DAC).

- Windows Server 2016 and Windows 10 include auditing policies that you can use to help prevent certain types of attacks, including audits of Plug and Play device insertions and group memberships.

- Windows PowerShell includes its own logging capabilities, which you can also enable using Group Policy.

- Microsoft Advanced Threat Analytics (ATA) is a security monitoring software package that uses information from domain controller events and captured traffic to develop a baseline of your network's behavior and identify suspicious activities that might indicate an attack in progress.

- The ATA architecture calls for a dedicated server running the ATA Center software and one or more gateways that feed information from domain controllers to the ATA Center computer for storage and processing.

- ATA includes two types of gateways. ATA Gateway runs on a standalone server and can service multiple domain controllers. ATA Lightweight Gateway runs on a domain controller itself.

- Configuration and result reports are available through the ATA console, which runs as an intranet web site on the ATA Center computer. ATA can also generate alerts in the form of emails and syslog messages when a suspicious activity occurs.

- Microsoft Operations Management Suite (OMS) is a cloud-based service that provides threat detection and log analytics, among other management services.

- OMS requires no on-premise infrastructure, other than an agent installed on each computer to be monitored. For cloud-based servers hosted by Microsoft Azure, you can link an OMS workspace to an Azure subscription.

- OMS analyzes log and other information received from its agents and packages the analyses as solutions, which appear as panes in the OMS portal. You select the solutions you want to add to the portal.

- Several of the OMS solutions provide information that can help administrators to detect and mitigate security threats. Solutions typically provide graphs and lists of computers, threats, updates, and other elements, along with recommendations for addressing any issues that arise.

- To ensure that OMS has access to the data it needs to perform the tasks you select, you must configure your monitored computers to compile logs for specific components, which you typically do using Group Policy.

Thought experiment

In this thought experiment, demonstrate your skills and knowledge of the topics covered in this chapter. You can find answer to this thought experiment in the next section.

You are an IT administrator at Contoso, Ltd. After a recent incident of credential theft that was nearly disastrous for the company, the IT director has asked you to evaluate network management products, and particularly their threat detection capabilities. The director has given you a list of questions that she wants answered for all of the solutions you are considering.

You decide to evaluate two products: Microsoft Advanced Threat Analytics (ATA) and Microsoft Operations Management Suite (OMS). Answer the following questions for each of these two products.

1. What on-premise hardware infrastructure does each of the considered products require?

2. Do the products you are considering require any external software products, such as SQL Server or Microsoft SharePoint?

3. The director is considering moving some of the organization's application servers to Microsoft Azure, in the cloud. Can the products you are considering evaluate threats originating on Azure servers?

4. Can the products you are considering capture and parse network packets for investigation?

5. Do the products you are considering require the installation of any special software on the computers to be monitored?

Thought experiment answers

This section contains the solution to the thought experiment.

1. ATA requires a minimum of one dedicated server to host the ATA Center application. ATA Gateways are also required, which can run on dedicated servers or be installed on domain controllers. Every domain controller must have access to a gateway. OMS requires no on-premise hardware at all, as it is a cloud-based service.

2. ATA is a self-contained program, which includes a database manager and a web interface, so there is no external software required. However, the ATA Center computer must run the Internet Information Services role supplied with Windows. OMS is a cloud-based service that runs on Microsoft's computers. It is not an application that runs on your own Azure server, so there is no software to install and maintain.

3. ATA can monitor Azure, as well as on-premise, servers. You must configure your Azure servers with access to an ATA Gateway, just as if they were physical servers on your network. OMS runs in the cloud and can link to an Azure subscription, as well as connect to agents installed in on-premise servers.

4. ATA captures all network traffic transmitted to and from your domain controllers, parses it, and examines the contents for security threats and behavioral anomalies. OMS includes a Wire Data solution that examines network traffic metadata, but it does not capture actual network packets.

5. ATA requires domain controllers to have access to a gateway, which can be installed on the domain controller itself, but the gateways can also run on external servers. OMS requires that every computer being monitored have the Microsoft Monitoring Agent installed, which is supplied with the product.

CHAPTER 6

Implement workload-specific security

Windows Server 2016 has a variety of features that can help administrators create working environments that are protected against attacks. Nano Server is a new Windows Server installation option that creates an operating system with a tiny resource footprint that greatly reduces the possible attack vectors. Containers are virtual instances of the operating system that provide software developers with a clean installation environment in seconds. Dynamic Access Control (DAC) is an Active Directory-based methodology for automatically assigning permissions to users, based on their roles in the organization.

Skills in this chapter:

- Secure application development and server workload infrastructure
- Implement a secure file services infrastructure and Dynamic Access Control

Skill 6.1: Secure application development and server workload infrastructure

The Nano Server installation option and the two implementations of containers in Windows Server 2016 Windows Containers and Hyper-V Containers are intended to provide server and application environments that are more isolated and therefore more resistant to attack than standard Windows Server installations. Nano Server is isolated by its reduced overhead of processes, services, and open ports, and containers provide a separate operating system environment for an application that is unaffected by other services and applications running on the same physical computer.

Determine usage scenarios, supported server workloads, and requirements for Nano Server deployments

In the Windows Server 2008 release, Microsoft introduced Server Core, a scaled-down installation option with reduced memory, storage, and maintenance requirements and a minimized attack surface. Server Core has no Windows Explorer shell, so the system is administered using the command and PowerShell prompts, and by remote management. In Windows Server 2016, Microsoft released Nano Server, another operating system installation option that is scaled down even further. Nano Server is headless; it has no local user interface, no 32-bit application support, and only the most basic configuration controls. There is no support for Remote Desktop; to administer the system, you use remote PowerShell, Windows Remote Management, and Windows Management Interface (WMI) tools.

Nano Server is designed to provide cloud-based infrastructure services with a minimal resource, management, and attack footprint. The two basic scenarios for Nano Server deployments are as follows:

- Server cloud infrastructure services, such as Hyper-V, Failover Clustering, Scale-Out File Servers, DNS, and Internet Information Services (IIS)
- Born-in-the-cloud applications running on virtual machines, containers, or physical servers, using development platforms that do not require a graphical interface

Nano Server's extremely small footprint enables the server to boot dramatically faster than Windows Server or Server Core, requires fewer updates, and provides a much smaller attack surface. By default, Nano Server runs less than half as many services and processes as a full Windows Server installation, and far fewer than Server Core, as well as maintaining fewer open ports.

Microsoft's commitment to cloud-based services—whether public, private, or hybrid—has led to the need for highly-efficient servers dedicated to specific tasks. One of the largest obstacles in this pursuit was the relatively large size of the Windows Server resource footprint, even in Server Core. Nano Server is designed to provide a more efficient virtual machine-based infrastructure with lower memory and storage requirements, minimal downtime, and simplified maintenance.

When running as a Hyper-V virtual machine, Nano Server is remarkably efficient. By empirical standards, a Nano Server VM uses much less than half the assigned memory of a lightly loaded member server running the full Windows Server Desktop Experience, and less than a Server Core system as well. For demonstration purposes, Microsoft was able to run over 3,400 128 MB VMs on a single computer with eight 20-core processors and 1 terabyte of RAM.

The headless nature of the Nano Server design does not mean that administrators are limited to PowerShell and Command Prompt management tools, although these are certainly available. You can connect to a Nano Server remotely using the standard Windows graphical tools, if desired, including Hyper-V Manager and other Microsoft Management Console (MMC) snap-ins, Server Manager, and even System Center.

The main shortcoming of the Nano Server design, at least at this point in its development, is its relatively limited utility. The server supports only a small subset of the roles and features in the full Windows Server product. However, the roles that are supported in Nano Server are particularly well-suited to cloud deployments. You can run IIS web servers, file servers, and Hyper-V servers, and, with the clustering and container support provided, these services are both resilient and highly scalable.

Install and configure Nano Server

There is no wizard for installing Nano Server, as there is for Windows Server and Server Core. You install the operating system by creating a Virtual Hard Disk (VHD) on another computer, from the PowerShell command line. Then you use the VHD to create a Hyper-V virtual machine or a boot drive for a physical server.

Windows Server 2016 includes a Nano Server directory on its installation disk or image file, which contains the Nano Server image, a PowerShell module, and a subdirectory containing the package files for the roles and features the operating system supports. Importing the PowerShell module provides the cmdlets you use to create and edit Nano Server images. The package files contain specially-created versions of the roles and features you can install directly to the VHD file. Despite their similarity to the versions used by Windows Server and Server Core, the roles are not interchangeable. You cannot install roles from the full Windows Server product on a Nano Server system.

Creating a Nano Server image

To create a new Nano Server image, open a PowerShell session with administrative privileges on a computer with the Windows Server 2016 installation media loaded or mounted. Then, switch to the NanoServer folder on the installation disk and import the Windows PowerShell module required to provide the cmdlets for Nano Server, using the following command:

```
Import-Module .\NanoServerImageGenerator -Verbose
```

Importing the module provides you with access to the New-NanoServerImage cmdlet, which you use to create a Nano Server VHD file.

To run the New-NanoServerImage cmdlet, use the following basic syntax:

```
new-nanoserverimage -deploymenttype guest|host -edition standard|datacenter -mediapath
root -targetpath path\filename -computername name
```

The required parameters for the New-NanoServerImage cmdlet are as follows:

- **DeploymentType**   Specifies whether the image file is used on a Hyper-V virtual machine (Guest) or a physical server (Host).

- **Edition**   Specifies whether to install the Standard or Datacenter edition of Nano Server.

- **MediaPath**   Specifies the path to the root of the Windows Server 2016 installation disk. or mounted image.

- **BasePath**   Specifies a path on the local system where the cmdlet creates a copy of the installation files from the location specified in the -MediaPath parameter. Once the copy is created, you can use the BasePath parameter only for future NewNanoServerImage commands and omit the MediaPath parameter. This parameter is optional.

- **TargetPath**   Species the full path and filename of the new image to be created. The filename extension (.vhd or .vhdx) specifies whether the new image should be Generation 1 or Generation 2.

- **ComputerName**   Specifies the computer name that should be assigned to the new image.

An example of the command to create a standard, Generation 2 Nano Server image with the computer name Nano1, for use on a virtual machine, would be as follows:

```
new-nanoserverimage -deploymenttype guest -edition standard -mediapath d:\ -targetpath
c:\temp\nanoserver1.vhdx -computername nano1
```

As the command runs, it prompts you for a password that is applied to the Administrator account in the Nano Server image. The output generated by the cmdlet appears as shown in Figure 6-1.

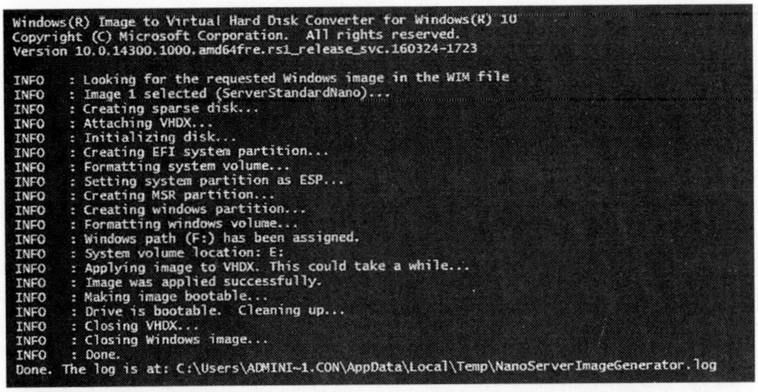

FIGURE 6-1 PowerShell output from New-NanoServerImage cmdlet

After the cmdlet creates the VHD file, it adds any packages you specified in the command. For example, the Guest drivers specified by the DeploymentType parameter are provided as a package, which the cmdlet installs to the VHD file. To install additional packages provided with Nano Server, you can add optional parameters to the NewNanoServerImage command line.

The optional parameters for the NewNanoServerImage cmdlet are as follows:

- **Compute**   Installs the Hyper-V role on the image specified by the TargetPath variable.
- **Clustering**   Installs the Failover Clustering role on the image specified by the TargetPath variable.
- **OEMDrivers**   Add the basic drivers included in Server Core to the image specified by the TargetPath variable.
- **Storage**   Installs the File Server role and other storage components on the image specified by the TargetPath variable.
- **Defender**   Installs Windows Defender on the image specified by the TargetPath variable.
- **Containers**   Installs host support for Windows Containers on the image specified by the TargetPath variable.
- **Packages**   Installs one or more Nano Center packages from among the following:
    - **MicrosoftNanoServerDSCPackage**   Installs the Desired State Configuration (DSC) package on the image specified by the TargetPath variable.
    - **MicrosoftNanoServerDNSPackage**   Installs the DNS Server role on the image specified by the TargetPath variable.
    - **Microsoft-NanoServer-IIS-Package**   Installs the IIS role on the image specified by the TargetPath variable.
    - **Microsoft-NanoServer-SCVMM-Package**   Installs the System Center Virtual Machine Manager agent on the image specified by the TargetPath variable.
    - **Microsoft-NanoServer-SCVMM-Compute-Package**   Installs the Hyper-V role on the image specified by the TargetPath variable, so that is it manageable with System Center Virtual Machine Manager. Do not use with the Compute parameter.
    - **Microsoft-NanoServer-NPDS-Package**   Installs the Network Performance Diagnostics Service on the image specified by the TargetPath variable.
    - **Microsoft-NanoServer-DCB-Package**   Installs Data Center Bridging on the image specified by the TargetPath variable.
    - **Microsoft-NanoServer-SecureStartup-Package**   Installs Secure Startup on the image specified by the TargetPath variable.
    - **Microsoft-NanoServer-ShieldedVM-Package**   Installs the Shielded Virtual Machine package on the image specified by the TargetPath variable (Datacenter edition only).

Joining a Domain

To create a new Nano Server image that is a member of a domain, you are essentially performing an offline domain join. To do this, you must have access to the domain the Nano Server joins so that you can harvest a domain provisioning file (called a *blob*) and apply it to the newly created VHD file.

The NewNanoServerImage cmdlet supports a DomainName parameter, which you can use when you are creating the image on a computer that is a member of the domain, and you are logged on using an account that has the privileges needed to create domain computer accounts. You specify the DomainName parameter on the NewNanoServerImage command line with the name of the domain the new image joins, as in the following example:

```
new-nanoserverimage -deploymenttype guest -edition standard -mediapath d:\ -targetpath
c:\temp\nanoserver2.vhdx -computername nano2 -domainname contoso
```

Once the command processing completes and the new image is created, a new Computer object appears in Active Directory, as shown in Figure 6-2.

```
PS C:\temp\NanoServer\Packages> get-adcomputer -identity nano2

DistinguishedName : CN=NANO2,CN=Computers,DC=contoso,DC=com
DNSHostName       : nano2.contoso.com
Enabled           : True
Name              : NANO2
ObjectClass       : computer
ObjectGUID        : e4f20dc6-0889-4e01-b5ee-bf485269a70b
SamAccountName    : NANO2$
SID               : S-1-5-21-862777183-1904649731-2918963198-1104
UserPrincipalName :
```

FIGURE 6-2 New Nano Server computer account in Active Directory

> ***NOTE*** **REUSING A DOMAIN COMPUTER NAME**
>
> If a computer account with the name specified in the ComputerName parameter already exists in Active Directory, you can configure a Nano Server image to reuse that account by adding the ReuseDomainNode parameter to the NewNanoServerImage command line.

It is possible to join a new Nano Server image to a domain when creating it on a computer that is not a domain member, but the process is more complicated. In this case, you have to harvest the blob file on a domain member computer, and then copy it to the computer where you intend to run New-NanoServerImage.

You create a blob file with the Djoin.exe tool included with Windows Server 2016, using the following syntax:

```
djoin /provision /domain domainname /machine computername /savefile filename.txt
```

An example of a Djoin provisioning command would be as follows:

```
djoin /provision /domain contoso /machine nano3 /savefile nano3blob.txt
```

Provisioning the computer in this way creates the computer account in the domain and creates a text file using the name you specified in the Djoin command. Although the blob is a text file, the information it contains is encoded, as shown in Figure 6-3.

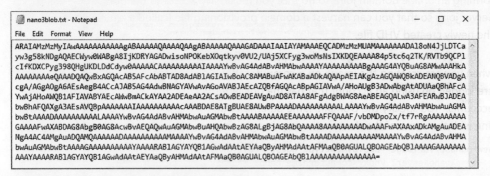

FIGURE 6-3 Contents of a blob file created by Djoin.exe

After you copy the blob file to the computer where you create the new Nano Server image, you run the NewNanoServerImage cmdlet with the DomainBlobPath parameter, specifying the location of the blob file, as in the following example:

```
new-nanoserverimage –deploymenttype guest –edition standard –mediapath d:\ –targetpath
c:\temp\nanoserver2.vhdx –computername nano2 –domainblobpath c:\temp\nano3blob.txt
```

Creating a Nano Server VM

Once you have created a Nano Server VHD or VHDX image file, using the NewNanoServerImage cmdlet, you can proceed to deploy it. In the case of a virtual machine (for which you specified Guest in the DeploymentType parameter), you create a new VM in Hyper-V, using the Nano Server VHD or VHDX image file instead of creating a new one.

If you create the VM using the New Virtual Machine Wizard in Hyper-V Manager, you select the Use an Existing Virtual Hard Disk option on the Connect Virtual Hard Disk page, and select the Nano Server image file you created, as shown in Figure 6-4.

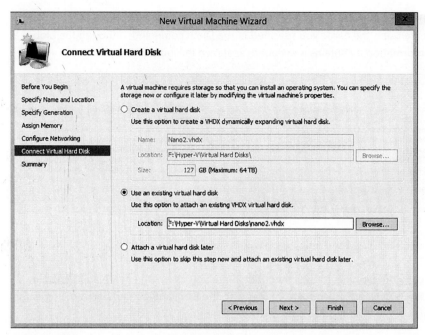

FIGURE 6-4 Using a Nano Server VHDX image file to create a virtual machine

If you use the New-VM PowerShell cmdlet to create the virtual machine, you use the VHDPath parameter to specify the name and location of the Nano Server image file, as in the following example:

```
new-vm -name "Nano2" -generation 2 -memorystartupbytes 1GB -vhdpath "f:\hyper-v\virtual
hard disks\nano2.vhdx"
```

> **NOTE CREATING THE CORRECT GENERATION VM**
>
> As mentioned earlier, the file extension you supply in the TargetPath parameter specifies whether the NewNanoServerImage cmdlet creates a Generation 1 or Generation 2 image. When creating the new virtual machine in Hyper-V, be sure to specify a Generation 1 VM for a VHD file or a Generation 2 VM for a VHDX file.

Logging on to a Nano Server

Once you have deployed the VHD image in a virtual machine and started the Nano Server system, a simple, character-based authentication screen appears, as shown in Figure 6-6.

FIGURE 6-5 The Nano Server authentication screen

After you log on, the Nano Server Recovery Console screen appears, as shown in Figure 6-6. This screen provides only the minimal controls you might need to configure the system's remote administration client capabilities.

```
                        Nano Server Recovery Console
==========================================================================
Computer Name: NANO2
Domain:          contoso.com
OS:              Microsoft Windows Server 2016 Standard Technical Preview 5
Local date:      Friday, September 23, 2016
Local time:      12:40 PM
Time zone:       Pacific Standard Time
--------------------------------------------------------------------------
> Networking
  Inbound Firewall Rules
  Outbound Firewall Rules
  WinRM
```

FIGURE 6-6 The Nano Server Recovery Console screen

You can configure the network interfaces, set Windows Firewall rules, and configure Windows remote Management (WinRM). Once the system is ready to listen for calls from remote management tools, there is nothing more to do from the Nano Server console. All subsequent administration occurs remotely.

Configuring a Nano Server IP address

As with the other Windows Server installation options, Nano Server has its Dynamic Host Configuration Protocol (DHCP) client enabled by default. If you have a DHCP server on your network, Nano Server obtains an IP address from it and configure the system's network adapter. If no DHCP server is available, you can configure the network adapter manually, using parameters in the NewNanoServerImage command line, or using one of the few functions available in the Nano Server Recovery Console.

You can configure a network adapter in a Nano Server as you create the VHD image file, by specifying the IP configuration settings on the NewNanoServerImage command line. The parameters to use are as follows:

- **InterfaceNameOrIndex**   Identifies the network adapter in the Nano Server to which the settings in the following parameters should be applied. In a machine with a single network interface adapter, the value Ethernet should be sufficient.

- **Ipv4Address**   Specifies the IPv4 address to be assigned to the network adapter identified by the InterfaceNameOrIndex parameter.

- **Ipv4SubnetMask**   Specifies the Subnet Mask value associated with the IP address specified in the Ipv4Address parameter.

- **Ipv4Gateway**   Specifies the IP address of a router on the local network where the IP address specified in the Ipv4Address parameter is located, that provides access to other networks.

- **Ipv4Dns**   Specifies the IP address of the DNS server that the system should use to locate resources.

An example of the NewNanoServerImage command line including these parameters would be as follows:

```
new-nanoserverimage -deploymenttype guest -edition standard -mediapath d:\ -targetpath
c:\temp\nanoserver4.vhdx -computername nano4 -domain contoso.com -interfacenameorindex
ethernet -ipv4address 192.168.10.41 -ipv4subnetmask 255.255.255.0 -ipv4gateway
192.168.10.1 -ipv4dns 192.168.10.2
```

To manually configure the network adapter to use a static IP address from the Nano Server Recovery Console, after the image has been created and deployed, use the following procedure:

1. Select the Networking item and press Enter.

> **NOTE** **USING THE NANO SERVER RECOVERY CONSOLE INTERFACE**
>
> The Nano Server Recovery Console has no support for the mouse, and even its keyboard support is limited. Number pads are not supported, nor are CapsLk and NumLk keys. To navigate the interface, you use the cursor keys or the Tab key to highlight an option and press Enter to select it. The legend at the bottom of the screen specifies additional key combinations.

2. On the Network Settings screen, select a network adapter and press Enter.
3. On the Network Adapter Settings screen, shown in Figure 6-7, press F11 to configure the IPv4 settings for the adapter.

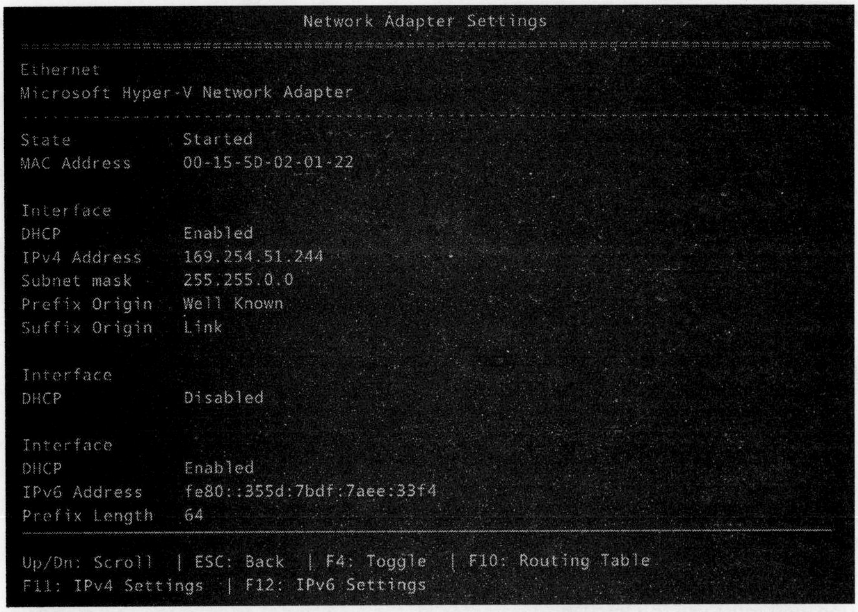

```
                    Network Adapter Settings
================================================================
Ethernet
Microsoft Hyper-V Network Adapter
................................................................

State           Started
MAC Address     00-15-5D-02-01-22

Interface
DHCP            Enabled
IPv4 Address    169.254.51.244
Subnet mask     255.255.0.0
Prefix Origin   Well Known
Suffix Origin   Link

Interface
DHCP            Disabled

Interface
DHCP            Enabled
IPv6 Address    fe80::355d:7bdf:7aee:33f4
Prefix Length   64
_____
Up/Dn: Scroll  | ESC: Back  | F4: Toggle  | F10: Routing Table
F11: IPv4 Settings  | F12: IPv6 Settings
```

FIGURE 6-7 The Network Adapter Settings screen in the Nano Server Recovery Console

4. On the IP Configuration screen, press F4 to toggle the DHCP client to Disabled, as shown in Figure 6-8.

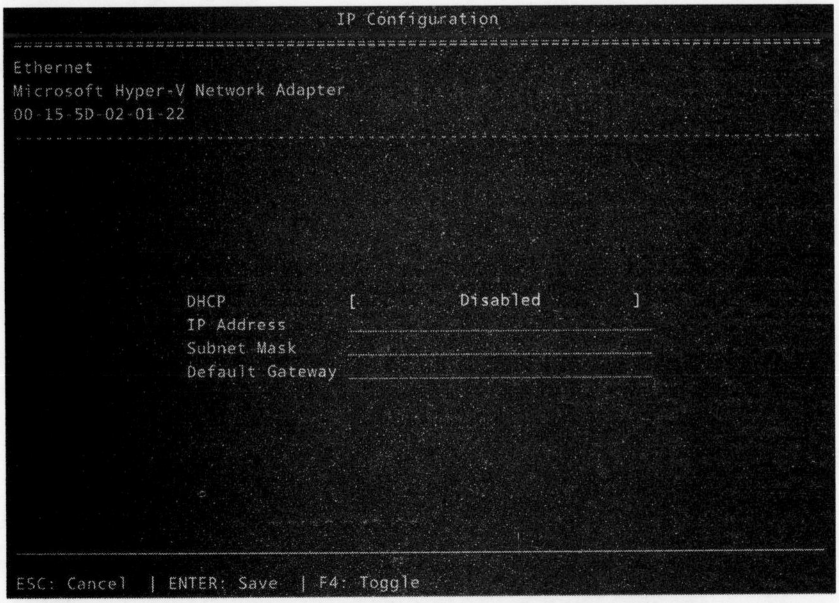

```
                       IP Configuration
================================================================
Ethernet
Microsoft Hyper-V Network Adapter
00-15-5D-02-01-22
................................................................




            DHCP            [        Disabled        ]
            IP Address      _____
            Subnet Mask     _____
            Default Gateway _____





_____
ESC: Cancel  | ENTER: Save  | F4: Toggle
```

FIGURE 6-8 The IP Configuration screen in the Nano Server Recovery Console

5. Press the Tab key to advance to the IP Address field and type an IP address for the adapter.

6. Press the Tab key to advance to the Subnet Mask field and type the mask associated with the IP address.

7. Press the Tab key to advance to the Default Gateway field and type the address of a router on the network.

8. Press Enter to save your settings.

9. Press Enter again to confirm the Save.

10. Press Esc to return to the Network Adapter Settings screen.

11. Press F12 to configure IPv6 Settings or F10 to modify the routing table, if necessary.

12. Press Esc twice to return to the Nano Server Recovery Console.

> **NOTE   CONFIGURING A DNS SERVER ADDRESS**
>
> Unusually, there is no way to specify a DNS server address in the Nano Server Recovery Console interface. To configure the DNS server address for an initial Nano Server configuration, you must use the Ipv4Dns parameter on the NewNanoServerImage command line or use DHCP to supply the address.

Configuring Firewall rules

Depending on what remote tools you intend to use to manage Nano Server, you might have to work with Windows Firewall rules to provide appropriate access to the computer. The local interface on Nano Server enables you to enable or disable existing firewall rules, both inbound and outbound, to open and close ports as needed.

On the Nano Server Recovery Console screen, when you select Inbound Firewall Rules or Outbound Firewall Rules, you see a scrollable screen containing all of the default rules on the system, as shown in Figure 6-9.

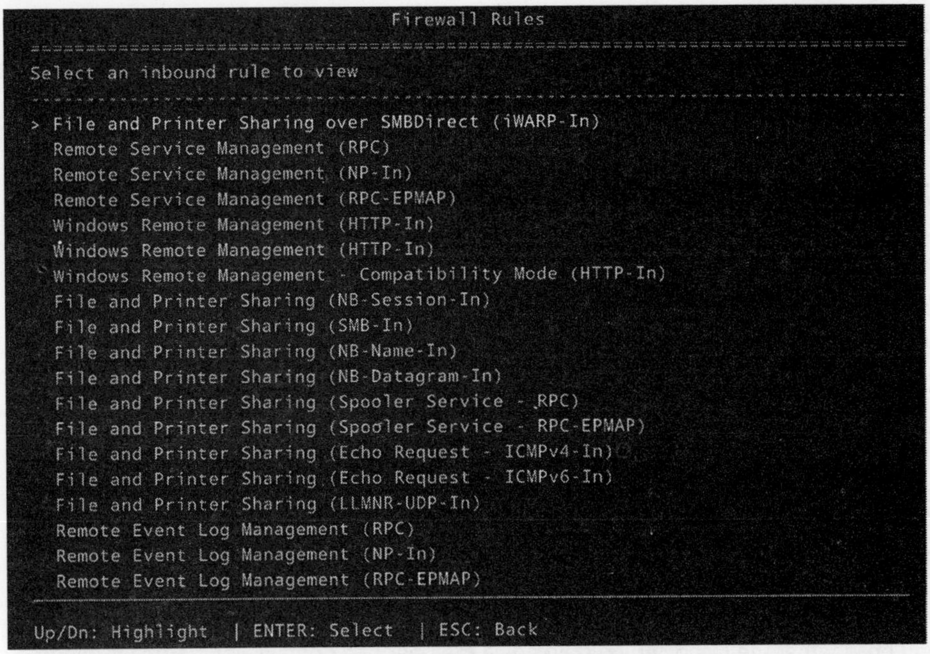

```
                        Firewall Rules
=================================================================
Select an inbound rule to view
-----------------------------------------------------------------
> File and Printer Sharing over SMBDirect (iWARP-In)
  Remote Service Management (RPC)
  Remote Service Management (NP-In)
  Remote Service Management (RPC-EPMAP)
  Windows Remote Management (HTTP-In)
  Windows Remote Management (HTTP-In)
  Windows Remote Management - Compatibility Mode (HTTP-In)
  File and Printer Sharing (NB-Session-In)
  File and Printer Sharing (SMB-In)
  File and Printer Sharing (NB-Name-In)
  File and Printer Sharing (NB-Datagram-In)
  File and Printer Sharing (Spooler Service - RPC)
  File and Printer Sharing (Spooler Service - RPC-EPMAP)
  File and Printer Sharing (Echo Request - ICMPv4-In)
  File and Printer Sharing (Echo Request - ICMPv6-In)
  File and Printer Sharing (LLMNR-UDP-In)
  Remote Event Log Management (RPC)
  Remote Event Log Management (NP-In)
  Remote Event Log Management (RPC-EPMAP)
-----------------------------------------------------------------
Up/Dn: Highlight  | ENTER: Select  | ESC: Back
```

FIGURE 6-9 The Firewall Rules screen in the Nano Server Recovery Console

Selecting a rule displays a Firewall Rule Details screen containing information about the rule, including the port affected by the rule and whether it is currently enabled, as shown in Figure 6-10. You can then press the F4 key to enable or disable the rule.

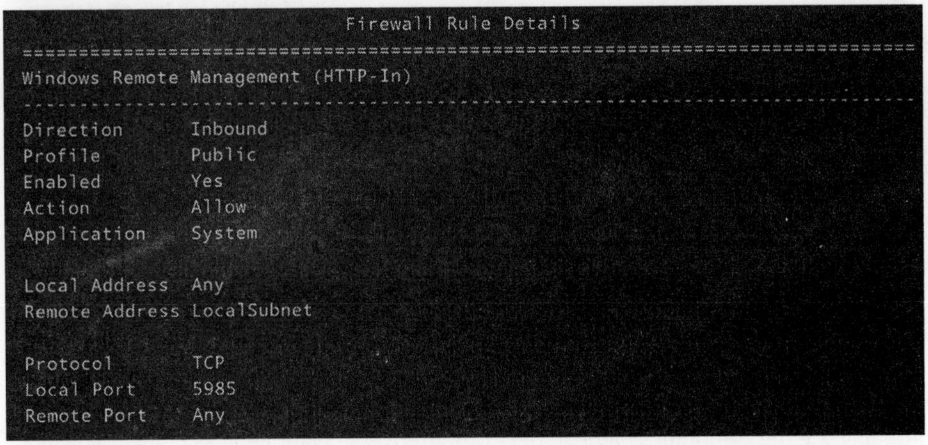

```
                     Firewall Rule Details
=================================================================
Windows Remote Management (HTTP-In)
-----------------------------------------------------------------
Direction       Inbound
Profile         Public
Enabled         Yes
Action          Allow
Application     System

Local Address   Any
Remote Address  LocalSubnet

Protocol        TCP
Local Port      5985
Remote Port     Any
```

FIGURE 6-10 The Firewall Rule Details screen in the Nano Server Recovery Console

This interface does not provide full administrative access to Windows Firewall. It is intended only to provide you with sufficient control to gain remote access to the Nano Server. You can activate or deactivate an existing rule, but you cannot modify rules themselves or create new ones. Once you have remote access to the Nano Server, you can use standard tools, such as the Windows Firewall with Advanced Security console or the Windows PowerShell cmdlets, to exercise complete control over the firewall.

Configuring Windows Remote Management

The WinRM entry on the Nano Server Recovery Console screen provides only a single function, the ability to reset the WinRM service and firewall to their default settings, in the event that the Nano Server's configuration is preventing you from establishing a connection with a remote management tool.

Connecting to a Nano Server using PowerShell

In most cases, a newly-installed Nano Server with a proper network adapter configuration should be ready to listen for incoming connection requests from remote management tools. For example, to connect to a Nano Server using Windows PowerShell, you create a PowerShell session using the NewPSSession cmdlet, using following basic syntax:

```
new-pssession -computername name -credential domain\username
```

The values you use for the ComputerName and Credential parameters in this command depend on whether the Nano Server is already a member of a domain. For a domain-joined Nano Server, you should be able to connect by specifying the fully-qualified domain name of the Nano Server and a domain account name, as in the following example:

```
new-pssession -computername nano4.contoso.com -credential contoso\administrator
```

The cmdlet prompts for a password for the administrator account and creates a new session, as shown in Figure 6-11. The output from the cmdlet specified the ID for the session, which you use to connect to it.

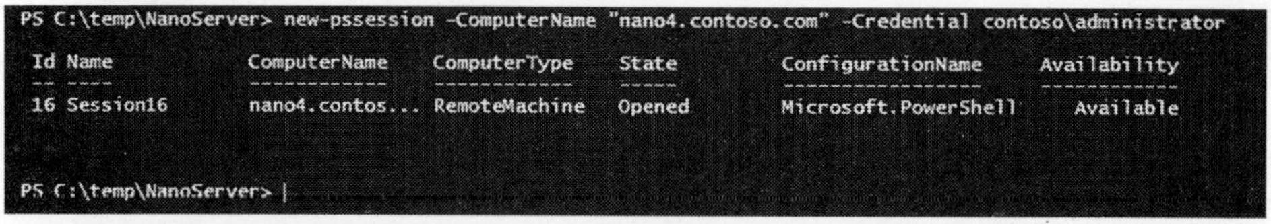

FIGURE 6-11 Creating a PowerShell session to a Nano Server

When the Nano Server is not joined to a domain, the process of creating a new session can be more complicated. First, you must consider whether or not the computer name of the Nano Server can be resolved. If the network adapter has been configured by DHCP, you can probably use the computer's name in the ComputerName parameter, as in the following example:

```
new-pssession -computername nano4 -credential -\administrator
```

Omitting the domain name from the Credential parameter causes the cmdlet to prompt you for the local account password.

If you have manually configured the network adapter, you might have to use the Nano Server's IP address instead of its computer name, as in the following example:

```
new-pssession -computername 192.168.10.41 -credential -\administrator
```

Second, you have to add the Nano Server to the computer's Trusted Hosts list in the Windows Remote Management implementation. Otherwise, the cmdlet tries to use Kerberos to authenticate the session, which fail in the case of a non-domain-joined host.

To add a computer to the Trusted Hosts list using PowerShell, you specify its name or IP address in the Set-Item cmdlet, as in the following example:

```
set-item wsman:\localhost\client\trustedhosts "192.168.10.41"
```

You can also use the Winrm.exe tool from the command prompt, as follows:

```
winrm set winrm/config/client @{TrustedHosts="192.168.10.41"}
```

Once you have successfully created a PowerShell session, you can connect to it using the EnterPSSession cmdlet, specifying the ID displayed in the New-PSSession output, as in the following example:

```
enter-pssession -id 16
```

When you successfully connect to the session, the command prompt changes to include the remote computer name, as shown in Figure 6-12.

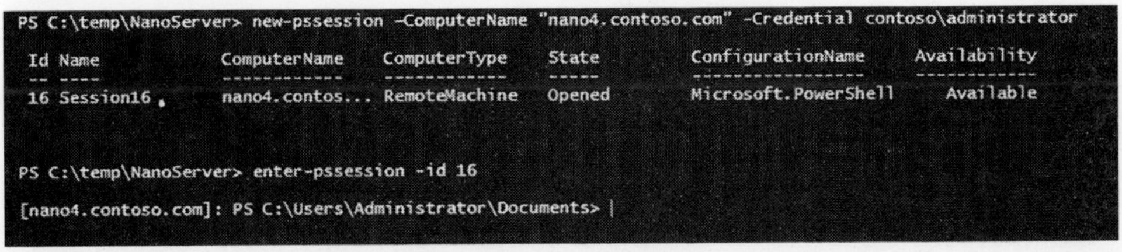

```
PS C:\temp\NanoServer> new-pssession -ComputerName "nano4.contoso.com" -Credential contoso\administrator

Id Name        ComputerName    ComputerType    State   ConfigurationName      Availability
-- ----        ------------    ------------    -----   -----------------      ------------
16 Session16   nano4.contos... RemoteMachine   Opened  Microsoft.PowerShell   Available


PS C:\temp\NanoServer> enter-pssession -id 16

[nano4.contoso.com]: PS C:\Users\Administrator\Documents> |
```

FIGURE 6-12 Connecting to a PowerShell session on a Nano Server

Once you have connected to the session, you are working with the Nano Server's PowerShell resources. The Windows PowerShell 5.1 version included in Windows Server 2016 now exists in two editions: Desktop and Core. The full version of Windows Server 2016 and Server Core both include the Desktop edition. Nano Server includes the PowerShell Core edition, as displayed in the $PSVersionTable variable, shown in Figure 6-13.

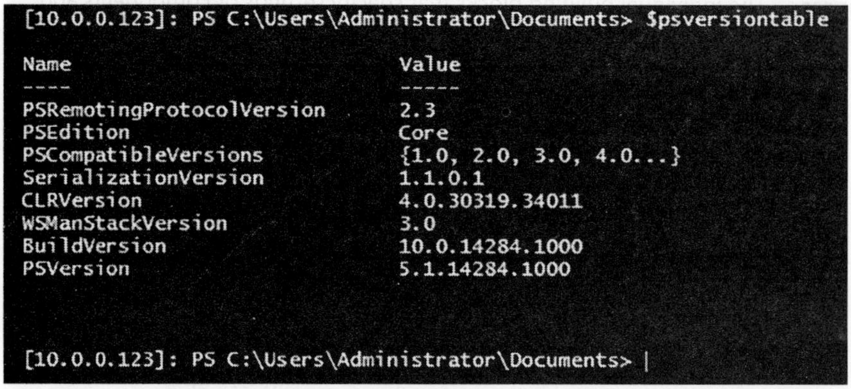

```
[10.0.0.123]: PS C:\Users\Administrator\Documents> $psversiontable

Name                          Value
----                          -----
PSRemotingProtocolVersion     2.3
PSEdition                     Core
PSCompatibleVersions          {1.0, 2.0, 3.0, 4.0...}
SerializationVersion          1.1.0.1
CLRVersion                    4.0.30319.34011
WSManStackVersion             3.0
BuildVersion                  10.0.14284.1000
PSVersion                     5.1.14284.1000


[10.0.0.123]: PS C:\Users\Administrator\Documents> |
```

FIGURE 6-13 Contents of the $PSVersionTable variable

PowerShell Core is a subset of PowerShell Desktop, omitting many of its features. Administrators and developers with existing PowerShell code should test it on a PowerShell Core implementation.

NEED MORE REVIEW? **POWERSHELL CORE FEATURE OMISSIONS**

For a list of the features not included in PowerShell Core, see *https://technet.microsoft.com/en-us/windows-server-docs/compute/nano-server/powershell-on-nano-server.*

To disconnect from a connected session, you can use the ExitPSSession cmdlet, or just type Exit. The command prompt returns to its original form, and you are back working with the host computer.

Implement security policies on Nano Servers using Desired State Configuration

As discussed earlier, remote management is an essential part of maintaining Nano Server installations, and it is possible for administrators to use most of their familiar tools—graphical and textual—to connect to a Nano Server and access its functions. However, Nano Server is particularly well-suited to high-density installations. Microsoft has created test deployments with thousands of Nano Server virtual machines running on a single Hyper-V host. In an environment like this, administering each VM individually would be an enormous task. One possible solution is to use the Windows PowerShell Desired State Configuration (DSC) feature to deploy standardized configurations to multiple Nano Servers.

As mentioned in Chapter 4,"Manage Privileged Identities," *Desired State Configuration (DSC)* is a Windows PowerShell feature that uses script files to apply, monitor, and maintain a specific system configuration. DSC consists of three components, as follows:

- **Configurations** PowerShell scripts that contain node blocks specifying the names of the computers to be configured and resource blocks specifying the property settings to be applied

- **Resources** The individual building blocks that specify settings or components and the values that the configuration should assign to them
- **Local Configuration Manager (LCM)** The engine running on the local system that receives configurations and applies them to the computer

To use DSC, administrators create configuration script files containing resource blocks, compile them into modules, and deploy them on a central file or web server. The LCM then receives the configuration modules from the server, using a push or pull relationship, and applies them to the system. The LCM also maintains the system configuration by monitoring the system, ensuring that the required resource settings are maintained and reapplying them if necessary. DSC configurations are idempotent, meaning that the scripts can be applied to a system repeatedly without generating errors or other undesirable results.

The Nano Server product in Windows Server 2016 includes a DSC package that you can install from the New-NanoServerImage command line by adding the Packages Microsoft-NanoServer-DSC-Package parameter. As with most of Nano Server's components, the DSC implementation is a subset of the full featured one in Windows Server 2016.

For example, you can configure a Nano Server to pull configurations from a DSC server, or receive configurations pushed from a server, but a Nano Server cannot function as a pull server for other clients. The Nano Server DSC implementation does include all of the cmdlets from the full version.

> **NEED MORE REVIEW? NANO SERVER DSC CAPABILITIES**
>
> For a complete list of what the Nano Server Desired State Configuration feature can and cannot do, see *https://msdn.microsoft.com/en-us/powershell/dsc/nanodsc*.

Creating DSC Configuration Scripts

A simple DSC configuration script to configure the DNS server address might appear as shown in Listing 6-1.

LISTING 6-1 Sample DSC Configuration Script

```
Configuration DnsClient
{
      Import-DscResource -ModuleName "xNetworking"
      Node ("ServerA","ServerB")
      {
            xDnsServerAddress DnsServer
            {
                  Address        = 10.0.0.1
                  AddressFamily  = "Ipv4"
                  InterfaceAlias = "Ethernet"
            }
      }
}
```

In this script, the configuration, called DnsClient, ensures that the two computers, ServerA and ServerB, have their DNS Server Address setting configured. The Import-DscModule command loads a module called xNetworking. The Node block specifies the names of the computers. The xDnsServerAddress statement specifies the resource in the module to be configured, and Address, containing the DNS server address, is the property for that resource. When the configuration is applied to a client, its LCM checks to see if the Ipv4 DNS Server Address for the specified network adapter is configured correctly. If it is, then nothing happens. If it is not, then the LCM configures it.

This particular script is appropriate for a Nano Server, because of the issues with DNS server configuration discussed earlier in this chapter. However, this is only the basic model for a configuration. Configuration scripts are often vastly more complicated than this. To configure security settings on a Nano Server, you can create a configuration that specifies registry key values to be applied, or that uses any of the hundreds of DSC resources available in modules downloadable from Microsoft's PowerShell Gallery (at *http://powershellgallery.com*). The xNetworking module used in the sample script is available there.

Compiling DSC configurations

When you run the configuration script, PowerShell creates a Management Object Format (MOF) file for each computer specified in the Node block. The output created by running the sample script shown earlier appears in Figure 6-14.

FIGURE 6-14 Output of a configuration script

The MOF files are the actual scripts that are distributed to the DSC clients.

Deploying DSC configurations

To deploy a DSC configuration module, the administrator must decide between implementing a pull or a push architecture. In a pull architecture, the MOF files are stored on a Pull Server, which is an SMB server or an IIS web server with an OData interface, set up with its own DSC configuration.

Once you have published the MOF files on the Pull Server, you must configure the LCM on the client computers with a local configuration script that provides the URL of the Pull Server and creates a scheduled task. When both the DSC server and the client are properly configured, the LCM on the client periodically checks the Pull Server for configurations and examines the local system for compliance. When necessary, the LCM downloads configuration files from the Pull Server and applies them to the local system.

In a push architecture, the administrator runs the Start-DscConfiguration cmdlet on the server, specifying the location where the MOF files are stored in the -Path parameter. By default, the cmdlet pushes the specified configuration to all of the clients that have MOF files in the specified path. However, you can also select individual computers for deployment, using the -ComputerName parameter, as in the following example:

```
start-dscconfiguration -path c\dsc\dnsclient -computername servera -credential contoso\
administrator -wait -verbose
```

Determine usage scenarios and requirements for Windows Server and Hyper-V containers

Hyper-V enables you to create virtual machines with processor, memory, and storage resources that appear to be isolated from the host computer and from other virtual machines. Windows Server installation options, such as Server Core and Nano Server, are designed to make these virtual machines smaller and more efficient. Containers are another form of virtualization, which provide multiple, isolated instances of the operating system on a single physical computer.

Like virtual machines, containers provide what appear to be separate instances of the operating system, each with its own processor, memory, and storage resources. Unlike virtual machines, however, which run completely separate copies of the operating system, containers actually share the operating system of the host system. There is no need to install a separate instance of the operating system for each container, nor does the container have to perform a boot sequence, load libraries, or devote memory to the operating system files. Containers start in seconds, and you can create more containers on a host system than you can virtual machines.

To users working in containers, what they appear to see is a clean operating system installation, ready for applications. The environment is completely separated from the host, and from other containers, using namespace isolation and resource governance.

Namespace isolation means that each container only has access to the resources that are available to it. Files, ports, and running processes all appear to be dedicated to the container, even when they are being shared with the host and with other containers. The working environment appears similar to that of a virtual machine, but unlike a virtual machine, which maintains separate copies of all of the operating system files, a container is actually sharing these files with the host, not copying them. It is only when a user or application in a container modifies a file that a copy is made in the container's file system.

Resource governance means that a container has access only to a specified amount of processor cycles, system memory, network bandwidth, and other resources, and no more. An application running in a container has a clean sandbox environment, with no access to resources allocated to other containers or to the host.

The ability to create new containers in seconds, and the isolated nature of each container, make an ideal platform for application development and software testing.

Two flavors of containers

Windows Server 2016 supports two types of containers: Windows Server Containers and Hyper-V containers. The difference between the two is in the degree of container isolation they provide. Windows Server Containers share everything with the host computer, including the operating system kernel and the system memory.

Because of this, it is conceivable that an application, whether accidentally or deliberately, might be able to escape from the confines of its container and affect other processes running on the host or in other containers. This option is therefore presumed to be preferable when the applications running in different containers are basically trustworthy.

Hyper-V provide an additional level of isolation by using the hypervisor to create a separate copy of the operating system kernel for each container. The containers also have their own memory assigned to them and isolated storage and network I/O. This provides a container environment that is suitable for what Microsoft calls "hostile multi-tenant" applications, such as a case in which a business provides containers to clients for running their own code, which might not be trustworthy. Thus, with the addition of Hyper-V containers, Windows Server 2016 provides three levels of isolation, ranging from the separate operating system installation of Hyper-V virtual machines, to the separate kernel and memory of Hyper-V containers, to the shares kernel and other resources of Windows Server Containers.

Windows Server 2016 and Docker

Windows Server 2016 includes a Containers, which you must install before you can create either type of container in Windows. However, the tool you use to create and manage containers is a third-party product called Docker. Docker consists of APIs, a Windows service, and a client program, which enable you to create containers out of existing image files.

Docker is an application that was originally created for the creation and management of containers on Linux systems. Now ported to Windows, you use Docker to create and manage both Windows Server Containers and Hyper-V containers. In fact, the two types of containers are interchangeable. You can create an image for a Windows Server Container and later run it in a Hyper-V container without modification.

> ***NOTE*** **CONTAINER PORTABILITY**
>
> While Windows-based containers are interchangeable between Windows Server Containers and Hyper-V containers, Windows containers are not interchangeable with Linux containers. You cannot run a Linux container in Windows, nor can you run a Windows container on a Linux machine. This is because the kernel APIs of the two operating systems are not compatible.

Install and configure Hyper-V containers

To install support for containers in Windows Server 2016, you must first add the Containers feature, either by running the Add Roles and Features Wizard in Server Manager, or by using the Install-WindowsFeature cmdlet in a Windows PowerShell session with administrative privileges, as follows:

```
install-windowsfeature -name containers -restart
```

The Containers feature provides operating system support for both Windows Server Containers and Hyper-V containers, but it does not include the Docker application. You must download and install this yourself.

Docker consists of two files, as follows:

- **Dockerd.exe** The Docker service, which runs in the background on the Windows computer

- **Docker.exe** The Docker client, a command line tool that you use to create and manage containers

There is no automatic installer for these files. You must create a folder on your computer called C:\Program Files\Docker and use the following two Invoke-WebRequest commands in PowerShell to download them.

```
invoke-webrequest -uri https://aka.ms/tp5/b/dockerd -outfile "c:\program files\docker\
dockerd.exe"
invoke-webrequest -uri https://aka.ms/tp5/b/docker -outfile "c:\program files\docker\
docker.exe"
```

With the Docker program files in place, you can then register the Dockerd program as a service by performing the following command from a Command Prompt with administrative privileges:

```
dockerd --register-service
```

> **NOTE** **PERFORMING DOCKER COMMANDS**
>
> Note that this, and other, Docker commands sometimes use double hyphens to proceed command line parameters.

Finally, start the docker service using the PowerShell Start-Service cmdlet, as follows:

```
start-service -name docker -force
```

With the docker service running, you can now use the docker client to download the images needed to create a new container. For example, the following command downloads the latest Nano Server container image from the Docker repository.

```
docker pull microsoft/windowsservercore
```

Once the download is complete, it is time to create a new container from the image. The following docker command creates a new Windows Server Container from the Nano Server image

```
docker run -it microsoft/windowsservercore cmd
```

This command creates a container from the windowsservercore image you downloaded and executes the cmd command in the container, opening a command prompt window. If you examine the files displayed by the `dir` command, you can see that you are interacting with a clean OS installation inside the container, not the host computer.

Type exit to return to the PowerShell session on the host computer, and you can use the following command to display the containers running on the system, as shown in Figure 6-15.

```
docker ps
```

FIGURE 6-15 Output of the docker ps command

To create a Hyper-V container, you must have the Hyper-V role installed on the host computer. Then, you execute the same command, with the addition of the isolation parameter, as in the following example:

```
docker run -it --isolation=hyperv microsoft/windowsservercore cmd
```

Once you have created a container, you can use the following Docker commands to manage it. The commands typically take the form of a keyword, followed by the container ID, and then any other necessary parameters. To display the help screen for a command, run the command with the help parameter.

- **Docker stop** Stops a running container
- **Docker start** Starts a stopped container
- **Docker restart** Restarts a container
- **Docker exec** Executes a command in a running container
- **Docker commit** Creates a new image from a modified container
- **Docker cp** Copies files between the container operating system and the host operating system

Skill 6.2: Implement a Secure File Services infrastructure and Dynamic Access Control

File sharing is one of the primary functions of the data network. While Windows has provided file system security since its inception, in the form of permissions, it is only relatively recently that Windows has gone beyond that, to provide a more secure and more flexible file services infrastructure. File Server Resource Manager is a tool that administrators can use to apply storage quotas to users, screen files, and generate reports on storage use.

Dynamic Access Control (DAC) is a system by which administrators can assign permissions to users based on predefined sets of rules. For example, a user in a management role might be granted access to files that other users cannot. In addition, that same user might be able to access the files from an office computer, but not from a home computer. By creating rules of this type, you can build a self-sustaining system of permission assignments, to accommodate users as they change jobs and files as their security requirements change.

This section covers how to:

- Install the File Server Resource Manager role service
- Configure quotas
- Configure file screens
- Configure storage reports
- Configure file management tasks
- Configure File Classification Infrastructure using FSRM
- Implement Work Folders
- Configure user and device claim types
- Create and configure resource properties and lists
- Create and configure Central Access rules and policies
- Implement policy changes and staging
- Configure file access auditing
- Perform access-denied remediation

Install the File Server Resource Manager role service

File Server Resource Manager (FSRM) is a Microsoft Management Console (MMC) snap-in that enables administrators to monitor and regulate the storage resources consumed by network users. Although the price of hard disk storage continues to decrease, network users still have a tendency to consume all of the storage space that administrators allocate to them. In addition, the increasingly common use of high definition audio and video files means that single files can be several gigabytes in size, adding to rapid disk space consumption.

In an enterprise environment, it is important for administrators to monitor and regulate the amount of storage space consumed by users, so that server resources are not over-whelmed by irresponsible user storage practices.

When you install the File Server Resource Manager role service in the File and Storage Services role, Windows Server 2016 installs a graphical tool that enables file server adminis-trators to monitor and regulate their server storage, by performing the following tasks:

- Establish quotas that limit the amount of storage space allotted to each user
- Create screens that prevent users from storing specific types of files on server drives
- Create templates that simplify the process of applying quotas and screens
- Automatically send notifications to users and/or administrators when quotas are ex-ceeded or nearly exceeded
- Generate reports providing details of users' storage activities

To install File Server Resource Manager, you can use the Add Roles and Features Wizard in Server Manager. By default, Windows Server 2016 installs the File Server and Storage Services role services, which are part of the File and Storage Services role, as shown in Figure 6-16. File Server Resource Manager is another role service in that role, which you can add using the wizard by selecting the appropriate checkbox.

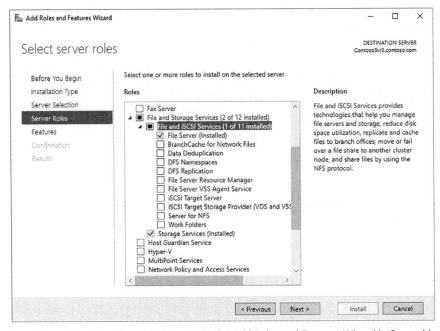

FIGURE 6-16 The Select Server Roles page in the Add Roles and Features Wizard in Server Manager

To install File Server Resource Manager using Windows PowerShell, you can open a PowerShell session with administrative privileges and run the Install-WindowsFeature cmdlet, specifying the role service using the -Name parameter, as in the following example:

```
install-windowsfeature -name fs-resource-manager
```

The resulting output of a successful installation is shown in Figure 6-17.

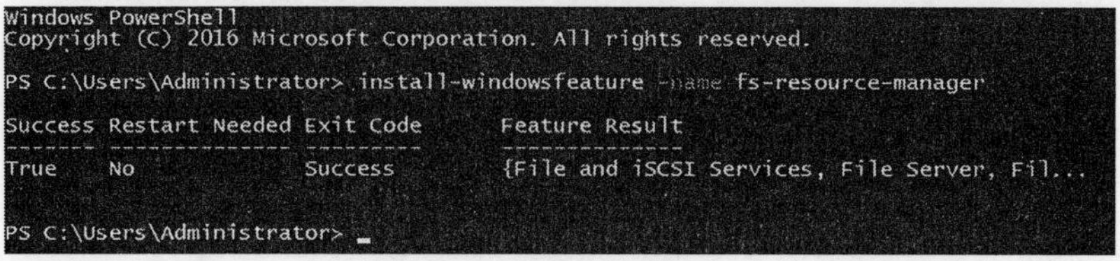

```
Windows PowerShell
Copyright (C) 2016 Microsoft Corporation. All rights reserved.

PS C:\Users\Administrator> install-windowsfeature -name fs-resource-manager

Success Restart Needed Exit Code      Feature Result
-------  -------------- ---------      --------------
True     No             Success        {File and iSCSI Services, File Server, Fil...

PS C:\Users\Administrator> _
```

FIGURE 6-17 Output of a PowerShell feature installation

> **NOTE** **DISPLAYING POWERSHELL FEATURE NAMES**
>
> To display the PowerShell names for the Windows roles and features that are available for installation, run the Get-WindowsFeature cmdlet.

Configure quotas

Quotas, in File Server Resource Manager, are settings that can warn administrators of trends in excessive storage utilization, or they can apply hard restrictions on the storage available to user accounts. A quota is simply a limit on the storage space a user is permitted to consume in a particular volume or folder.

Quotas are based on file ownership. Windows automatically makes a user the owner of all files that he or she creates on a server volume. The quota system tracks all of the files owned by each user and calculates their total size. When the total size of a given user's files reaches the quota specified by the server administrator, the system takes action, also specified by the administrator.

The actions the system can take when a user approaches or reaches a quota are highly configurable. For example, administrators can configure quotas to be hard or soft. A hard quota prohibits users from consuming any storage space beyond the allotted amount, while a soft quota allows the user additional storage space and just sends a notification to the user and/or administrator. Administrators can specify the thresholds at which the system should send notifications and configure the server to generate event log entries and reports in response to quota thresholds.

Creating quota templates

While it is possible to create a quota from scratch for each individual user, this is not a practical solution for an enterprise networks. Instead, FSRM enables you to create quota templates, to manage quota assignments on a large scale. A quota template is a collection of settings that defines the following:

- Whether a quota should be hard or soft

- What thresholds FSRM should apply to the quota
- What actions FSRM should take when a user reaches a threshold

The File Server Resource Manager console includes several predefined templates, which you can use to create your own template. To create a quota template, use the following procedure.

1. Using an account with administrator privileges, open File Server Resource Manager from the Tools menu in Server Manager. The File Server Resource Manager console appears, as shown in Figure 6-18.

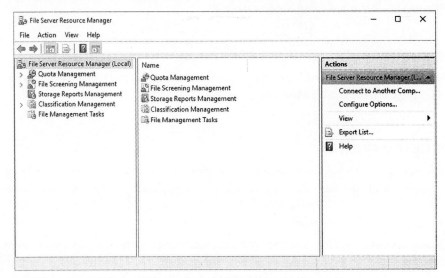

FIGURE 6-18 The File Server Resource Manager console

2. Expand the Quota Management node and select Quota Templates to display the predefined templates included with FSRM, as shown in Figure 6-19.

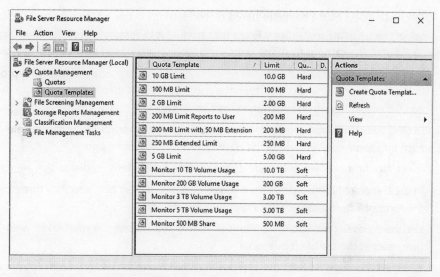

FIGURE 6-19 Predefined Quota Templates

3. Right-click the Quota Templates node and, from the context menu, select Create Quota Template. The Create Quota Template dialog box appears, as shown in Figure 6-20.

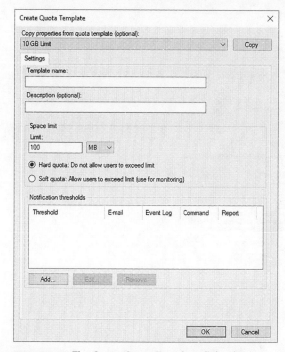

FIGURE 6-20 The Create Quota Template dialog box

4. To create a new quota template based on the settings in one of the existing templates, select the template in the Copy Properties from Quota Template drop-down list and click Copy. The settings from the template appear in the dialog box, so that you can modify them as needed.

5. In the Template Name text box, type the name you use to identify the template. Type additional identifying information in the Description text box, if desired.

6. In the Space Limit box, specify the amount of storage space you want to allocate to each individual user and select the Hard Quota or Soft Quota option.

7. In the Notification Thresholds box, click Add. The Add Threshold dialog box appears.

8. In the Generate Notifications When Usage Reaches (%) text box, specify a threshold in the form of a percentage of the storage quota you specified.

9. Use the controls on the following tabs to specify the actions you want taken when a user reaches the specified threshold:

   ■ **Email Message** Select the appropriate checkboxes to specify whether you want the system to send an email message to an administrator, to the user, or both, as shown in Figure 6-21. For administrators, you can specify the email addresses of one or more persons separated by semicolons. For the user, you can modify the text of the default email message.

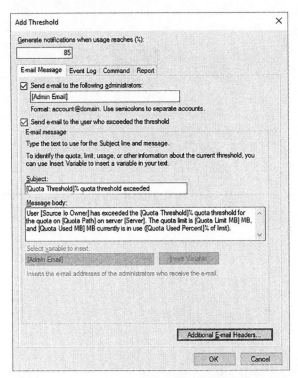

FIGURE 6-21 The Email Message tab in the Add Threshold dialog box

To send email messages, the Windows Server 2016 computer must be running the Simple Mail Transfer Protocol (SMTP) service. To install SMTP, you can use Server Manager to add the SMTP Server feature or use PowerShell to install the SMTP-Server feature with the InstallWindowsFeature cmdlet.

- **Event Log** Select the Send Warning to Event Log checkbox to create a log entry when a user reaches the threshold, as shown in Figure 6-22. You can modify the wording of the log entry in the text box provided.

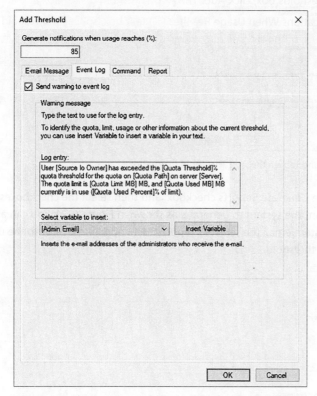

FIGURE 6-22 The Event Log tab on the Add Threshold dialog box

- **Command** Select the Run This Command or Script checkbox to specify a program or script file that the system should execute when a user reaches the threshold, as shown in Figure 6-23. You can also specify command arguments, a working directory, and the type of account the system should use to run the program or script.

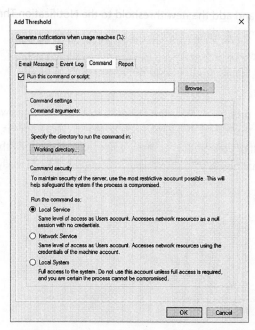

FIGURE 6-23 The Command tab on the Add Threshold dialog box

■ **Report** Select the Generate Reports checkbox, and then select the checkboxes for the reports you want the system to generate, as shown in Figure 6-24. You can also specify that the system email the selected reports to an administrator or to the user who exceeded the threshold.

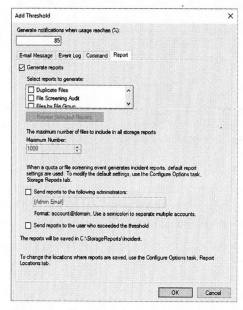

FIGURE 6-24 The Report tab on the Add Threshold dialog box

10. Click OK to close the dialog box and add the new threshold to the Notification Thresholds list on the Create Quota Template dialog box.

11. Repeat steps 7–10 to create additional thresholds, if desired. When you have created all of the thresholds you need, click OK to create the quota template.

12. Close the File Server Resource Manager console.

Using quota templates simplifies the process of managing quotas, in much the same way as assigning permissions to groups, rather than users. If you use a template to create quotas, and you want to change the properties of all of your quotas at once, you can simply modify the template, and the system applies the changes to all of the associated quotas automatically.

Creating quotas

After you have created your quota templates, you can create the quotas themselves. To create a quota, use the following procedure.

1. In the FSRM console, expand the Quota Management node, right-click the Quotas folder and, from the context menu, select Create Quota. The Create Quota dialog box appears, as shown in Figure 6-25.

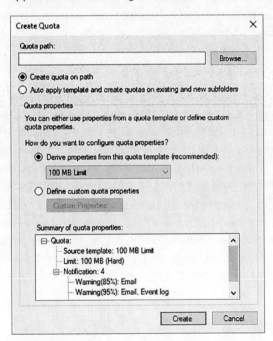

FIGURE 6-25 The Create Quota dialog box

2. In the Quota Path text box, type or browse to the name of the volume or folder for which you want to create a quota.

3. Select one of the following application options.

- **Create quota on path**   Creates a single quota for the specified volume or folder.
- **Auto apply template and create quotas on existing and new subfolders**   Causes FSRM to automatically create a quota, based on a template, for each subfolder in the designated path, and for every new subfolder created in that path.

4. Select one of the following properties options:

   - **Derive properties from this quota template**   Configures the quota using the settings of the template you select from the drop-down list.
   - **Define custom quota properties**   Enables you to specify custom settings for the quota. Clicking the Custom Properties button opens a Quota Properties dialog box for the selected volume or folder, which contains the same controls as the Create Quota Template dialog box.

5. Click Create. The new quota appears in the console's details pane.

Even if you do not install the File Server Resource Manager role service, a different type of quota is available on NTFS volumes. However, these *NTFS quotas* are limited to controlling storage on entire volumes, on a per-user basis. When you create FSRM quotas for volumes or folders, they apply to all users. NTFS quotas are also limited to creating event log entries only, while FSRM quotas can also send email notifications, execute commands, and generate reports, as well as log events.

Configure file screens

FSRM, in addition to creating storage quotas, enables administrators to create file screens, which restrict access to storage by preventing users from saving specific types of files on a server drive. Administrators typically use file screening to keep large audio and video files off of server drives because they can consume a lot of space and most users do not need them to complete their work. Obviously, in an organization that utilizes these types of files, screening them would be inappropriate, but you can configure FSRM to screen files of any type.

The process of creating file screens is similar to that of creating storage quotas. You choose the types of files you want to screen and then specify the actions you want the server to take when a user attempts to store a forbidden file type. As with quotas, the server can send emails, create log entries, execute commands, and generate reports. Administrators can also create file screen templates that simplify the process of deploying file screens throughout the enterprise.

To create a file screen, use the following procedure.

1. In FSRM, expand the File Screening Management node and select File Screens. Then, right-click the File Screens container and, from the context menu, select Create File Screen. The Create File Screen dialog box appears, as shown in Figure 6-26.

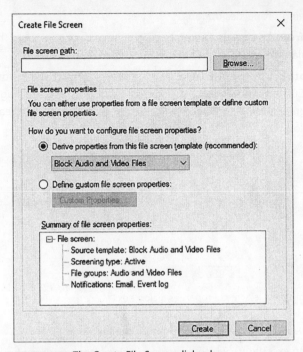

FIGURE 6-26 The Create File Screen dialog box

2. In the File Screen Path text box, type or browse to the name of the volume or folder you want to screen.

3. Select one of the following properties options:

   - **Derive properties from the file screen template** Configures the file screen using the settings of the template you select from the drop-down list.

   - **Define custom file screen properties** Enables you to specify custom settings for the file screen. Clicking the Custom Properties button opens a File Screen Properties dialog box for the selected volume or folder, which contains the Settings tab shown in Figure 6-27, plus the same Email Message, Event Log, Command, and Report tabs as the Quota Properties dialog box.

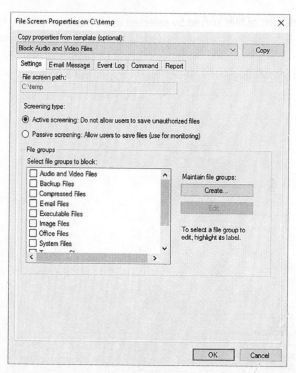

FIGURE 6-27 The Settings tab of a File Screen Properties dialog box

4. Click Create. The new file screen appears in the console's details pane.

You can also create file screen exceptions, which override the file screening rules inherited from a parent folder. For example, if you are screening out audio and video files from a particular volume, and you need to store these types of files in one folder, you can create an exception only for that folder.

Configure Storage Reports

Reporting is one of the most important tools for efficient storage management. File Server Resource Manager can generate a variety of reports that enable administrators to examine the state of their file server volumes and identify transgressors of company storage policies.

FSRM can create the following report types:

- **Duplicate Files** Creates a list of files that are the same size and have the same last modified date.

- **File Screening Audit** Creates a list of the audit events generated by file screening violations for specific users during a specific time period.

- **Files By File Group** Creates a list of files sorted by selected file groups in the File Server Resource Manager console.

- **Files By Owner**   Creates a list of files sorted by selected users that own them.
- **Files by Property**   Creates a list of files sorted by the values of a specified classification property
- **Folders By Property**   Creates a list of folders sorted by the values of a specified secure classification property
- **Large Files**   Creates a list of files conforming to a specified file spec that are a specified size or larger.
- **Least Recently Accessed Files**   Creates a list of files conforming to a specified file spec that have not been accessed for a specified number of days.
- **Most Recently Accessed Files**   Creates a list of files conforming to a specified file spec that have been accessed within a specified number of days.
- **Quota Usage**   Creates a list of quotas that exceed a specified percentage of the storage limit.

Using the FSRM console, you can generate reports on the fly or schedule their creation on a regular basis. To schedule a report, use the following procedure.

1. Select the Storage Reports Management node. Then right-click Storage Reports Management and, from the context menu, select Schedule a New Report Task. The Storage Reports Task Properties dialog box appears, as shown in Figure 6-28.

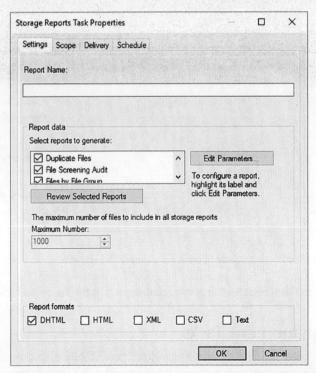

FIGURE 6-28 The Settings tab of the Storage Reports Task Properties dialog box

2. On the Settings tab, in the Report Data box, select the reports that you want to generate. When you select a report and click Edit Parameters, a Report Parameters dialog box appears, in which you can configure the parameters for that specific report.

3. In the Report Formats box, select the checkboxes for the formats you want FSRM to use when creating the reports.

4. On the Scope tab, select the checkboxes corresponding to the data types you want the report to include.

5. Click Add and, in the Browse For Folder dialog box that appears, select the volume or folder on which you want a report. Repeat this step to select multiple volumes or folders, if desired.

6. If you want FSRM to send the reports to administrators via email, click the Delivery tab and select the Send Reports To The Following Administrators checkbox. Then enter one or more email addresses (separated by semicolons) in the text box.

7. Click the Schedule tab and select the time when you want FSRM to run the reports. Then, select the frequency of the reports by selecting Weekly or Monthly, and/or the days of the week to run the report.

8. Click OK to close the Storage Reports Task Properties dialog box and add the new report to the schedule, as shown in Figure 6-29.

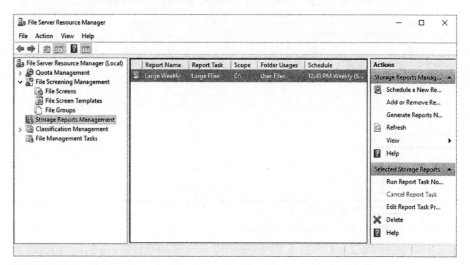

FIGURE 6-29 The Storage Reports Management node with a report scheduled

The report is now added to the schedule. The system generates it at the specified time.

Configure File Management Tasks

The File Management Tasks folder in FSRM enables administrators to schedule actions to occur on specific files and folders based on specific criteria. For example, you can create a task that cause all files in a specific folder that have not been accessed in six months to be moved to an archive location. FSRM calls this File Expiration. You can also configure selected files to be encrypted, or execute a custom task on them.

To create a file management task, use the following procedure.

1. In FSRM, select the File Management Tasks node. Then right-click File Management Tasks and, from the context menu, select Create File Management Task. The Create File Management Task dialog box appears.

2. On the General tab, specify a Task Name and (optionally) a Description. Make sure the Enabled checkbox is selected.

3. On the Scope tab, shown in Figure 6-30, specify the files or folders you want to manage, by selecting from the file type checkboxes and/or clicking Add to add files or folders to the list.

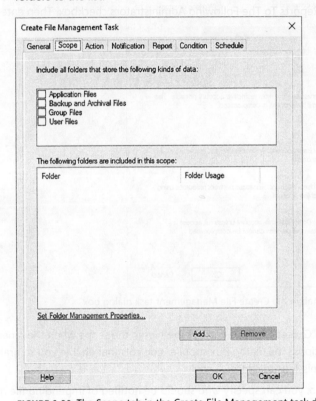

FIGURE 6-30 The Scope tab in the Create File Management task dialog box

4. On the Action tab, use the Type drop-down list to select one of the following actions to be taken on the files in the scope. Each selection presents a different set of the controls on the tab.

- **File Expiration** Causes the files in the scope to be moved to a specified location when they meet the selected conditions.

- **Custom** Enables you to configure an external program to run against the files in the scope when they meet the selected conditions. The dialog box supplies controls (shown in Figure 6-31) that enable you to specify an executable to run and command line arguments, as well as select the account the system should use to execute the program.

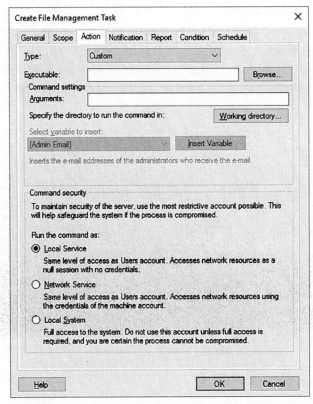

FIGURE 6-31 The Action tab in the Create File Management task dialog box

- **RMS Encryption** Causes FSRM to encrypt the files in the scope when they meet the selected conditions. The dialog box supplies controls that enable you to grant access control permissions to specific users.

5. On the Notification tab, you can specify who should be notified of impending file management actions, using email messages, event log entries, or external commands.

6. On the Report tab, you specify the types of logs and reports FSRM should maintain on the file maintenance task.

7. On the Condition tab, shown in Figure 6-32, you specify the criteria the system uses to select files in the scope for management. You can create conditions based on classification properties you have created in FSRM; file creation, modification, and last accessed dates; or file name patterns using wildcard characters.

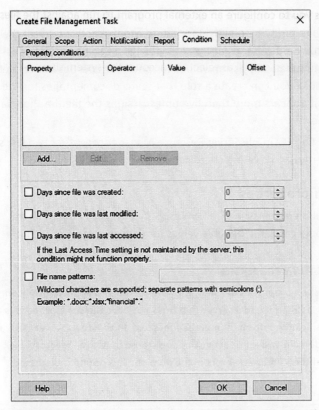

FIGURE 6-32 The Condition tab in the Create File Management task dialog box

8. On the Schedule tab, you select the time when you want FSRM to execute the file maintenance task and the frequency when the task should be repeated, by selecting Weekly or Monthly, and/or the days of the week.

9. Click OK to close the dialog box and create the new file management task.

The task appears in the File Management Tasks pane, and execute according to the schedule you specified.

Configure File Classification Infrastructure using FSRM

Since long before Windows, files have had properties that contain information about them, such as who created them and the date they were created and last modified. The File Classification Infrastructure (FCI) in FSRM enables administrators to create additional properties for files, based on the specific needs of the organization. You can, for example, create a classification property called Security Level and assign it the values High, Medium, and Low. By classifying your files using these property values, you can run a file management task in FSRM to encrypt all documents with a High Security Level.

FCI is more than just additional properties that you can manually configure on individual files, however. It would hardly be practical for administrators to have to set the Security Level property value on thousands of files individually. FCI also includes classification rules, which can automatically assign values to specific properties based on the contents of a file. For example, you can create a rule that scans document files for the word "confidential" and, if it appears more than five times, assigns the file the High value for the Security Level property.

The process of implementing FCI in File Server Resource Manager consists of two steps: creating classification properties and creating classification rules.

Creating classification properties

When you create a classification property in FSRM, you specify the type of data that the property contains and, in some cases, the possible values for the property.

> **NOTE** **LOCAL CLASSIFICATION PROPERTIES**
>
> When you create classification properties in FSRM, they are stored and applied locally on the server. If you move a classified file to a server that does not have the same properties configured, then any classification information in the file is lost. In Windows Server 2016, it is also possible to create domain-wide properties that are stored in Active Directory, making them available to all of the Windows servers in the domain. This option is discussed later in the chapter.

To create a local classification property in FSRM, use the following procedure:

1. In FSRM, expand the Classification Management node and select Classification Properties. Three default properties appear in the console.

2. Right-click Classification Properties and, from the context menu, select Create Local Property. The Create Local Classification Property dialog box appears.

3. Specify a Name and Description for the new property, and use the Property Type drop-down list (shown in Figure 6-33) to select from the following types:

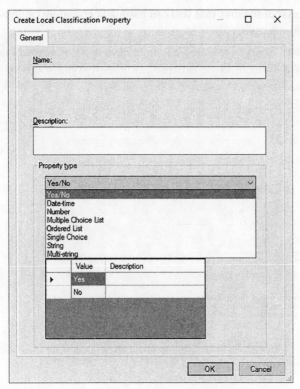

FIGURE 6-33 The Create Local Classification Property dialog box

- **Yes/No** Indicates that the property value contains only the value Yes or the value No.

- **Date-time** Indicates that the property value contains only a timestamp specifying the date and time of an event.

- **Number** Indicates that the property value contains only a simple number.

- **Multiple Choice List** Specifies a list of values that the property can contain, with the ability to choose multiple values, such as a list of file types, several of which can apply to a single file.

- **Ordered List** Specifies a list of values that the property can contain, with priorities established by a specific order, such as High, Medium, and Low for a property indicating a security level.

- **Single Choice** Specifies a list of values that the property can contain, with the ability to choose only one value, such as a list of countries of origin, only one of which can apply to a single file.

- **String** Indicates that the property contains only a specified text string, such as the contact email address of the person responsible for the security of the file.

- **Multi-String** Indicates that the property contains a list of specified text strings, such as multiple email addresses.

4. Depending on the Property Type you choose, you might have to enter the possible values for the property. For example, in the Ordered List property type, you enter the range of values in the array provided, as shown in Figure 6-34.

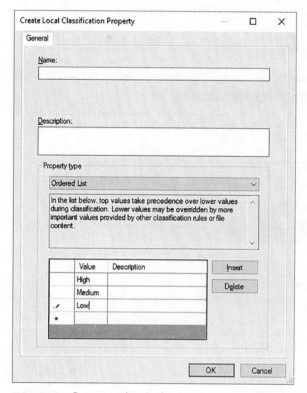

FIGURE 6-34 Property values in the Create Local Classification Property dialog box

5. Click OK to create the property and add it to the console.

Creating classification rules

Creating classification properties specifies the type of data that the new file properties contain and, in some cases, the property values themselves. However, that process does not specify how the system determines what property value (or values) it should assign to a particular file. For this to occur, you must create classification rules in FSRM.

To create a classification rule, use the following procedure.

1. In FSRM, select the Classification Rules node. Right-click Classification Rules and, from the context menu, select Create Classification Rule. The Create Classification Rule dialog box appears.

2. Specify a Rule Name and Description for the new rule.

3. On the Scope tab, specify the files or folders to which you want to apply the rule, by selecting from the file type checkboxes and/or clicking Add to add files or folders to the list.

4. On the Classification tab, you select a Classification Method. Then, you specify the property, and the value for that property, that you want to apply with the rule, as shown in Figure 6-35.

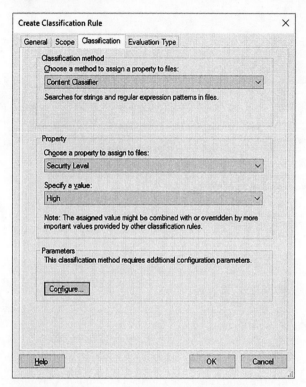

FIGURE 6-35 The Create Classification Rule dialog box

5. Click Configure to open the Classification Parameters dialog box. This is where you specify how the system should identify a file as conforming with the property value you selected. In this example, the organization always inserts the word Confidential in the header and footer on each page of all sensitive documents. Therefore, this rule uses the Content Classifier method to scan the files in the scope for the word Confidential. If the word appears five or more times in a file, the Security Level property is assigned the value High.

6. In the Parameters area, in the Expression text box, type the word Confidential and set the Minimum Occurrences value to 5, as shown in Figure 6-36. Then click OK to close the Classification Parameters dialog box.

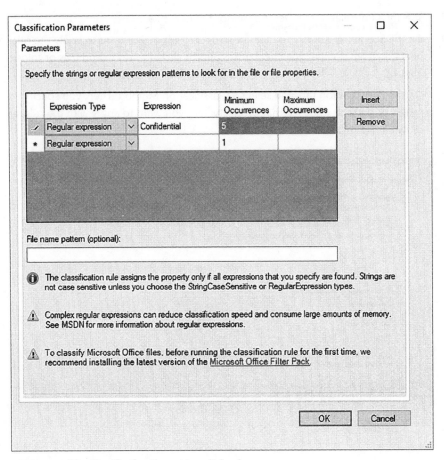

FIGURE 6-36 The Classification Parameters dialog box

7. Click OK to create the rule and close the Create Classification Rule dialog box.

Once you have created your properties and rules, you can select Configure Classification Schedule in the FSRM console's Action pane to specify when the classification should occur. You can also select Run Classification With All Rules Now to execute the classification process immediately.

Once the classification is completed, every file in the scope should list the properties you created on the classification tab of its Properties sheet. For files that conform to the parameters of the rule you created, the Security Level property is assigned the value High, as shown in Figure 6-37.

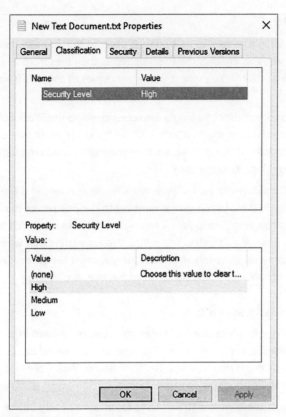

FIGURE 6-37 Classification properties assigned to a file

Implement Work Folders

Work Folders is a Windows Server 2016 role service that enables users to synchronize their work documents with a central server. This enables the users to access their files from any device, anywhere, and enables administrators to protect the server copies of the files from accidental deletion or other damage.

A simple Work Folders deployment consists of a single file server running the Work Folders role server, on which you have created a sync share, which is where the users' work files are located. Onsite users configure their workstations to access the sync share, or administrators configure the workstations remotely using Group Policy.

In a more complex deployment, there might be multiple Work Folders servers at different sites, in which case you must see to it that each user is directed to the one server that contains his or her files. You can do this with Group Policy settings, or have users search for the correct server by supplying their email addresses. You might also have users that want to access their work files from home or while traveling, in which case you must set up a reverse proxy, so that they can connect to the Work Folders server from the Internet.

Installing the Work Folders role service

To install the Work Folders role service, you use the Add Roles and Features Wizard in Server Manager. Work Folders is part of the File and Storage Services role, and is located under File and iSCSI Services. The installation prompts you to install the IIS Hostable Web Core feature, which is a minimal version of Internet Information Services (IIS).

To use Work Folders in a production environment, you have to obtain a Secure Sockets Layer (SSL) certificate for the server and bind it to the Default Web Site created by the IIS Hostable Web Core. You do this using the Internet Information Services (IIS) Manager console on another computer to connect to the Web Folders server.

To install Work Folders using PowerShell instead, you use the Install-WindowsFeature cmdlet, as follows:

```
install-windowsfeature -name fs-syncshareservice
```

Creating Work Folders Groups

Work folders requires dedicated domain security groups, as follows:

- **User groups**   For each sync share you plan to create, create a domain security group whose members are the users that are permitted to use that share
- **Administrator group**   If you plan to deploy multiple Work Folders servers on your network, create a domain security group whose members are the Work Folders administrators. The members of this group are able to modify a user object attribute specifying the server that each user uses.

You can create the groups using Active Directory Administrative Center, Active Directory Users and Computers, or the New-ADGroup cmdlet in Windows PowerShell.

Creating sync shares

Once you have installed the Work Folder role service, you can create a sync share on the server using Server Manager. To create a sync share, use the following procedure.

1. On the Server Manager Dashboard, click File and Storage Services\Work Folders. The Work Folders pane appears.

2. From the Task menu, select New Sync Share. The New Sync Share Wizard appears.

3. On the Server and Path page, select the local server. Under Location, select Enter a Local Path and type the path to the folder on a local drive where you want to create the work folders.

4. On the User Folder Structure page, select one of the following options to specify the format of the folders that Work Folders creates for each user:

   ■ **User Alias** Creates folder named for the user account only. This provides compatibility with other data storage solutions, such as Folder Redirection.

   ■ **User Alias@domain** Creates folder named for the user account with the domain name. This eliminates problems caused by duplicate account names in different domains.

5. On the Sync Share Name page, specify a Name and Description for the sync share.

6. On the Sync Access page, add the user groups you created that contain the individuals who use Work Folders.

7. On the PC Security Policies page, specify whether you want to encrypt the Work Folders and whether you want to secure users' devices by locking their screens after fifteen minutes and requiring a six-character password unlock it again. This setting also implements a device lockout after ten unsuccessful unlock attempts.

8. Review your settings on the Confirmation page and click Create.

9. When the sync share is created, click Close.

You can also create a sync share using the NewSyncShare cmdlet in Windows PowerShell, as in the following example:

```
new-syncshare "work" c:\work -user "domain users"
```

Configuring Work Folders clients

Once the Work Folders server is configured, you can set up the client half of the application on your workstations. The Windows workstation operating systems include a Work Folders application in the Control Panel, which users can employ to set up Work Folders themselves. To perform a mass deployment, administrators can use Group Policy settings.

To configure Work Folders client manually, use the following procedure:

1. Open Control Panel and, in System and Security, launch the Work Folders application.

2. Click Set Up Work Folders. The Enter Work Email page appears, as shown in Figure 6-38.

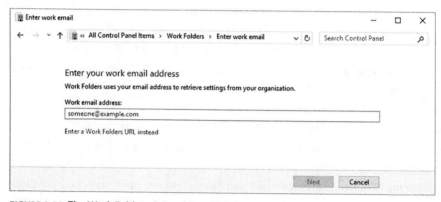

FIGURE 6-38 The Work Folders Control Panel application

3. Type the email address of a user that is a member of the users group you created earlier. Alternatively, you can click the Enter a Work Folders URL Instead link and type the URL of the Work Folders server to use. The format for the server's URL is *https:// servername.domain.com.*

4. After authenticating as the user, on the Introducing Work Folders page, you can click Change to modify the default location of the Work Folders directory on the local drive.

5. The Security Policies page lists the changes that administrators can make to the PC through the Work Folders feature. Select the I Accept These Policies On My PC checkbox.

6. Click Set Up Work Folders. The Work Folders Has Started Syncing With This PC page appears.

The setup process creates a folder on both the client and the server, the contents of which are synchronized. At this point, when there are no changes to the files in the client's Work Folders directory, the client attempts to sync with the server every ten minutes, seeking modifications to its folder on the server. Adding or modifying a file in the client Work Folder directory triggers an immediate sync. When the client initiates a sync with the server, the server informs the client of any changes to files in the server folder, and transfers them as needed.

A user can then log on from any workstation, set up Work Folders, and establish a sync relationship with the Work Folders server. The folders on the servers and the workstations and then remain synchronized.

Configure user and device claim types

File Server Resource Manager enables you to classify the files stored on a server by creating classification properties and applying property values using classification rules. Dynamic Access Control (DAC) is an Active Directory technology that take this concept farther. Using DAC you can configure Active Directory to automatically assign access control permissions based on more complex scenarios than were ever possible using just NTFS and share permissions, and which extend to an entire domain, rather than a single server.

DAC components

DAC is based on three components that work together to define these scenarios: resource properties, claim types, and central access rules.

For example, you might have confidential files stored on a server that are flagged as such using *resource properties*. These are similar to the classification properties in FSRM, except that they are stored in Active Directory. Windows Server 2016 includes a large collection of resource properties that you can assign to files, or you can create your own. You then deploy them to your file servers using Windows PowerShell.

These confidential files are to be accessible only by corporate users at the director level or above. Those users are identified by *user claims*, which are attributes that specify characteristics of the network users, such as their ranks in the corporate hierarchy.

The confidential files must also be accessible only by users working in the corporate home office in Chicago. The company workstations, therefore, can be identified by *device claims* that specify their locations. User and device claims are Active Directory attributes associated, in this case, with the user and computer objects. You can create claim types based on existing object attributes, or you can extend the Active Directory schema to create new ones.

The third component, *central access rules*, ties the DAC components together by defining the conditional statements that govern the access control assignments. To define the conditions for access to the confidential files mentioned earlier, you might create a central access rule that states that access to the confidential files is to be granted only when the following conditions are met:

- File resource property: Security = High
- User claim: Rank = Director
- Computer claim: Location = Chicago

In other words, the central access rule states that when the Security resource property of a file is High, access is granted only when the Rank user claim is at least Director and the Location computer claim is Chicago.

This is a simple example of the types of scenarios you can define using DAC. You can create any number of resource properties, user claims, and device claims, and combine them in central access rules that are far more complex than this one. A collection of central access rules is called a *central access policy* (CAP), which you deploy using Group Policy settings.

EXAM TIP

When preparing for the 70-744 exam, be sure to remain conscious of the differences in scope between the local properties and rules that you create in File Server Resource Manager and the domain-based Dynamic Access Control elements that you create in Active Directory Administrative Center, such as claim types, resource properties, and central access rules. The DAC elements are global and available to all of the file servers in the domain. The FSRM rules and properties affect only the local file system. If you want to deploy FSRM rules and properties throughout your network, you must create them on each file server individually.

Creating claim types

To create claim types, and the other DAC elements, you use the Active Directory Administrative Center console, as in the following procedure.

1. Open the Active Directory Administrative Center from Server Manager's Tools menu.
2. In the left pane, click the Dynamic Access Control arrow and select Claim Types. The Claim Types pane appears, with only a single claim type listed.
3. In the Tasks pane, click New | Claim Type. The Create Claim Type dialog box appears.
4. Under Source Attribute, select an Active Directory attribute from the list, using the Filter search box to locate one, if necessary, as shown in Figure 6-39.

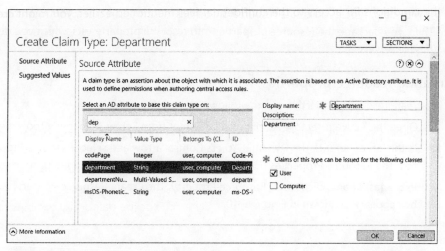

FIGURE 6-39 The Create Claim Type dialog box

5. In the Display Name text box, specify a friendly name for the claim type.

6. Select the User or Computer checkbox to specify the object type to associate with the claim.

7. In the left pane, click Suggested Values and select the The Following Values Are Suggested option.

8. Click Add. The Add a Suggested Value dialog box appears.

9. In the Value text box, type one of the possible values for the attribute you selected. In the Display Name text box, type the name by which you want the value to appear. For example, if you are creating a claim type from the Department attribute, you might want to add suggested values such as Sales, Marketing, and IT.

10. Click OK to add the suggested value and repeat steps 8 to 9 to create additional values.

11. Click OK to close the dialog box and create the claim type.

Create and configure resource properties and lists

Resource properties are similar in function to the classification properties you can create in File Server Resource Manager. They contain metadata that you can add to files and folders. The primary difference is that resource properties are stored in Active Directory, and are therefore available to any file server in the domain. This prevents you from having to create the same classification properties in FSRM on every file server.

Later, you can create central access rules that associate user and device claims with resource properties, to determine what permissions should be applied to the files.

As with claim types, you create resource properties in Active Directory Administrative Center. Then, you package the resource properties into resource property lists, which you deploy to your file servers.

Creating resource properties

To create resource properties, use the following procedure.

1. Open the Active Directory Administrative Center from Server Manager's Tools menu.

2. In the left pane, click the Dynamic Access Control arrow and select Resource Properties. The Resource Properties pane appears, with a list of 16 predefined properties.

3. In the Tasks pane, click New | Resource Property. The Create Resource Property dialog box appears, as shown in Figure 6-40.

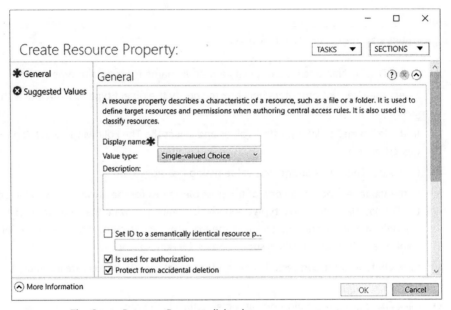

FIGURE 6-40 The Create Resource Property dialog box

4. In the Display Name text box, type a name for a property.

5. In the Value Type drop-down list, select an option that controls the nature of the property's values. The Value Type options are essentially the same as the Property Types in FSRM.

6. In the Suggested Values box, click Add. The Add a Suggested Value dialog box appears.

7. In the Value text box, type one of the possible values for the property. In the Display Name text box, type the name by which you want the value to appear. For example, if you are creating a resource property called Security Level, you might want to add suggested values such as High, Medium, and Low.

8. Click OK to add the value to the property.

9. Repeat steps 6 to 8 to create additional property values

10. Click OK to create the new resource property and add it to the list.

Newly-created resource properties are enabled by default, however, the predefined resource properties are not. To use one of the existing properties in the list, select it and click Enable in the Tasks list. You can also click Properties to open the Properties sheet for the selected resource property and modify it, such as by adding values.

For example, if you enable the Department resource property and examine its properties, you find that is already populated with a list of standard department names as values. To use this resource property, you might want to modify this list by adding or removing department name values.

Creating resource property lists

All of the resource properties you create are stored in the Active Directory database. To propagate them to the File Server Resource Manager console on your file servers, you must package them into *resource property lists*.

To create a new resource property list, use the following procedure.

1. Open the Active Directory Administrative Center from Server Manager's Tools menu.

2. In the left pane, click the Dynamic Access Control arrow and select Resource Property Lists. The Resource Property Lists pane appears, with one predefined list.

3. In the Tasks pane, click New | Resource Property List. The Create Resource Property List dialog box appears, as shown in Figure 6-41.

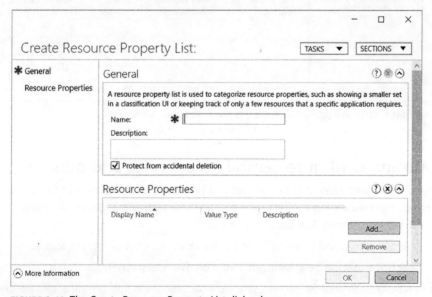

FIGURE 6-41 The Create Resource Property List dialog box

4. In the Name text box, type a name for the list.

5. Click Add. A Select Resource Properties dialog box appears.

6. In the list provided, select each property you want to add to the list and click the right arrow to add it to the Add the Following Resource Properties box.

7. Click OK to add the selected properties to the list.

8. Click OK to close the Create Resource Property List dialog box and create the new list.

Once you have created a resource property list, you can deploy it to a file server by opening a Windows PowerShell session with administrative privileges on the file server and running the following cmdlet, with no parameters.

```
Update-FSRMClassificationPropertyDefinition
```

Now, if you open FSRM and look at the Classification Properties pane, you see that the resources properties you created in Active Directory Administrative Center appear on the file server with a Global scope, as shown in Figure 6-42. You can now use these properties as you would the local ones you created in FSRM, assigning them to files and folders manually or by using local classification rules.

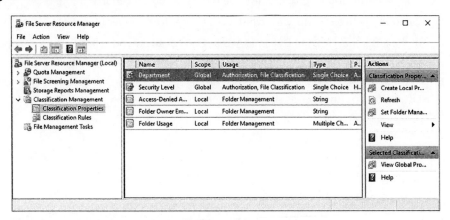

FIGURE 6-42 Global properties in the File Server Resource Manager

Create and configure central access rules and policies

Once you have created claim types and resource properties and have classified your files and folders, you can create central access rules that tie these elements together. A *central access rule* (CAR) has two primary functions, as follows:

- Selects the classified files and folders to which access control lists are applied
- Selects the users to be authorized, based on their claim types

To deploy CARs to your file servers, you must package them into central access policies (CAPs), which you add to Group Policy Settings.

Creating Central Access Rules

To create a central access rule, use the following procedure.

1. Open the Active Directory Administrative Center from Server Manager's Tools menu.

2. In the left pane, click the Dynamic Access Control arrow and select Central Access Rules. The Central Access Rules pane appears.

3. In the Tasks pane, click New | Central Access Rule. The Create Central Access Rule dialog box appears, as shown in Figure 6-43.

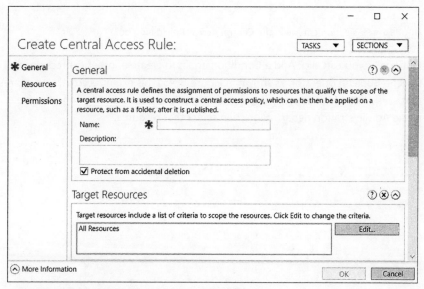

FIGURE 6-43 The Create Central Access Rule dialog box

4. In the Name text box, type a name for the rule.

5. In the Target Resources box, click Edit to open a Central Access Rule dialog box.

6. Click Add a Condition. Five drop-down lists appear, in which you select the criteria by which the rule selects the files and folders to which it assigns permissions. These drop-down lists are populated with the resource properties you have created and their values.

7. Select criteria from the drop-down lists to define an expression identifying the resources you want the rule to modify. For example, if you select the Security Level property in the second drop-down list, the values you defined for that property appear in the fifth drop-down list, as shown in Figure 6-44. If you select the value High, you are creating an expression that says "If the file's Security Level property value is equal to High, then select that resource."

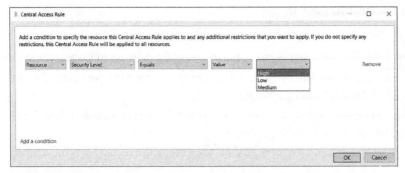

FIGURE 6-44 Selecting criteria in the Central Access Rule dialog box

8. Optionally, you can click Add a Condition again to create another expression, and select a Boolean operator, as shown in Figure 6-45. This example creates an expression that says, "If the file's Security Level property value is equal to High and the file exists in the Administration department, then select that resource."

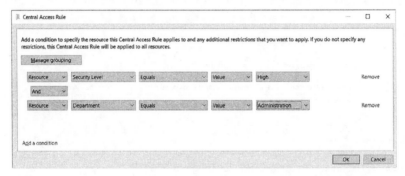

FIGURE 6-45 Creating a compound expression in the Central Access Rule dialog box

9. Click OK to close the dialog box and add the expression to Target Resources box.

10. In the Permissions box, select the Use the Following Permissions as Current Permissions option.

11. Click Edit to open the Advanced Security Settings for Permissions dialog box.

12. Click Add to add users or groups and specify the permissions they should receive to the files or folders selected by the target resources expression. For example, you might grant the Managers group the Allow Read and Allow Write permissions, and the Directors group the Allow Full Control permission, as shown in Figure 6-46.

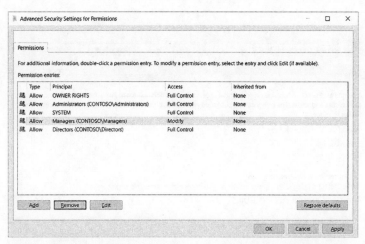

FIGURE 6-46 The Advanced Security Settings for Permissions dialog box

13. Click OK to add the permissions you created to the Permissions list.

14. Click OK to close the dialog box and add the new rule to the Central Access Rules pane.

Creating central access policies

A central access policy (CAP) is simply a package that contains one or more central access rules for deployment. To create a CAP, use the following procedure.

1. Open the Active Directory Administrative Center from Server Manager's Tools menu.

2. In the left pane, click the Dynamic Access Control arrow and select Central Access Policies. The Central Access Policies pane appears.

3. In the Tasks pane, click New | Central Access Policy. The Create Central Access Policy dialog box appears, as shown in Figure 6-47.

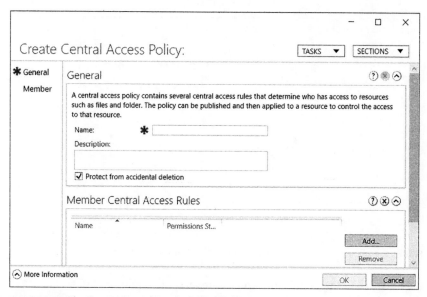

FIGURE 6-47 The Create Central Access Policy dialog box

4. In the Name text box, type a name for the policy.

5. In the Member Central Access Rules box, click Add to open a Create Central Access Policy dialog box.

6. Select the rules you want to add to the policy and click the right arrow to add them to the Add the Following Central Access Rules list.

7. Click OK to add the rules you selected to the Member Central Access Rules box.

8. Click OK to close the dialog box and create the CAP.

Deploying central access policies

As with claim types and resource properties, central access rules and central access policies are stored in Active Directory. To deploy the CAPs you have created to the file servers in your domain, you use Group Policy settings.

The select the CAPs for deployment, use the following procedure:

1. Open a Group Policy object in the Group Policy Object editor console and browse to the Computer Configuration/Policies/Windows Settings/Security Settings/File System/Central Access Policy folder.

2. Right-click the folder and, from the context menu, select Manage Central Access Policies. The Central Access Policies Configuration dialog box appears.

3. In the Available Central Access Policies list, select the CAPs you want to deploy and click the Add button, as shown in Figure 6-48.

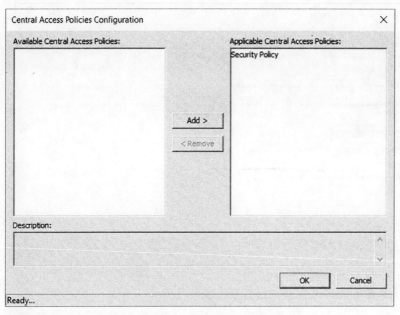

FIGURE 6-48 The Central Access Policies Configuration dialog box

4. Click OK to create settings for the CAPs you selected.

5. Link the GPO to appropriate domain, site, or organizational unit objects, so that it is deployed to all of your file servers.

6. In the Default Domain Controllers GPO, browse to the Computer Configuration/Policies/Administrative Templates/System/KDC folder.

7. Open the Properties sheet for the KDC Support for Claims, Compound Authentication and Kerberos Armoring policy setting.

8. Select the Enabled option, and in the drop-down list, select Supported and click OK.

9. Run the `gpupdate /force` command on your domain controllers and your file servers, to apply the Group Policy objects.

To confirm that your selected CAPs have been applied to your file servers, do the following:

1. On your file server, open the Properties sheet for a file which the CAR should have selected.

2. Click the Security tab.

3. Open the Advanced Security Settings dialog box.

4. Click the Central Policy tab. Your CAP should be available in the Central Policy drop-down list, as shown in Figure 6-49.

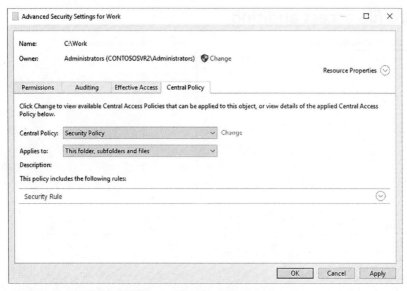

FIGURE 6-49 The Advanced Security Settings dialog box

Implement policy changes and staging

Creating and managing all of the different elements required for a DAC implementation can be complicated, and any system that automatically manipulates access control lists has the potential for disaster if it is incorrectly configured. For this reason, DAC includes a staging capability, which enables you to deploy central access policies without actually modifying the permissions involved.

When you create a central access rule, the default option in the Permissions section is Use Following Permissions as Proposed Permissions. Leaving this option selected in your CARs causes the resulting CAPs to generate access requests for the targeted resources and log them in the system's event logs. You can then examine the logs in Event Viewer to determine whether the correct resources have been targeted and the correct permissions proposed.

In addition to leaving the staging option selected in your CARs, you must also enable auditing for the proposed permissions by configuring Group Policy settings in a GPO deployed to your file servers. In the GPO, browse to the Computer Configuration/Policies/Windows Settings/Security Settings/Advanced Audit Policy Configuration/Audit Policies/Object Access container and enable Success and Failure auditing for the following two policies:

- Audit Central Access Policy Staging
- Audit File System

Once the auditing policies are in place, and you have enabled auditing of the files or folders on the Auditing tab of their Advanced Security Settings dialog boxes, you should monitor the Security event log for Auditing Event 4818: Proposed Central Access Policy Does Not Grant the Same Access Permissions as the Current Central Access Policy.

Configure file access auditing

Monitoring resource usage, and attempted usage, is a critical part of maintaining a secure workplace, and the auditing capabilities of Windows Server 2016 enable administrators to configure granular targets for resource monitoring. This prevents the need for administrators to pore over thousands of event log entries looking for the ones that indicate a potential problem.

You have already studied the process of enabling specific audit policies in Group Policy objects elsewhere in this book. However, Dynamic Access Control can contribute to these auditing capabilities. You can use the claim types and resource properties you create in Active Directory Administrative Center to control the circumstances under which file system resources generate auditing events.

To audit file access activities, you must first enable the Audit File System setting in the Computer Configuration/Policies/Windows Settings/Security Settings/Advanced Audit Policy Configuration/Audit Policies/Object Access container of a Group Policy object. Then, you must enable auditing in the properties of the files and folders that you want to monitor.

You enable auditing of a file or folder by opening its Properties sheet, clicking the Security tab, and opening the Advanced Security Settings dialog box. On the Auditing tab of this dialog box, you create auditing entries in which you select a security principal—that is, a user or group—that you want to audit, specify whether you want to audit success or failure or both, and select the specific permissions that you want to audit for that principal.

Beneath the Basic Permissions list, however, is an often-ignored box that enables you to add a condition that limits the scope of the auditing entry. These conditions take the form of expressions that you create, much as you did when creating central access rules, as described earlier in this chapter. Clicking the Add a Condition link causes a series of drop-down lists to appear that, as in Active Directory Administrative Center, are populated with the DAC claim types, resource properties, and values you have created.

For example, the first drop-down list enables you to select Device, Resource, or User, as shown in Figure 6-50. When you select one of these, the other drop-down lists are populated with the values of the element you select. For example, when you select Resource in the first list, the second list contains the resource properties you have created. When you select a resource property, the last list contains the values you configured for that property.

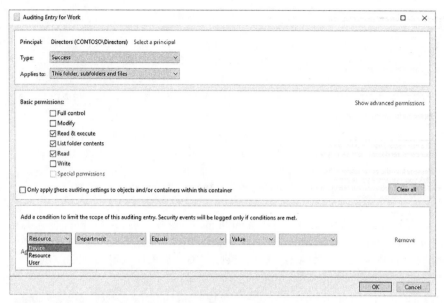

FIGURE 6-50 Creating Auditing Entry Expressions

This enables you to create expressions that specifically define the elements that the system audits. Instead of auditing all file accesses to a particular folder by everyone in the Managers group, for example, you can create an expression that audits only members of the Managers group that have the value High in their Security Level claim type. As with central access rules, you can also create multiple conditions and join them with Boolean operators, to create compound expressions.

Perform access-denied remediation

When a user attempts to open a file and is denied access because of insufficient permissions, there was a time when he or she had no recourse but to give up or try to locate an administrator responsible for that file. Windows Server 2016 includes a feature called *access-denied remediation* (also called *access-denied assistance*) that addresses this issue by enabling administrators to customize the message displayed to users when they are denied access.

To enable access-denied remediation, you can use File Server Resource Manager to configure a single file server, or use Group Policy settings for a domain-wide solution. To configure access-denied remediation on a single server with FSRM, use the following procedure.

1. Open File Server Resource Manager and, in the Actions pane, click Configure Options. The File Server Resource Manager Options dialog box appears.

2. Click the Access-Denied Assistance tab, as shown in Figure 6-51.

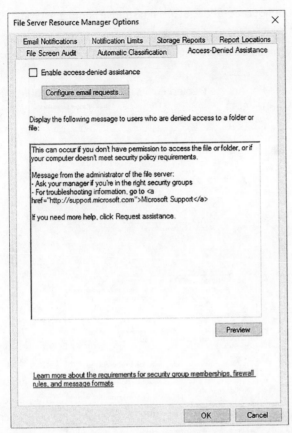

FIGURE 6-51 The File Server Resource Manager Options dialog box

3. Select the Enable Access-Denied Assistance checkbox.

4. Optionally, modify the Access Denied message that appears, to provide users with specific instructions for gaining access to the resource.

5. If you want to enable users to request assistance by generating emails, Click Configure Email Requests. The Access-Denied Assistance dialog box appears.

6. Select the Enable Users to Request Assistance checkbox.

7. Enter email addresses in the Recipient List text box and select or clear the Folder Owner and Administrator checkboxes, to specify who should receive the emails.

8. Optionally, modify the message included in the emails.

9. Click OK to close the Access-Denied Assistance dialog box.

10. Click OK to close the File Server Resource Manager Options dialog box.

To configure access-denied assistance for multiple file servers, you must enable settings in a Group Policy object, as in the following procedure.

1. Open a GPO in the Group Policy Management Editor.

2. Browse to the Computer Configuration\Policies\Administrative Templates\System\ Access-Denied Assistance folder.

3. Open the Enable Access-Denied Assistance On Client For All File Types dialog box and enable the policy setting.

4. Open the Customize Message For Access-Denied Errors dialog box and enable the policy setting, as shown in Figure 6-52.

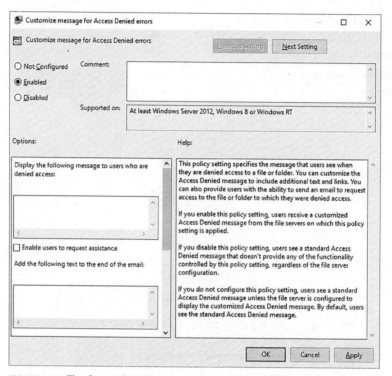

FIGURE 6-52 The Customize Message For Access-Denied Errors dialog box

5. Enter text to be displayed in the Access Denied message that users receive.

6. To allow users to send emails from the Access Denied message, select the Enable Users To Request Assistance checkbox.

7. Optionally, modify the message included in the emails.

8. Enter email addresses in the Additional Recipients List text box and select or clear the Folder Owner and File Server Administrator checkboxes, to specify who should receive the emails.

9. Click OK to close the dialog box.

10. Deploy the GPO to domain, site, or organizational unit objects containing your file servers.

Chapter summary

- Nano Server is a Windows Server 2016 installation option that creates a server with a smaller footprint than Server Core, designed for cloud and virtual machine use.

- Nano Server has no user interface beyond a rudimentary network configuration capability; you install it by creating a VHD file from a Nano Server image and deploying it on a virtual or physical machine.

- Containers are virtual operating system environments that enable software developers and other users to create clean installation environment in seconds, using resources shared with the host system.

- Windows Server 2016 includes two container implementations: Windows Server Containers, which share the host system kernel; and Hyper-V containers, which have individual kernels provided by the hypervisor, making them more secure.

- Using File Server Resource Manager, you can create quotas, to limit user storage space; file screens, to prevent users from storing specific file types; storage reports, to track storage-based activities; and file management tasks, to take action on files based on their contents.

- The File Classification Infrastructure enables you to assign properties values to files and folders based on rules that evaluate their contents.

- Using Work Folders, you can configure user workstations to sync files to file servers, enabling users to access their files from any device and administrators to protect the files with server-based backup and encryption.

- Dynamic Access Control is an Active Directory-based technology that enables administrators to define claim types and resource properties, and use them to create central access rules that automatically assign file system permissions.

- Access-Denied Remediation enables administrators to customize Access Denied messages, to provide users with assistance in accessing files to which they lack permissions.

Thought experiment

In this thought experiment, demonstrate your skills and knowledge of the topics covered in this chapter. You can find answer to this thought experiment in the next section.

The Human Resources department at Tailspin Toys has a great many documents containing employee Social Security numbers on their file server. You have been asked by your director to implement a solution that encrypts the files.

How can you do what the director asks?

Thought experiment answers

This section contains the solution to the thought experiment.

To do as the director asks, you must locate the document files that contain social security numbers and then encrypt them. You can do all of this using File Server Resource Manager on the file server.

1. Install the File Server Resource Manager role service on the file server.

2. In the FSRM console, create a Yes/No classification property called SSN. This property indicates files that contain Social Security numbers.

3. Create a classification rule with the following parameters:

    ■ Specifies a scope that includes all of the document folders on the file server

    ■ Uses the Content Classifier method to assign the Yes value to the SSN property of a file when it contains the regular expression \d{3}-\d{2}-\d{4}. This is the standard regular expression for a string containing 3 digits, then 2 digits, then 4 digits, separated by hyphens.

4. Create a classification schedule that runs weekly and allows continuous classification for new files.

5. Create a file management task with the following parameters:

    ■ Specifies a scope that includes all of the document folders on the file server.

    ■ Uses the RMS Encryption action.

    ■ Contains the condition that the SSN property has the value Yes.

    ■ Contains a schedule that runs weekly and runs continuously on new files.

Index

A

access control. *See also* Dynamic Access Control; *See also* File Server Resource Manager (FSRM)
  central access rules 298–300
access control lists (ACLs) 114, 179, 206
access-denied assistance 306
access-denied remediation 306–308
activation requests 148
Active Directory (AD)
  architecture
    clean source principles in 135–138
  modifying, for LAPS 178–180
Active Directory (AD) administrative tiers 133–134
Active Directory Certificate Services (AD CS) 15
Active Directory Domain Services (AD DS)
  recovery password retrieval from 12–13
Add-HgsKeyProtectionCertificate cmdlet 67
Address Space Layout Randomization (ASLR) 35
administrative architecture
  clean source for 137–138
administrative credentials 40
administrative forests 131–138
  AD administrative tiers 133–134
  bastion forests 139–144
administrative privileges 134–135
Administrator account
  changing name of 183
administrator groups 290
administrator logons
  restrictions on 172–173
admin-trusted attestation 63–67
Advanced Audit Policy Configuration folder 193–198
Advanced Threat Analytics (ATA) 213–229

alerts configuration 224–226
architecture 217
ATA Center 215, 220–221, 224–226
deployment requirements 215–219
event forwarding 220
gateways 216–218, 222–224
installation and configuration 220–224
port mirroring 218–220
Timeline page 227–229
usage scenarios 213–214
  compromised credentials 214–215
  domain dominance 214
  lateral movement 214
  privilege escalation 214
  reconnaissance 213
AES-128 algorithm 7
AES-256 algorithm 7
alerts
  configuration of 224–226
  mail 225–226
  notification settings 226–227
  syslog 226
Allow BitLocker Without A Compatible TPM setting 6
antimalware assessment 236–237
antimalware solutions 26–40
Application Identity service (AppIDSvc) 32
application-specific firewall rules 105–107
AppLocker
  policies
    implementing 33–34
    testing and monitoring 34–35
  rules
    implementation of 31–35
    types 31–33

X

About the authors

TIMOTHY WARNER is an IT professional and technical trainer based in Nashville, TN. A computer enthusiast who authored his first BASIC program in 1981, Tim has worked in nearly every facet of IT, from systems administration and software architecture to technical writing and training. He can be reached via Twitter at @TechTrainerTim.

CRAIG ZACKER is the author or co-author of dozens of books, manuals, articles, and web sites on computer and networking topics. He has also been an English professor, an editor, a network administrator, a webmaster, a corporate trainer, a technical support engineer, a minicomputer operator, a literature and philosophy student, a library clerk, a photographic darkroom technician, a shipping clerk, and a newspaper boy. He lives in a little house with his beautiful wife and a neurotic cat..

Free ebooks

From technical overviews to drilldowns on special topics, get *free* ebooks from Microsoft Press at:

www.microsoftvirtualacademy.com/ebooks

Download your free ebooks in PDF, EPUB, and/or Mobi for Kindle formats.

Look for other great resources at Microsoft Virtual Academy, where you can learn new skills and help advance your career with free Microsoft training delivered by experts.

Microsoft Press

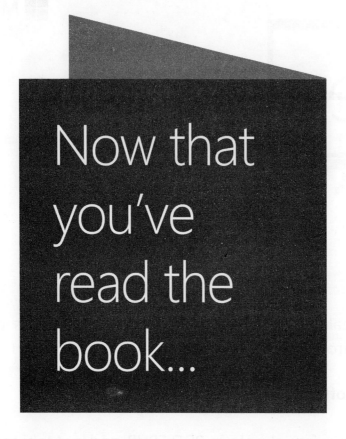

Now that you've read the book...

Tell us what you think!

Was it useful?
Did it teach you what you wanted to learn?
Was there room for improvement?

Let us know at http://aka.ms/tellpress

Your feedback goes directly to the staff at Microsoft Press,
and we read every one of your responses. Thanks in advance!

 Microsoft